BLACK AND GOLD

In BLACK AND GOLD Anthony Sampson
provides an original insight into a critical frontier
of the South African crisis – the relationship
between big business and the black political
movements on which the country's future
depends.

Drawing upon his special knowledge of the
workings of multinationals as well as rare insight
gained from personal contact with black leaders,
including Nelson Mandela and Oliver Tambo, he
traces the problem from the first confrontations,
when early diamond and gold millionaires
employed black miners, creating a new kind of
urban black nationalism. He shows how the
multinationals which arrived in the sixties were
seen by blacks as apologists and paymasters,
following ferocious Afrikaner apartheid.

Finally, he brings the reader up to date, telling
the inside story of business attempts to defuse the
crisis and come to terms with black resistance –
attempts which have culminated in two
emergencies, lobbying and passionate arguments
over disinvestment and sanctions.

CRITICAL ACCLAIM FOR
BLACK AND GOLD

'Miraculously up-to-date . . . a valuable and timely book'

Financial Times

'Sampson has a long acquaintance with South Africa, has mulled long and thoughtfully over its history, and has a particularly sharp eye for the way in which the South African political economy reacts upon – and is reacted upon – by the great multinationals. What else would one expect of someone who has written so well about the politics of airlines, oil companies, banks and arms dealers? . . . He sheds light on a number of key recent events'

New Society

'Sampson offers a brilliant and concise account of the rise of Afrikaner Nationalist power since the present Government was elected in 1948 . . . Superbly researched, grimly fascinating tour of the battlefront'

Hampstead and Highgate Express

'It is difficult to see the situation with any clarity . . . which is why Anthony Sampson's account becomes useful. He has the right credentials . . . Interesting'

The Times

'Sampson's story could hardly be more topical'
The New Statesman

'Shows uncanny foresight . . . Sampson tells his story in the same easy-to-read way as when he was anatomising Britain . . . Fascinating insights . . . Essential reading'

The Independent

'Anthony Sampson is uniquely qualified to assess past and present relationships between international businessmen and their government. More significantly, he is also uniquely qualified to advise on the future possibilities and implications of relationships between businessmen everywhere and the black majority in post-apartheid South Africa. Sampson knows the key decision-makers personally'

The Observer

'One cannot fault his homework. BLACK AND GOLD is a professional job. Mr Sampson is an experienced practitioner on the anatomy of national situations'

The Sunday Telegraph

'Sampson is a powerful reporter . . . his book is itself the message. It is the money men, the company men, the faceless men of the IMF who can, if they choose, change the course of history in South Africa'

The Guardian

About the Author

Anthony Sampson spent four years in Johannesburg in the early 1950s as editor of the black magazine *Drum*. He witnessed the emerging black resistance at first hand and knew most of the black leaders including Nelson Mandela and Oliver Tambo, with whom he has maintained contact. He has visited the country several times since the fifties.

Anthony Sampson's ANATOMY OF BRITAIN was first published in 1962 and has been followed by many highly acclaimed and successful books on business. In 1973 he wrote THE SOVEREIGN STATE: THE SECRET HISTORY OF ITT, a study of the political power of a multinational corporation, and he has since pursued his interest in global companies with THE SEVEN SISTERS (about oil corporations), THE ARMS BAZAAR (about the international arms companies), THE MONEY LENDERS (about the power of international bankers) and, most recently, EMPIRES OF THE SKY (about airline companies).

Also by the same author,
and available from Coronet:

THE ARMS BAZAAR
THE CHANGING ANATOMY OF BRITAIN
EMPIRES OF THE SKY
THE MONEY LENDERS
THE SEVEN SISTERS
THE SOVEREIGN STATE

Black and Gold

Anthony Sampson

CORONET BOOKS
Hodder and Stoughton

Copyright © 1987 by Anthony
Sampson

First published in Great Britain in
1987 by Hodder and Stoughton
Limited

Coronet edition 1987

British Library C.I.P.

Sampson, Anthony
   Black and gold: tycoons,
revolutionaries and apartheid. –
Rev. and updated ed.
1. Apartheid – South Africa 2.
Corporations Foreign – South
Africa
I. Title
323.1′68   DT763

ISBN 0-340-41853-2

Printed and bound in Great Britain
for Hodder and Stoughton
Paperbacks, a division of Hodder
and Stoughton Limited, Mill Road,
Dunton Green, Sevenoaks, Kent
(Editorial Office: 47 Bedford
Square, London WC1B 3DP) by
Richard Clay Ltd. Photoset by
Rowland Phototypesetting
Limited, Bury St Edmunds, Suffolk.

Contents

Introduction

Oh I will sit me down and weep
For bones in Africa

A E Housman

No one can pretend to be wholly dispassionate about South Africa, so it is wiser to declare interests beforehand. I felt pressed to write this book from two very contrasted experiences. On the one side I had been fascinated by the South African problem ever since I worked for four years from 1951 as editor of the black magazine *Drum* in Johannesburg. It was a job which provided an almost unique opportunity to get to know black South Africans, including such political leaders as Albert Luthuli, Nelson Mandela and Oliver Tambo; and I was able to spend much of my time in Soweto, Sophiatown and black shebeens at a time when there were few bridges across the colour bar. After returning to London to work on the *Observer* I took every excuse to report on South Africa, including visits for the Treason Trials in 1957 (about which I wrote a book, *The Treason Cage*), for Macmillan's visit and the Sharpeville emergency in 1960, for Mandela's trial in 1964, for the elections of 1970, for the Muldergate scandals of 1978. And in London I was able to keep in touch with black politicians in exile.

But I have also had a long curiosity about the relationship between corporations and politics, which may have originated in my childhood when my father worked as a research chemist in ICI. After studying the broader national power structure in my book *Anatomy of Britain* in 1962 I became more intrigued by the political involvements of multinational corporations, which I then explored in a succession of books: about ITT, the oil companies, arms companies and airlines. In each of them I came up against the recurring problem of where corporate loyalties lie when confronted with dictatorships or potential enemies; and when revisiting South Africa I became more interested in business attitudes and dilemmas over apartheid.

When the South African crisis became more acute two years ago I was editing my own international newsletter which enabled me to keep in touch through the telephone with South African friends including Nadine Gordimer, Winnie Mandela, Gatsha Buthelezi, Helen Suzman and Oliver Tambo. I found that international direct-dialling could sometimes give easier access to a range of information and opinions, including banned politicians, than communications inside South Africa. Through Tambo and other black leaders I tried to learn more about the attitudes of the black opposition; while at the same time businessmen both in London and New York were becoming more concerned about their future in a black South Africa, and I tried to ease the communications between the two sides. As the crisis worsened I returned to South Africa twice, at the beginning of each of the two emergencies, to talk both to black leaders and to businessmen.

In this book I have tried to trace the erratic relationships between these two groups of actors in the South African drama – the international business leaders and the black politicians – since they first encountered each other a century ago. I try to show how the story developed from both sides, to explore some of the characters and their motivations on the way, and to convey the flavour of each period without hindsight. I do not attempt to analyse with the same closeness the changing attitudes of Afrikaners and their governments, except insofar as they affected the whole climate and legislation of the country. But from 1978, when P W Botha became prime minister, I look at the story in more detail, to try to trace the stages towards the current tragic deadlock and to show the viewpoint from America and Europe as well as South Africa.

I have far too many debts and obligations, and too many discreet or reluctant sources and helpers, to list. I am grateful to several journalists in Johannesburg and London who have been generous with their advice; I appreciate the trust and assistance of black politicians; and I have had long talks partly in confidence with many of the bankers and businessmen involved. I am grateful to my American publisher Andre Schiffrin of Pantheon for invaluable editorial suggestions; to my London publishers Hodder & Stoughton and my editor Ion Trewin for their continuing efficiency and support; to my two agents Michael Sissons in London and Sterling Lord in New York; to Joe Bullman for useful research; to Bettie du Toit for patiently listening, and advising on difficult chapters; and to Carla Shimeld for helping through the last stages of editing.

I hope this book may interest and help those who like me believe that it is still possible to avert a catastrophe in that marvellous and resilient country, and that businessmen, as well as politicians, can use their influence and foresight to prepare for a democratic future.

Anthony Sampson, *London, November 1986*

For this paperback edition I have added a postscript chapter bringing the story up to the South African general election in May 1987.

1

Looking Across the Abyss

If we really want to lose everything, then we must hang on to everything now.

Donald Masson (retired president of the Afrikaner
Institute of Commerce), June 1986

In the big garden of Marlborough House in London in August 1986, seven Commonwealth prime ministers were attending a cocktail party before having a final argument about South Africa. It was a poignant setting, down the Mall from Buckingham Palace, in the former royal mansion which used to house only King George V's widow: it was now turned into the headquarters of the Commonwealth of forty-nine countries, run by its Guyanan Secretary-General, Sonny Ramphal, from Queen Mary's old bedroom. The South African fires six thousand miles away had rekindled all the smouldering emotions about black and white, about order and chaos, appeasement and confrontation. Marlborough House had become the central battleground: conservatives had been attacking Ramphal for trying to lure the Queen herself away from Britain's true interests, while across the street demonstrators had been yelling all day, 'Free Mandela!' Inside Marlborough House the prime ministers had spent two days arguing with Margaret Thatcher about the report of their 'eminent persons' who had warned them that unless

they took effective measures South Africa could turn into
'the worst bloodbath since the Second World War'. They
had had some of the most acrimonious exchanges they
could remember: the room, said one participant, was 'flowing with vitriol'.

But at the garden party Ramphal was welcoming everyone with the same jolly laugh, and the multiracial Commonwealth still showed some life. Brian Mulroney from
Canada, with his boyish chin, was joking with a
lugubrious-looking Kenneth Kaunda from Zambia who
was staring upwards with his horror-movie eyes. Robert
Mugabe from Zimbabwe was gesturing intently at Bob
Hawke from Australia. Malcolm Fraser, the former Australian prime minister, was restraining his emotional outbursts and beaming down like a beacon. They were nearly
all talking about sanctions from the perspective of their
own interests and oceans. Bob Hawke was determined on
stopping air traffic; but the Australian airline Qantas had
long ago stopped flying to South Africa. Mulroney was
pressing for wider sanctions, including minerals; but the
Canadian uranium producers would benefit. Rajiv Gandhi
wanted to stop all trade; India had (officially) stopped
trading twenty years ago. They all preferred to discuss the
long term rather than the short term: Mulroney insisted
that the world must see 'the sweep of history'; Fraser
explained that every country must be seen to be on the
right side in this historic crisis.

They were all gunning for Britain, which was by far the
biggest investor in South Africa; and the British isolation
was very visible. The senior officials stood round the edge
of the lawn speculating about the effects of a real Commonwealth split, while their prime minister, looking for once
exhausted, arrived late and kept her distance. She listened
patiently, with a puzzled expression, while an Asian diplomat discussed a prize for Nelson Mandela, but before
long burst out against the hypocrisy of sanctions and the
ignorance of other prime ministers: 'They think that we
could close down the South African tourist office just like

that . . . they don't understand about bank loans . . . they
don't realise there are 800,000 South Africans with British
passports.' The timing of this summit could hardly be
worse, she told me, just before Botha was due to make
another big speech to his people. She would have liked to
talk to him herself, but this was not the right time.

Everyone talked about national interests, but everyone
had their own emotional involvement; and few more than
Mrs Thatcher. To her, South Africa seemed partly like a
nightmare caricature of the dangers within Britain, from
Brixton to Belfast, with terrorists threatening to induce
chaos, and rioters and strikers undermining commercial
stability. She sympathised with the embattled Afrikaners
and their fighting spirit, encouraged by her husband Denis
– who had been back in South Africa in March – and by
her Afrikaner friend the writer Laurens van der Post: she
saw them as stubborn, ready to fight to the bitter end,
thriving in isolation. As she described them, she might be
talking about herself; for at this summit she seemed to
gain new energy from being alone. But she also believed
that British voters were behind her: that they too were fed
up with being lectured by black autocrats who had made
a mess of their own countries and had locked up their
opposition in jail.

At the conference inside Marlborough House she had
slapped down the black prime ministers, rubbing in their
dependence on British aid, and explaining how Botha was
dismantling apartheid and how South African blacks had
higher standards of living and education than most others.
When Mugabe protested, she replied: 'But weren't you
educated in South Africa?' The prime ministers were predictably exasperated. Kaunda maintained that she 'cut a
pathetic picture'. Gandhi complained that she had given
up the moral leadership of the Commonwealth. Mugabe
protested that 'Britain has let the people of South Africa
down.' She seemed impervious to them all – except perhaps
to General Obasanjo, the bulky former Nigerian president
who had been co-chairman of the Commonwealth Group,

who was heaving himself round the garden party in a genial mood. Thatcher held the general in unusual respect, and had exchanged friendly letters with him about the Afrikaner character in which the general had insisted that, though Afrikaners were stubborn, they would not commit suicide: but now he ended the correspondence with a despairing open letter to 'my dear Margaret': he was appalled, he wrote, by her ignorance of conditions inside South Africa, her absurd hopes of Botha's reforms, her apparent faith in his policy of dividing the tribes. 'Such was our discussion that I must ask: "Did you even read our report?"' He warned her that 'many people around the world view your continued opposition to sanctions as founded in instinct, not logic, and as displaying a misguided tribal loyalty and myopic political vision . . . Not only does the mental laager of the Boer seem to be mirrored in your own attitudes, but his fatal concessions of too little, too late, are paralleled in your actions.'*

But it was now Washington rather than London that was making the running, where the South African fires were arousing even higher emotions. President Reagan himself shared many of Mrs Thatcher's instincts, dreading revolution and terrorism and always hopeful that the Afrikaners would liberalise themselves; while his White House contained ideologues who naturally equated South Africa with Nicaragua, Iran or the Philippines, including his speech-writer Pat Buchanan who had hoped to be ambassador to South Africa. But the Congress, aroused by black protests and massive television coverage, had taken up the cause of black South Africans with rare bi-partisan unity; and when President Botha declared a second state of emergency the State Department under George Shultz was determined to send a strong signal of disapproval to Pretoria. Then Reagan decided to make his first major speech about South Africa, which soon became a trial of strength among his advisers. Buchanan had already

* *Financial Times*, August 7, 1986

interested Reagan in an article in *Commentary* magazine
by Paul Johnson, the British right-wing journalist whose
books Buchanan admired (Johnson was later told that
Reagan had read the article three times). Johnson had
recently been to South Africa to write a book for Consolidated Goldfields, and his article argued that blacks were
better off in South Africa than elsewhere in the continent
and that disinvestment was 'a cruel absurdity'. The State
Department prepared its own draft for the President's
speech, very critical of Botha and insisting on more
thorough reforms; but Buchanan got a look at it, complained that it was 'relentless Boer-bashing', and quickly
substituted his own version, with several quotations from
Paul Johnson about the improvement of black conditions
in South Africa compared to the rest of Africa, and with
lurid warnings against communism and terrorism.* Many
officials complained it would now only give comfort to
Botha, but Reagan went ahead to deliver his speech, based
on Buchanan's version, on July 22. It read like a catalogue
of doubts and hesitations about South Africa, swinging
from but to but, from however to nevertheless. The President agreed that apartheid was morally wrong and politically unacceptable; but agreed with Mrs Thatcher that
punitive sanctions were also immoral and repugnant. Pretoria was not obliged to negotiate with terrorists; but
Mandela should be released, to participate in the political
process. The strongest allies of blacks, Reagan insisted,
were the Western businessmen who brought in their own
ideas of social justice: 'capitalism is the natural enemy of
such feudal institutions as apartheid.'

The speech rapidly achieved the opposite of what the
State Department had intended. President Botha welcomed it in support of his anti-communist crusade, while
black South Africans were outraged. 'The West, for my
part, can go to hell,' said Bishop Tutu in Johannesburg.
But it also appalled much of Washington. George Shultz

* *New Republic*, September 15, 1986; and private information

soon explained he was flexible about sanctions and wanted
to speak to black leaders, while Senators and Congressmen
were now determined to rescue America's reputation, as
they saw it, by pushing through a bill for sanctions. Three
weeks after Reagan's speech the Senators held an historic
debate, re-stating their fears about apartheid, and the
Republican Senator Richard Lugar put forward his bill for
sanctions – against South African steel, coal, airlines,
textiles and new investment. 'We believe it is time to send
a blunt message to President P W Botha's government',
said Lugar; and his bill was passed with an emphatic
majority. President Reagan vetoed it, saying once again
that sanctions would hurt blacks most of all; but finally
Congress used its two-thirds majority to override the veto,
by seventy-eight votes to twenty-one, in the biggest foreign
policy reversal of Reagan's presidency.

In London Mrs Thatcher had also been compelled to
modify her own stand under pressure from the Commonwealth and the European Community; and in September
the twelve European nations had their own wrangle, with
the Danes and the Dutch most determined on maximum
sanctions and the Germans and Portuguese turning against
a ban on South African coal. But by September 17 they
had agreed to ban imports of iron, steel, gold coins or any
new investment. The Western sanctions were much less
biting and unambiguous than the complete mandatory
sanctions which black South Africans had asked for. Yet
they marked a tragic cross-roads: the end of a long open
road of growing investment and trade, stretching back over
a century, during which the Western billions had helped
to transform the bottom of the continent into an industrial
power-house. Sanctions ended the hopes that investment
and wealth could in themselves undermine apartheid. But
their economic consequences could prove less important
than their signal that the West had finally dissociated itself
from Pretoria, and begun to change sides.

The long Western debate about sanctions had highlighted all the conflicting images of South Africa, but

without much relevance to the real inhabitants. To Western conservatives it stood for the disciplined white world in contrast to the chaos and disintegration in the black North: however awful the system, any revolutionary alternative must be more awful. Marxists saw South Africa as the ultimate case study of the class conflict, with workers painted black and capitalists white, whose origins had helped Lenin to form his theories about imperialism. To many American liberals it was the last replay of their own revolution, an assertion of inalienable human rights: to American blacks it was an extension of the civil rights campaign. To ageing European liberals it was the last of the liberation epics, the bottom line after all the false accountings through Africa, which called for an agonising reappraisal of what kind of freedom the early liberations had really achieved.

South Africa seemed not so much a real country as a map of the mind in which anyone could find his own place. The blacks, who had so often since Rousseau's Noble Savage been receptacles for liberal imaginations, now appeared as the last of the underdogs, fighting battles which had long ago been won elsewhere. Idealists could still find reassurance in their half-biblical world, where words like crucifixion and persecution still had a literal meaning, and where protest still had a kind of innocence, uncorrupted by power. Many Western conservatives, like Mrs Thatcher, identified themselves with the Afrikaners as the extreme exponents of will-power and survival in a world threatened by chaos; while others saw them as the reincarnations of Nazis, bringing back the horrors of racialism and genocide.

White South Africans heard the Western theorising with wry smiles. They noticed that while Americans enjoyed self-righteously attacking the brutalities of apartheid, they preferred not to consider the consequences of a black majority as in the rest of Africa. They noticed the ignorance of their critics, explaining: 'We know the Bantu'. But behind that confident singular did they really know him – or them? Most whites had never been inside a black

township; few had talked to any of them except as servants.
It was a country of dialogues of the deaf, of leaders who
had never met each other: the censored television and
newspapers gave South Africans less news of key events
in their own country than could be gained by a casual TV
viewer in the West; and many foreign correspondents knew
far more about black politics than South African members
of parliament. Was South Africa really a nation at all?
Some British politicians speculated whether they could not
rescind the Act of Union which created it 75 years ago;
and even the Pretoria government had its doubts. 'We are
not really one nation,' the ambassador to London, Denis
Worrall, told British MPs: 'and do not have a single perceived history or one single set of shared heroes.'*

. Behind all these black-and-white images South Africa
was always a much greyer area than the theorists described:
far more industrialised and detribalised than the rest of
the continent. For over a century – before the nation had
been invented – the mills of industry round Johannesburg
and elsewhere had been grinding away at the old tribal
structures, drawing still more people into its disciplines
and motivations. Sowetans had as little in common with
Ugandans as British factory workers had with Polish
peasants, and the rural myths of the Afrikaners had more
to do with their reaction against the harsh facts of industrialisation than with their enduring characteristics. The
makers of this modern state were as much the industrialists, miners and bankers as the politicians and tribal
chiefs, whether Afrikaners or blacks. And while Western
politicians were arguing about interests, ideologies and
strategic importance, the businessmen were contending
with much more practical worries about who they could
do business with in the future, and whether their companies
could survive.

* Evidence to Foreign Affairs Committee Report on South Africa,
June 30, 1986

Down in South Africa, the view was much more detailed, but much more fragmented, like a cracked telescope. Johannesburg, its commercial hub, had always been a city of money and business, or nothing, and had transformed everyone it had drawn into its field – white, black and brown. Unlike other African cities it had been started from scratch, built up on a bleak landscape 400 miles from the sea, with no river or trees, with no tribal or rural traditions to modify its intense urban character, and gold as its only reason for existence. It was soon driven by its gold-wealth and ambition, until it became the biggest industrial complex in the continent. Now in its centenary year its glittering white suburbs stretched twenty miles to the north, linked by a brand-new freeway system which seemed to promise indefinite expansion; while some of the palatial old mansions, complete with white-suited black servants, seemed to be competing as sets for *Gone With The Wind*. Their peace and security was still undisturbed by black dwellings which had been largely contained in the vast township of Soweto in the south, where the houses were a quarter of the size. Every day the white executives drove to work from the north, while the black workers poured in by train or bus from the south, combining their energies which had built up the city's prosperity. Every evening they all separated out again, like unravelled knitting, to their opposite areas.

But by June 1986, Johannesburg and its hidden twin Soweto were at the core of the crisis, the immediate cause of the state of emergency which President Botha had declared, just before the planned celebrations of the tenth anniversary of the Soweto uprising. I had flown out there just beforehand, to see again the magnetic city where thirty years ago I had moved without much difficulty between the black and white worlds. Now it seemed almost as if war had been declared between them. On the Monday of the anniversary the city centre was like a ghost-town, with shut shops, empty streets and young blue-capped police reservists fingering their rifles: only a gun-shop was doing much business. Newspaper and television news offered government propaganda and extended sports coverage. The *Financial Times* arrived from London with its front-page story blacked out. All the roads to Soweto, only ten miles away, were blocked by police who searched every car, while the telephone lines to Soweto went dead, 'for technical reasons'. The only journalists admitted were flown in by helicopter, and driven briefly round in a barred van. It seemed more remote from white Johannesburg than East Berlin from the West. President Botha had just declared apartheid outdated: but in the geographical sense it had never been so effective.

The state had mobilised its resources to enforce the most thorough clampdown in South Africa's history, with the strongest army in Africa to reinforce the police: they had been given almost limitless powers of arrest and detention, and were deliberately trying to terrify the blacks by making people disappear; what they called 'the Argentine option'. 'I can't find out about my black clients', said an Indian defence lawyer: 'whether they're detained, or are hiding, or have left the country – or are dead'. 'That's the worst part of it,' said a young Sowetan writer, 'not knowing what's happened to your friends.' There was no legal means of public protest: only a special service at the cathedral where Bishop Tutu warned that there would be 'greater and greater repression with smaller and smaller results'. At dinner at his house next evening I found the bishop subdued and depressed by a talk with President Botha who seemed as committed as ever to his apartheid policy of homelands; but he talked with the same passion in private as in public: 'Why don't people understand the pain in our hearts? How many more thousands must be killed?'

Yet with all the government's show of strength the blacks seemed almost absurdly uncowed and confident of victory. I was reminded of the words of the Afrikaner political scientist, Hermann Giliomee: 'The most serious failing is the inability of each side to assess the other's real strength.'

The Afrikaners put their confidence in money and guns; the blacks in ideas and world opinion. Each had tragically underestimated the other, in this ultimate non-meeting of minds.

Certainly the blacks had some reason to question the power of the state. Their oldest black political organisation, the African National Congress, had been banned since 1960, its members exiled or imprisoned; yet its leader, Nelson Mandela, was far more famous than when he was jailed twenty-four years ago, and the ANC never had more support. The more the government denounced its exiled president Oliver Tambo the more he was admired in the townships. The government had just distributed 70,000 copies of a free booklet about the ANC, to warn the whites about its communist influences; but the blacks gobbled it up in the townships, quoted the speeches and pinned up Mandela's photograph (the next edition left out the photograph). At the weekend before June 16 a car-bomb had exploded on the Golden Mile beachfront in Durban, close to popular nightspots such as Magoos and the Why Not bar, killing three white women. The police immediately blamed it on the ANC, and the whites were united in horror: the government called it 'despicable and cowardly'; the opposition leader Colin Eglin said it was 'cowardly and despicable'. But most blacks preferred not to comment on it.

Ironically the only black political leaders who were easily accessible were twenty-two who were already in prison, being tried for treason in the small town of Delmas, forty miles east of Johannesburg. When I went out there with their defence attorney we found the accused waiting behind bars in the cells below the courtroom, where they had been on trial for months and could face life imprisonment. Yet they seemed more exuberant and optimistic than most people outside, and they were preparing for a wedding of one of the accused in the courtroom next day: I began to understand why white liberals who visited black prisoners often found they needed the visits to revive their own spirits. The prisoners were full of questions about Western politics: would Mrs Thatcher agree to a coalition? Would Chester Crocker keep his job in the State Department? The thirty-four-year-old activist Popo Molefe was one of the generation who had been politicised by the Soweto revolt ten years before, who had become the general secretary of the United Democratic Front: 'it was the voice,' he insisted, 'to say that there was still a chance to bring about change without great loss of life. Now the state of emergency can't contain the anger of the people.' But he still put much hope on international pressure. 'This is a moment of truth for the West: they've run out of excuses. We don't expect countries to ignore their self-interest. We know we won't get complete sanctions. But they can be selective, to show they mean business. What are the interests you have in this minority government? You know, we're aware of these things.'

Talking to black journalists, I found them all the more convinced of their strength by the government's reaction. 'The emergency was a deadly mistake,' said Percy Qoboza of City Press, 'the leadership is already regrouping, and the jungle telegrams are still working.' 'If Botha had reformed from a position of strength the black people might have been grateful,' said Stanley Motjuwadi, the editor of *Drum* magazine: 'but they know that it's pressure that made him move . . . The more people he detains, the greater the armies of his enemies.'

But to a white lunch-party in northern Johannesburg, on a brown lawn under that marvellous bright winter sun, this black confidence seemed merely pathetic; and the turmoil in Soweto seemed as distant as another continent. How could this solid material city, with all its Western technology and communications, protected by the massed police and defence forces, be seriously threatened by in-competent terrorists, still riddled with informers, in-structed by a bunch of out-of-touch exiles in Zambia six hundred miles north? Was it more improbable, I ventured, than the confidence of the Ayatollah Khomeini, confront-

ing the military might of the Shah with only a mad idea?
Or even of the Afrikaners themselves when they took on
the might of the British Empire eighty years earlier? But
the Shah's army had none of the determination of the
Afrikaners, I was told, and the blacks in South Africa had
none of the fanatical unity of either the Islamic fundamen-
talists or the old Boers.

Yet the English-speaking whites were clearly less confident about everything than they had been when I last
visited Johannesburg a year earlier. Whatever new unity
they might have found from the emergency and the threat
of sanctions, they had no convincing future to look to: the
government's policy had shown no real consistency, and
no serious new political blueprint to take the place of
the grand apartheid of the past, with its homelands and
elaborate demarcations: the next homeland due to be
declared independent, KwaNdebele, was already in open
revolt, while the new three-chamber parliament, which
was President Botha's special creation, had been over-
ridden and discredited by the emergency. Whatever the
temporary boom the record numbers of emigrants (3,000
a month, according to British Airways) told their own
story, as they took the 'chicken-run' to escape from con-
scription and the prospect of a future civil war. Each batch
of emigrants made the eventual conflict look harsher and
more uncompromising.

And many people on both sides, black and white, were
now talking not so much about winning or losing, but
about chaos: a continuing loss of control from both sides,
as black and white violence fed on each other while relative
moderates, including both Mandela and Botha, were
pushed out of the way. In the townships the 'necklace' –
the tyre filled with petrol and set alight round the victim's
neck – had become the instrument of retribution from the
young 'comrades' providing their own counter-terrorism
to stamp out informers and collaborators. The rubber
necklace had become the symbol of anarchic power, the
subject of dark threats and jokes: 'You can have your

choice, Goodyear or Firestone.' Two months earlier
Winnie Mandela, the wife of the ANC leader who was now
a politician in her own right, had sent shivers down many
white spines by talking about blacks being armed with their
necklaces and matchboxes. Tambo and the ANC leaders
had told her to keep quiet: she was incommunicado for a
few weeks and then modified her remark, while Tambo
later emphasised that the ANC disapproved of necklaces –
'you can take a hint.' But the ANC's 'Radio Freedom' still
made bloodthirsty broadcasts, and the necklace remained
the image of black fury. To Western leaders it was the
portent of chaos: 'a barbaric atrocity', Reagan called it.
But to many radical young blacks it was their only demonstration of power, which had to be extended into the white
world. I asked a group of young Sowetans whether they
and their friends were worried by the implications of
Winnie's outburst. 'They didn't bat an eyelid,' said one of
them. 'They know in their heart of hearts that they must
go into the white suburbs – which epitomise all our
problems,' said another: 'They take the necklaces for
granted.' The only way to avoid far worse violence, they
all insisted, was sanctions: 'The right question isn't: do
you support sanctions? It's "Do you want to destroy
apartheid? If so, do you prefer sanctions or violence?"
But we know that the Iron Lady and the Cowboy will
be on the side of the Boers in the end. Violence will be
our only weapon.'

Both sides were making their own parallels with the
horrors of the Algerian War thirty years earlier. Was South
Africa, too, moving into a civil war in which another
million could be killed? Was it now like Algiers in early
1958, when the rebels had lost the battle but won international support? Would the Afrikaners, like the French
colonists, continue to give too little, too late, and to lock
up the only rebels they could negotiate with? Would the
Afrikaners fight to the bitter end, because they had nowhere else to go? Or was it because the French did have
somewhere to go that they fought so ferociously; while the

Afrikaners, who had to stay, knew that in the end they would have to do a deal?

Facing this vortex of violence, how could the businessmen who had built up this unique industrial society protect their own interests? Everyone was now looking towards them, whether as villains or potential saviours. 'There can be no real change until business takes the side of freedom,' Winnie Mandela had said to me with careful emphasis. 'At present we regard them as the government's allies. If they want real change with stability, they must identify themselves with the aspirations of our people.' 'Botha retains his power because of big business,' said Popo Molefe. And President Reagan said in his August speech that the Western business community should be the 'agents of change and progress and growth'; while Henry Kissinger had told the tycoon Harry Oppenheimer that 'business in South Africa may have a decisive role to play, because it can set an example and do unilaterally what would be very difficult for the political process to originate.'*

The business leaders in Johannesburg, in their sunny palaces surrounded by greenery, still have the confident, open-air style of men who are accustomed to developing half a continent; but they heard these conflicting messages with growing unease. They could not yet afford to get too caught up in ideologies and mythologies like the politicians: they had to be prepared in the end to do business with anyone. They longed for stability; yet they knew that they had to be prepared for unprecedented changes – perhaps even some kind of revolution. The giant Anglo-American Corporation which controlled half the gold mines and half the Johannesburg stock exchange was now openly divided. The bluff chairman Gavin Relly, who had earlier talked with the ANC revolutionaries, was now wary: 'Frankly, the uncertainty is driving some people bonkers.' But his more

* HFO: some personal perspectives. Privately printed for the Anglo-American Corporation, Johannesburg 1985

political director Zach de Beer was outspoken against
Botha's policies and the emergency: 'I'm extremely disappointed that it should be thought necessary . . . It's vital
for the government now to negotiate with legitimate black
leaders.' Gordon Waddell, the hearty chairman of Anglo's
subsidiary, Johannesburg Consolidated Investments, explained with his impenetrable bonhomie: 'Most businessmen think that the government had to restore law and
order. But the trouble is that business never really changes
until it feels the impact. Let's face it, we're not much good
at politics.'

Botha, like Hitler in 1933, was confident that he could
rally businessmen to his side against the threatened 'communist onslaught'. On the first morning of the emergency
he had summoned eighteen of his favoured conservative
businessmen, including Julian Ogilvie Thompson, the head
of Anglo's sister-company De Beers, to explain the need
for tough measures. Most businessmen agreed about the
necessity. 'Both the internal and external image of the
country is one of being out of control,' said Fred du Plessis,
the chairman of the Afrikaner conglomerate Sanlam who
also presides over the SA Foundation, a major spokesman
for business: 'The state of emergency was therefore a
necessary step.' 'Drastic security action was necessary,'
said the chief executive of Trust Bank, Chris van Wyk,
'but it must be accompanied by an ambitious, bold, imaginative and accelerated programme of reform.'

A few younger businessmen resisted all Botha's pressures, and even talked openly about the ANC eventually
coming to power. Tony Bloom, the young entrepreneur
who runs the Premier group of mills, bakeries and stores,
insisted in his last chairman's report that 'Negotiations
with the ANC are an historic inevitability. The question is
not whether, but rather when such negotiations will take
place.' Chris Ball, the forty-four-year-old managing director of Barclays National, the biggest bank, maintained that
most so-called extremists were 'decent people wanting the
same as the rest of us' and was on friendly terms with

Winnie Mandela. 'The only way to get away from a per-
petual state of emergency,' he told me, 'is to extend the
process of conciliation rather than restrict it.' The
supermarket-owners and retailers who depended both on
black customers and black trade unionists were openly
outraged by the arrest of union leaders with whom they
were negotiating. The most outspoken business critic of
all was Bob Tucker, the young chief executive of the SA
Permanent Building Society, who was exposed to black
conditions as legal adviser to the Urban Foundation. 'It's
tragic that business has been able to stay so aloof from
the blacks,' he said to me. 'South African capitalism is the
greediest, the most acquisitive, the most short-term, in the
world. We may be substituting economic domination for
racial discrimination – which could be even more perni-
cious.'

The emergency and the threat of sanctions had given
Botha most of the business support he had hoped for, in
his determination to stamp out the black revolt. In the
next two months the police detained over eight thousand
suspected black activists; the army moved into schools
and surrounded whole townships, while the press was
forbidden to report them. The military leaders and hawks
in the cabinet who had advised Botha to defy world opinion
had made their point, and many businessmen looked with
relief towards a new period of calm. Yet few had much
confidence that the military offensive could provide any
lasting solution. They knew that each new crackdown
would radicalise the blacks further. 'Blacks regard capitalism and the government as almost synonymous,' said
Robin Plumbridge, the conservative head of Gold Fields.
'Most of them haven't really got into the system: they're
terribly exposed to home-grown socialism.' Clive Menell,
the elegant and liberal vice-chairman of the Anglo-Vaal
group, had said that 'the vast majority of black South
Africans regard business, the government, apartheid, the
status quo and the devil as one.' 'We dare not allow the
baby of free enterprise,' said Zach de Beer, 'to be thrown

out with the bathwater of apartheid.' But many young
blacks looked forward to both baby and bathwater flooding
out; while anti-capitalist feeling in the townships was running higher than ever. 'The experience of the working class
dictates that it is too late to save the free enterprise system
in this country,' said the leader of the black mineworkers
Cyril Ramaphosa. 'The alliance between big business and
the apartheid regime has gone on too long and is soaked
with the blood of workers . . .'

The businessmen knew they were approaching an abyss,
and that they must find some way round it: but they could
not bring themselves to look down it for long. They knew
that they could not run their factories and mines for long
without the consent of the black workers, and that black
political ambitions could not be suppressed indefinitely.
Many even agreed that there could be a black government
in ten years' time. But they could not visualise any likely
transition between now and then. They were prepared to
offer blacks almost anything except the one thing they
demanded: one man, one vote. Most found it impossible
to contemplate majority rule, or to deal with the blacks
who were likely to command it.

Back in London the multinational executives, whose
companies had invested in South Africa for most of the
century, were now anxiously trying to rethink their policies
towards Pretoria; with more detachment than their
Johannesburg counterparts, but still with some dread.
'Businessmen are supposed to be trained to work with
uncertainty', said one of them at the Commonwealth
garden party, 'but we hate it.' The British Industry Committee on South Africa had just announced that 'South
Africa is approaching the edge of an abyss . . . unless
apartheid is ended soon South Africa could be plunged
into even greater chaos.' The British, like the South Africans, were very unsure how to get round the abyss, but
they were beginning to wonder more seriously: was there
really no alternative to Botha? Might they not be able to
work with a black government in the future?

Three weeks after the emergency was declared a group
of international businessmen sat down for lunch with the
African National Congress, at the Connaught Rooms in
London. It was a surprisingly relaxed encounter between
capitalists and revolutionaries who could never see each
other inside South Africa, meeting in the solidly respect-
able Masonic building dedicated to business lunches. Some
bombs had exploded that morning in central Johannesburg, but there was little sense of a tense confrontation.
Tambo had brought with him several members of the
ANC executive including Thabo Mbeki, the director of
information, and Mac Maharaj, who had spent several
years in jail on Robben Island. They sat between the
bankers and businessmen cheerfully discussing how they
might more effectively undermine apartheid and achieve
something together. At the head was Oliver Tambo, the
sixty-eight-year-old President of the ANC who looked less
like a terrorist than a reverend (which he nearly was)
or like a kindly uncle with his grey side-whiskers and
questioning eyes. Tambo was still desperately hoping that
sanctions and world pressure could avert a far more serious
bloodbath, by making apartheid unworkable: 'as the price
for maintaining the apartheid system rises', he had said the
day before, 'so will it be clear to many of these White
South Africans that the time for change has come.'* He
looked to Britain as the defender of freedom which had
stood out against Hitler and racialism; and he looked to
businessmen to bring their own pressure on both the South
African and foreign governments.

The bankers and businessmen each came with their own
perspectives and worries, as they tried to peer over the
abyss from their different viewpoints. The chairman of
the two biggest banks in South Africa, Lord Barber of
Standard and Sir Timothy Bevan of Barclays, were both
now at odds with their own prime minister and determined
to keep in touch with the black opposition. They took

* Speech to the Royal Commonwealth Society, June 23, 1986

turns to talk privately to Tambo ('do they *both* want to be bankers to the ANC?' asked one observer). Barclays had lent over a billion dollars to South Africa and had come under fire for supporting apartheid; but Bevan had been persuaded that they could not jeopardise their interests elsewhere, and he was now much more openly confronting Pretoria: Barclays would not lend a penny more, he insisted, until the bankrupt system of apartheid had been abolished. Lord Barber was a former conservative Chancellor of the Exchequer, and his bank had lent $1.5 billion, even more than Barclays, to South Africa;* but he had also been a member of the Commonwealth group reporting on South Africa, and had boldly stated that it was unreasonable to expect the ANC to renounce violence unconditionally.

The industrialists, stuck with their immovable assets on South African soil, were more cautious than the bankers. The two oil giants, Shell and BP, had built up refineries and chemical plants which had fuelled South African industry and defence over the last fifty years. BP were becoming much more concerned about Botha's policies, and had already made some contacts with the ANC. Shell was more cautious, but vulnerable, since the ANC had called for a boycott of all their filling-stations in America and Europe until they pulled out of South Africa. Only one percent of their profits came from there, against 25 percent from the United States: but Shell were proud of being able to do business in almost every country. They had been approached by a South African group to sell their interests, and were quite tempted; but they decided they should stay and 'keep chipping away' at apartheid. Shell was always reluctant to take political sides: 'We will always serve under the government, whatever it is,' said one of its top

* For details *see* John E Lind & Diane V Espaldon, *South Africa's Debt at the Time of Crisis*. San Francisco: California-Nevada Interfaith Committee on Corporate Responsibility, April 1986. *See also* next chapter

men. 'There's one thing you must never ask a multinational to do: to choose.'

Other companies at the lunch faced still more agonising choices. Consolidated Goldfields, Cecil Rhodes' old company, had been making profits for a century from its subsidiary Gold Fields of South Africa, which had friendly links with Pretoria: but the London parent had been extending its interests round the world and was now even interested in China: it had to take a longer perspective, wondering who might rule South Africa in ten years' time. The textile multinational Courtaulds had invested heavily in a wood-pulp plant to supply other Courtauld plants round the world; but it was a joint venture with the Pretoria government. Unilever, the soap-and-food group, preferred to stay aloof and take the lowest possible profile, conscious of their huge investments in black Africa and hoping that protesters would not notice their wide spread in South Africa. The Anglo-American Corporation, the most influential of all, was also lying very low; but the two most outspoken business leaders from Johannesburg, Tony Bloom of Premier and Chris Ball of Barclays National, had come to London to talk to the ANC, and to sense the British reaction.

At lunch Tambo talked quietly about the extremity of the crisis: he reminded them of President Botha's threat that he had not used a tenth of his forces, but he warned that the ANC had not, either. He explained how he and others had realised, when the first apartheid government came to power in 1948, that they were treated as foreigners in their own country. He described how they had tried to protest through passive resistance and strikes until the government used troops to break them up, and how they reluctantly decided that they could only respond with violence. But for thirty years they had been asking for sanctions to bring pressure to prevent a total confrontation. Unless the international community intervened, they would have to fight it out themselves. The businessmen must decide: would they serve apartheid, or serve the whole country?

The businessmen discussed with the ANC leaders what they might do: the two from South Africa looked to the British to help them, while the British looked to the South Africans. They asked whether the ANC could make common cause with other black leaders, particularly with the Zulu Chief Buthelezi. Lord Barber told Tambo about his talks with Mandela in jail, who had convinced him that he could bring black unity: Tambo, who had been Mandela's closest colleague in the 'fifties, interrupted him: 'Do you realise that you're the only person in this room who has met Mandela for twenty-five years?' The businessmen were clearly relieved that the revolutionaries were prepared to discuss their country's economic future calmly with Western capitalists. They all agreed that they wanted further meetings and issued a public statement saying they should all 'contribute what they can to help ensure that South Africa becomes a democratic and peaceful country'. The ANC leaders were still sceptical about the extent of the capitalists' change of heart: 'They always go running back to Botha in the end,' said one of them. But they recognised that it had been businessmen, more effectively than diplomats, who had opened up the bridge to the West; and during the lunch Tambo had arranged to see Lynda Chalker, the conservative minister in charge of Africa at the Foreign Office, later that day. It was a diplomatic breakthrough – the first time a British minister had talked with the ANC – and a few days later the State Department announced that it too was planning closer contacts. Three months later, Tambo was talking to both Sir Geoffrey Howe, the Foreign Secretary, and Chester Crocker from the State Department. It was the end of a quarter-century period when Britain and America had left the ANC out in the cold.

Across the Atlantic the big American corporations and banks were engaged in a more fundamental debate. They were under much heavier pressure from their shareholders to show that they were fighting apartheid, and to prove that capitalism was on the side of democracy and justice.

South Africa had become the new testing-ground for all the old arguments about the social responsibility of corporations. Mobil, the biggest investor, was bombarding Pretoria with statements and advertisements – its favourite artillery – and had offered a multi-million-dollar fund for black education. Coca-Cola, from its black stronghold in Atlanta, had promised another $10 million in trust funds for black welfare. General Motors, the biggest employer, had been losing money in South Africa for four years; but its chairman Roger Smith seemed committed to stick it out and show his company's concern for its black employees. But more and more corporations were giving up the two-way battle against both Afrikaners and shareholders, selling up and getting out.

Would the blacks begin to see capitalism as on the side of their freedom and democracy in this final showdown? Or would communists find the proof they had been looking for, to show that apartheid had always been the tool of the capitalists? It was a hundred-billion-dollar question, which could settle the future of half a continent. But it could not be answered in simple ideological or economic terms; for it had as much to do with people and perceptions as with hard statistics; and the story was full of twists and surprises. For years the Left had depicted the American bankers as the arch-villains who lent money to Pretoria for each new military build-up of apartheid; but it was the bankers who had made decisions, a year before Botha's crackdown, which had undermined South Africa's economic future much more drastically than any government's pressures, and as the banking crisis had unfolded it threw light on the whole relationship between South African money and politics.

2

Pulling the Plug

*The nationalist leader who is frightened of violence is
wrong if he imagines that colonialism is going to 'massacre all of us'. The military will of course go on playing
with tin soldiers which date from the time of the conquest,
but higher finance will soon bring the truth home to them.*

Frantz Fanon, *The Wretched of the Earth*, 1961

In the Chase Manhattan Plaza just off Wall Street the
chairman of the Chase, Willard Butcher, was an unlikely
choice to be the arch-enemy of apartheid in July 1985. It
had, after all, been the Chase under David Rockefeller,
the personification of capitalism, which had been reviled
by black South Africans when it had begun lending to the
Pretoria government after Sharpeville two decades earlier,
when protesters had chanted 'apartheid has a friend in
Chase Manhattan'. And when Butcher had taken over
from Rockefeller in 1981 he was seen as a more conservative and technical chairman, with none of his predecessor's
princely style. Bland and long-winded, he bored many
fellow bankers with his slow sporting clichés and saw
himself as 'an evangelist for the free market system'. He
was dedicated to catching up with Citibank, Chase's old
rival; and after the Mexican debt crisis of 1983 he was much
preoccupied with Chase's shaky loans to Latin America.
By comparison, the Chase's loans to South Africa of

$500 million, and their Johannesburg office with eighteen people, were much less important than the Latin exposure. And for Butcher and his board they were providing tiresome complications: withdrawals and shareholders' motions were damaging their business in Manhattan. Morgan Guaranty, the most aloof and discreet of all the New York banks, was already rapidly 'managing down' its South African exposure; and all the big banks were becoming more weary with the 'hassle factor' over apartheid. The Chase was the quintessential New York bank with a high visibility: South Africa accounted for less than half a percent of its total assets of $87 billion, and it was not worth the hassle.

Already by the end of 1984, as violence was building up in the black townships, the Chase was reducing its exposure to South Africa. When President Botha declared his first state of emergency on July 20 it was the last straw. The rand was already falling as investors pulled out; and New Yorkers were protesting more angrily. On July 31, the French government announced a ban on investment in South Africa: it was a hollow gesture, since the French had scarcely invested anything since the arms embargo had limited their chief exports. But on the same day Butcher and his chief executive Thomas Lebrecque decided to stop rolling over the loans to South African companies – so that they would recall credits as they came due – and to freeze all the unused lines of credit. The South Africans would thus have to repay a few hundred million dollars over the next year; and 85 percent of the American banks' loans were short-term, due to be repaid within a year.*

It was a deadly decision. 'There is no country in the world that can repay all its short-term debts, even when the proportion of short-term debts is much lower,' said the Swiss banker Fritz Leutwiler afterwards. 'That is absolutely impossible. And if one bank, such as a big American bank, starts the process then a chain reaction is almost

* Lind and Espaldon: *op. cit.*

inevitable . . . South Africa is much less important to the big US banks than a South American country. A US bank would have considered the matter many times before withdrawing from a big Latin American country.'*

It was Butcher's decision, and David Rockefeller himself (who was still chairman of the bank's advisory committee) was against it. He was concerned about apartheid, and had even talked to Oliver Tambo; but he was worried about the implications of withdrawal. Butcher's decision was taken on strictly technical grounds, with no indication of moral motives. The bank always insisted that public condemnations of foreign governments raised impossible precedents and parallels: what about loans to Russia, or Chile? South African businessmen quickly assumed that the pull-out was influenced by Hughlyn Fierce, the black banker at the Chase (whose brother worked for the Ford Foundation) who had recently been put in charge of Africa and the Middle East. But Fierce later assured them that he had nothing to do with it. Butcher continued to maintain a deadpan and technical posture; but soon afterwards he received a letter written on tattered toilet paper by a black political prisoner in South Africa, thanking the Chase. The sheets were carefully pieced together and Xeroxed, to be circulated round the bank.

When the news of the Chase's withdrawal appeared in the *Wall Street Journal* the bank never publicly confirmed, denied or explained it. While it had marched into South Africa a quarter-century earlier with a roll of drums, it now retreated in silence. But all South African businessmen knew what Butcher had done, and realised the implications: they called him the Butcher of the Rand. The currency, the rand, immediately began falling; and the Chase's decision had a snowball effect. Security Pacific followed suit immediately; other big banks, including Bankers Trust, Manufacturers Hanover and Bank of America, planned a 'phased reduction'. One big American

* Interview with *Leadership* magazine, Johannesburg, Vol. 5, 1986

bank dropped South Africa's credit-rating from B to D without stopping at C (E is bottom). The other New York banks, particularly Citibank, the biggest lenders, were furious with the Chase for 'pulling the plug' without warning. By getting out first the Chase had caused a stampede; 'they got their money', said a Citibank man, 'but at our expense. Everyone knew they could have done it gradually.' It was a bankers' saying that 'when everyone runs for the door, no one gets out'. But in the course of August the American banks withdrew about $400 million from South Africa – about a tenth of their loans.* The immediate impact was partly offset, it was thought, by Japanese banks who made short-term loans†; but the American withdrawal marked a massive loss of confidence.

American bankers were partly motivated by depositors and shareholders threatening to pull out, and by the danger of Washington imposing sanctions that could cripple their South African clients. Their worries had been compounded by the riots, raids and whippings in the townships which were being shown almost every night on the TV screens; while their children, wives and friends were adding to the chorus of protest, forcing them to talk and think about the connections between money and politics. Many politicians – particularly those opposed to government sanctions, including Reagan and Thatcher – would later point to the bankers' withdrawal as part of the wisdom of the market-place making its own judgment on apartheid. But that was a misreading of what happened. It was not the simple calculations of profit or loss, risk and reward, which had finally warned off the banks. It was the careful intervention of churches, foundations and shareholders' pressure groups which insisted, not that apartheid was unprofitable, but that it was morally intolerable. It may well have been in the banks' long-term commercial interest to withdraw: but it was the hassle, more than the numbers, which forced their decisions.

* Lind and Espaldon, p. 3
† *New York Times*, August 1, 1985

At the South African Reserve Bank at Pretoria, the donnish governor Gerhard de Kock was appalled. He rang up Butcher in New York, who seemed surprised by the furore he had caused and explained that it was part of the routine monthly revision of credit risks round the world. De Kock, he said later, 'tried to ride the storm.'* The European banks stayed in, and a few Swiss and Germans increased their loans at very high interest rates – as much as 4 percent above the normal interbank rate (LIBOR), a higher rate than Zaire. There were hopes that the falling currency would produce bargains which would attract foreign buyers back again: but they now seemed to be so worried about the political instability that they would not come back at any price. The South African banks began desperately buying dollars to repay the loans as they came due, which pushed down the rand further and made the loans more expensive; while the country's foreign currency reserves, including its gold, were falling perilously. Two years earlier Governor de Kock had been hailed as the great liberaliser of South Africa's financial markets, opening the windows to the world. Now the windows were letting in an icy gale.

As the rand fell further the South African bankers and businessmen put their faith in the promised speech of President Botha – who had so carefully cultivated them since 1979 – who was to address the opening of the National Party Congress in Durban on August 15. Rumours were circulated, and not denied, that he would make spectacular concessions including releasing Nelson Mandela. An American team, including Reagan's national security adviser Robert McFarlane and his African expert Chester Crocker, met beforehand with the South African foreign minister Pik Botha in Vienna and came away reassured and expectant. And the speech was transmitted live by satellite round the world, while brokers and exchange dealers listened to every word.

* To Charles Grant, in *Euromoney*, December 1985

It was a historic anti-climax, a harangue designed to reassure his Afrikaner supporters rather than black South Africans or the rest of the world. 'I am not prepared to lead white South Africans and other minority groups on a road to abdication and suicide,' said the President; and he reached a climax of finger-wagging by saying: 'Don't push us too far! Don't push us too far!' He talked about his country's economic health as if nothing was wrong: overspending eliminated, money supply under control, balance of payments in surplus, interest rates down, gold reserves up. He blamed the unrest on 'barbaric communist agitators' and on the foreign media, and slammed the door on Mandela.

To black South Africans the speech was an insult: 'I felt truly ashamed of being dominated and oppressed by a man of such poor quality,' Winnie Mandela complained to me afterwards. 'Can any human being imagine himself a separate entity from the rest of the world, to threaten everyone including the West? He has pushed *us* too far.' But to international bankers and businessmen the speech was equally exasperating, and the Mandelas seemed suddenly on the same side as the bankers. Overnight the speech caused a massive loss of confidence and a flight of capital; and the rand fell with a record drop.

The crunch did not come until some days after the speech on 'Black Tuesday', August 27. That morning de Kock had published his annual statement which explained how well the economy was doing: the current account surplus of R400 million (about $140 million at the morning's rate) could repay all foreign loans and other capital outflow. 'In several fundamental respects the underlying state of the economy is sounder than it was a year ago.' But during that Tuesday the Cape leader Allan Boesak had been arrested, more riots had broken out and confidence was fading further. It was impossible now to separate economic from political judgments.

That afternoon I happened by chance to be in the Johannesburg stock exchange, watching the white brokers

dealing and screaming on the floor, while three black men
on a platform chalked up the share-prices as the rand
was falling still faster. The most furious trading was in
gold-shares, which South Africans were buying to protect
themselves against the devalued currency, and which were
breaking new records. But my stockbroker companion
explained: 'The share values reflect what South Africans
are thinking: that everything is OK. The rand reflects what
the world thinks, and it's saying God Help You.' By the
close of trading on that Tuesday, the rand was worth half
its value against sterling compared to a year before. I asked
three stockbrokers just afterwards: how would the rand
react if the government were to release Mandela? One
said it would make no difference, the others insisted it
would rapidly increase confidence: 'Even the Afrikaner
brokers want him out.'

In Pretoria, while the rand was collapsing, Governor de
Kock was talking with the minister of finance Barend du
Plessis. They agreed there was only one solution: to close
the markets. 'We had to protect our banks,' de Kock
explained later. 'They did not know how many loans they
would have to repay. The German and Swiss banks were
loyally standing by us, but did not want to be the last in
the queue for repayment.' Just after trading stopped at the
stock exchange the government announced that all dealing
would be suspended for four days.

On the Sunday, September 1, du Plessis made the announcement that already seemed inevitable. South Africa
would freeze repayments on its foreign debts until the end
of the year, while still paying interest. The strict exchange
controls which Pretoria had only recently abandoned with
relief would be reintroduced, with the 'financial rand' –
through which shares were bought and sold – selling at a
discount compared to the 'commercial rand' for trade and
domestic transactions. South Africa, in spite of all its
economic prospects, gold exports and industrial resources,
was now suddenly in a state of virtual default like the most
unreliable Latin American debtor, with a credit-rating

near the bottom of the league. The President's confident claims two weeks earlier were meaningless. From now on, the Republic had lost nearly all its charms to foreign investors. 'The unrest is now so serious,' wrote the cold-blooded Lex in the *Financial Times* on September 2, 'that decisions to lend to, or invest in, South Africa are not just based on moral scruples: they are hard to justify by any measure of risk and reward.'

De Kock immediately set off on a thirteen-day tour of America and Europe, visiting nineteen bank chairmen, four central banks and the IMF and the State Department in Washington, to negotiate an emergency loan, falling back on gold reserves to provide extra credit. The spectacle of the central banker rushing round Western capitals cap in hand hardly accorded with the proud Afrikaner legend of defying foreign critics by retreating 'back to the laager'. And the worries in Pretoria about the economic collapse were already undermining the recurring arguments that sanctions would have no effect, or would simply compel South Africa to become self-sufficient. 'We will always need foreign capital,' said Clive Menell the vice-chairman of Anglo-Vaal, 'and the technology that it brings with it.' 'It's the lack of capital which really hurts us,' said Mike Rosholt the chairman of Barlow Rand. The 'capital boycott' by foreign bankers was soon proving more devastating and fast-acting than anything Western governments were planning: even Afrikaner capitalists could not ignore this harsh equation between politics and money.

It was a double irony. 'Those whom the far Left would call apartheid's best friends, the pillars of its financial entrenchment, have hit us where it hurts most,' said Nigel Bruce, the editor of the conservative *Business Day*: 'In our ability to finance immediate economic growth consistent with a rapidly rising black birth rate.'* And campaigners against apartheid were surprised to find that their old capitalist enemies were now their best allies. 'Who

* Nigel Bruce, *Leadership*, 1985

would have thought,' said the editor of *International Reports*, Andrew Hilton, giving evidence to the UN in New York, 'that decisions taken – probably in haste – by two US banks not to roll over trade lines would have forced the South African government on the defensive in a way that decades of pressure by this institution had failed to achieve?'*

On his world tour, de Kock soon painfully discovered how rapidly his country had become a bankers' pariah. In New York he first called on Citibank in Park Avenue on August 30, where he regarded Bill Rhodes, their tireless master-negotiator and rescheduler of debts, as his 'mentor and teacher'. But Citibank's chairman John Reed was wary of any public association: he himself, when he was running Citibank's consumer division under his right-wing predecessor Walter Wriston, had resisted pressure to expand in South Africa. Citibank was furious with Chase for having pulled the plug and started the whole panic; but as the biggest American lender to South Africa and the only bank which took local deposits it felt yet more vulnerable to New Yorkers' protests. The last thing Citibankers wanted was to be seen to help Pretoria out of its fix. 'We told him Pretoria must change its politics first,' said one of them; and soon afterwards two senior Citibankers, Hans Angermuller and Bill Koplowitz, went out to visit South Africa and came back more worried.

Nearly everywhere de Kock was treated as if he had the plague. In Washington de Larosiere of the IMF said that they were short of liquidity, and they could only lend for balance-of-payments problems. Even the Swiss cold-shouldered him: Pierre Languetin of the Swiss National Bank went to the extraordinary length of officially denying a report that he had seen him. In London no banker wanted to be seen at a meeting with him, and Rothschild's

* United Nations, New York: public hearings on the activities of Transnational Corporations in South Africa and Namibia, September 16, 1985

(whose chairman Evelyn de Rothschild was a director of De Beers) only met him very discreetly. The governor of the Bank of England, Robin Leigh-Pemberton, would not see him and the British government made it known that he had received no help. 'De Kock seemed to have been pole-axed,' said one senior Bank of England director. 'We thought he was quite internationally-minded when he was a director of the IMF. But he never seemed to have realised how isolated Pretoria had become.' And whenever de Kock or any South African officials were asked what kind of concessions the West wanted, the same words came back: release Mandela, release Mandela. It was a weird equation: the man who had been in jail for a quarter-century, whose party, writings and photograph were banned in the Republic, who was condemned by the State President as a terrorist and a communist, was now seen as the only key to unlock the billions on which the state depended for its future expansion.

On the face of it South Africa was in a far healthier state than most developing countries in debt: it had a current-account surplus of $2 billion a year, and its debts were not out of scale with its exports – half of them gold. But this performance was totally overshadowed by the political hazards for the bankers, both in the Republic and at home. 'Last year our political situation was good,' complained the finance minister du Plessis, 'but the economy was completely overheated . . . Yet in one morning I could borrow a billion dollars. This year it's just the opposite.'*

Back in Pretoria, de Kock faced many recriminations as the crisis revealed how inadequate were the central banks' controls and information. Two years before he had encouraged South African companies to borrow short-term in dollars abroad, at lower interest rates than locally: now the short-term debts were coming due, and proved bigger than he thought – $14 billion instead of $12 billion – while

* *Wall Street Journal*, October 22, 1985

the dollars were far more expensive to repay. De Kock had been praised for liberalising the financial markets; but now all the liberalisation had turned against him. The foreign branches of South African banks (as the Bank of England had warned him a year before) turned out to be raising loans for their headquarters banks, thus increasing the exposure. 'Ripples from the rest of the world,' said Chris van Wyk of Trust Bank, 'are tidal waves when they hit Johannesburg.' 'It's hard to find a banker in Johannesburg', wrote Charles Grant of *Euromoney*, visiting South Africa after the crash, 'who doesn't blame this fervent advocate of free enterprise markets for at least some of the debt crisis.' Nedbank, the biggest Afrikaner bank which a year before was admired as 'South Africa's international bank', was now in severe difficulties with its over-adventurous foreign branches. It had rashly banked on the rand recovering, to the point of reaching parity with the dollar; and as the rand sank further de Kock had to write a 'letter of comfort' promising that the Reserve Bank stood behind its branches – which meant providing more dollars. Nedbank never really recovered from the loss of confidence: its share-price collapsed, and its chief executive Rob Abrahamsen eventually resigned in March 1986.

De Kock was now desperate to find a respected negotiator who could mediate between his government and the twenty-nine main creditor banks, who were refusing to join any committee to deal directly with the South Africans. After an anxious search the Union Bank of Switzerland, which was much involved in gold deals with South Africa, proposed Fritz Leutwiler, the former president of the Swiss National Bank who had become chairman of the Swiss engineering group Brown Boveri. Leutwiler liked South Africa which he had first visited seven years before, and had become friendly with the former finance minister Owen Horwood. He asked the President of Switzerland, whom he knew well, whether negotiating for South Africa would damage his country; he said no, and Leutwiler agreed. Pretoria would pay expenses for him and two

assistants, which included work to be done for him by
Price Waterhouse and Partners.

Leutwiler was well-known as a very sound central
banker: his first job at the age of twenty-four had been as
secretary for the Association for a Sound Currency. But
his experience was limited to high finance, and he was not
politically sophisticated. He faced an appalling assignment
which he only accepted, said de Kock, 'out of a sense of
responsibility for the international banking system.' The
tensions between the bankers were hard enough: the Europeans were furious with the Chase and other Americans
for beginning the panic; the Swiss and Germans criticised
the British for political bias, while the Swiss were blamed
as usual for making money out of the crisis. The Swiss
were delicately but profitably placed. They were insistently
neutral, refusing to talk the language of morality, not
wanting to favour any one nation. But they were the biggest
lenders to South Africa per head of their population; and
their three biggest banks had lent one percent of their
assets to South Africa – as high a ratio as Barclays in
Britain.* The Swiss also profited from laundering South
African funds illegally leaving the country, thus easing the
capital flight which was a major part of Pretoria's problem.
They could make money both from the hole in the bucket,
and from filling it up. But even the Swiss were now forced
to make some political linkage; and Max Kuhne, managing
director of the Swiss Bank Corporation, said that the banks
were eager for genuine political reform in return for a
rescheduling agreement.† Nor was Leutwiler himself
altogether politically immune: the Brown Boveri Company
had important contracts in developing countries including
China; and Beijing had politely made clear that they had
noticed that the chairman was involving himself with white
South Africa.

Pretoria was now taking a high moral line. At the annual

* Lind and Espaldon, *op. cit.*, p. 16
† *International Herald Tribune*, November 16, 1985

IMF meeting in Seoul, South Korea, in October officials
explained that the West had a duty to continue lending,
for the sake of the blacks, and half of Africa was dependent
on them: 'There is no way in which sub-Saharan Africa
can develop in the next ten years,' warned de Kock, 'unless
the Republic of South Africa is part and parcel of the
action.' The finance minister du Plessis warned about 'the
threat to the integrity of the present international financial
system', and stressed the need for South Africa to develop.

> If ever there was a time when man's morality should
> match his technology, it is now. If ever his compassion
> was to be equal to his skills in material goods and wealth,
> the time is now. The challenge to those who have lies in
> caring sufficiently to share their knowledge and other
> resources and to materially assist developing nations on
> the road to sustainable economic growth, with due re-
> gard to their dignity and self-respect.

Leutwiler was soon in a hornet's nest. His first task was to
try to call a meeting of the twenty-nine main creditor banks
– who remained fearful even to be seen with a South
African – which he eventually fixed in London on October
23. The anti-apartheid protesters were now beginning to
see their old villains the bankers as potential allies who
could be lobbied individually. From London Father Trevor
Huddleston, as president of the Anti-Apartheid Movement, wrote personally from his office in Mandela Street
to the British banks to warn them that there could be no
peace and stability until apartheid was abolished, and to
ask them not to attend the meeting. From Johannesburg
Bishop Tutu and Beyers Naude of the South African
Council of Churches asked the bankers hopefully to 'make
rescheduling of South Africa's debt conditional upon the
resignation of the present regime and its replacement by
an interim government responsive to the needs of all South
Africa's people'. The bank chairmen all politely agreed
with Huddleston about the evils of apartheid, and several

explained how they were working for peaceful change. But they turned up to Leutwiler's meeting.

The bankers officially said nothing about politics, but in fact they made clear to Leutwiler that they 'expected some positive political signals from Pretoria' and he knew he could not evade politics.* The South African team headed by the Afrikaner Chris Stahls stressed that exporting capital would make the blacks poorer, and explained the impossibility of repaying $14.3 billion within a year. But the bankers could reach no agreement, and postponed any decision. 'Looking at this as an economist you'd say there's no problem,' de Kock said the next week in Pretoria. 'But because of political considerations it was a very difficult meeting to handle. The banks can't be seen as helping South Africa because it would be seen as propping up apartheid.'†

The bankers were now in a critical position. They had asserted their formidable negative power, by withdrawing support from the apartheid regime; could they go further and assert a positive power by encouraging a non-racial alternative? Some opponents of apartheid now thought they had a unique opportunity. 'Should they not say,' asked Robert McNamara, the former President of the World Bank, 'today we are very reluctant to put new funds at risk in that country, but we would take a quite different attitude were the government to move towards a more stable situation by beginning to negotiate with the blacks for their participation in the political process?'‡ All eyes were on Leutwiler, who now appeared to have more political leverage on Pretoria than all the world's governments and do-gooders; for he controlled the one thing that President Botha really needed – money. And Botha himself said that 'debt is our only problem', though he was still amazingly ignorant of the laws of economics. (When in

* *Leadership*, p. 14
† To Steve Mufson of the *Wall Street Journal*, October 30, 1985
‡ Interview with author, October 1985

October one economic journalist asked him how he explained the collapse of the rand he explained it was because of the strength of the dollar – even though the dollar had just suffered a precipitate decline.)

Leutwiler certainly seemed to be trying to bring his own pressure with an outspokenness unusual for a Swiss banker. On Swiss television he complained on November 15 that Pretoria's repression was 'the very opposite of what I had hoped for' and that restricting the media was 'the most stupid thing the government could have done.'* There was no prospect of an agreement, he told a Swiss newspaper, unless there was a 'positive statement at the highest level . . . If South Africa delays much longer certain clients, particularly those of American, British and other banks, will say they will be satisfied only by the principle of one man, one vote.'† And the bankers' pressure seemed to be taking some effect: in Johannesburg de Kock for the first time made a direct link between the financial and political crisis, telling a banquet of businessmen that foreign bankers were viewing South Africa as in the throes of 'an Iranian-type, pre-revolutionary situation', and warned that 'unless improvements are effected, South Africa may have to remain a capital-exporting country for some time'. De Kock was now vigorously defending the open international economy against Afrikaners who seemed prepared for South Africa to retreat into autarchy. 'All the measures that will contribute to South Africa's isolation and tend to turn it into a siege economy,' said de Kock, 'should be opposed.' The rand was falling again, but the South African team of bankers still hopefully put forward a proposal for a 'multi-year rescheduling', which meant that they would not repay any money until 1990. Leutwiler passed on their plan to the bankers in New York, who were appalled by the South Africans' arrogance and cross with Leutwiler for even distributing the

---

* *International Herald Tribune*, November 16, 1985
† Zurich: *Tages Anzeiger*, November 14, 1985

proposal. By the beginning of December the rand was down to thirty-five cents, close to its bottom on Black Tuesday: and Pretoria had to introduce new rules by which the Reserve Bank would pay the gold mines in rand, not dollars.

In the New Year Leutwiler went out to South Africa to try to persuade the South Africans to take a different approach. He insisted that Pretoria must repay some money quickly to show goodwill and must offer a generous interest rate of one percent above the existing high rate – particularly to satisfy the American banks – in view of the political risk. 'I could not run the risk of a refusal of my proposal by the banks,' he said later. He talked at length with the President who assured him that his next major speech, at the opening of parliament at the end of January, would propose much more definite reforms than his August 'Rubicon' speech. South African businessmen were once again waiting in hope for Botha, and the tobacco king Anton Rupert publicly pleaded with him, quoting the Swiss theologian-soldier Zwingli: 'For God's sake, do something brave.'

Leutwiler was now visibly turning. He said that Botha's reforms – which he had seen in a draft of the speech – were 'a helluva programme'. He had stopped warning Pretoria and was now trying to reassure his banker-clients. In South Africa he talked to twenty people chosen by de Kock, including the Zulu leader Chief Buthelezi whom he had already met in Switzerland. Leutwiler had some criticisms of apartheid, particularly of the long journeys which blacks had to make to get to the factories; but he refused to meet Oliver Tambo or any members of the African National Congress, arguing that they had admitted receiving arms from the Soviet Union, 'which doesn't make gifts for nothing'. 'I'm reluctant to shake hands with a communist without counting my fingers afterwards,' he said. 'I don't trust them. My impression of the ANC is that it does not represent the blacks.'* It was a surprising

* *Leadership*, p. 14

refusal, in the light of the insistence by many bankers, and even by Thatcher and Reagan, that releasing the leader of the ANC was a pre-condition for a peaceful settlement. Leutwiler even claimed that the businessmen who visited the ANC in Lusaka now regretted their visit, though one of them, Tony Bloom of Premier, promptly contradicted him: 'The talks were not a mistake, and the door remains open for future meetings.'

Leutwiler left South Africa convinced, he said, 'that positive signals will be given in the not-too-distant future', and he prepared optimistically for a further meeting of the creditor banks in February. He appeared now to have discarded his leverage and to have reversed the previous insistence of political reforms first, money afterwards. 'The world needs South Africa,' he explained, 'and South Africa needs a healthy economy as a prerequisite of further political reforms.'

Botha's speech to parliament in January was totally different in tone to his provocative harangue five months before: it might have been written for the bankers, and it confirmed some hopes for genuine reforms, including abolishing the hated pass-laws. The contrast between the two speeches in itself appeared a tribute to the power of the bankers. But it soon turned out to be much less promising and specific than Leutwiler had suggested, and it was followed by an open row with the foreign minister Pik Botha which made it look still less promising. Leutwiler was disappointed, particularly after the leader of the opposition Van Zyl Slabbert had precipitately resigned in despair of the white parliament. But he partly blamed the media: 'One thing is clear. South Africa should improve its PR.' He prepared new proposals for the next meeting in London on February 20 with the bankers, who were now anxious to settle and receive at least some money up front; and he sent the proposals to them ten days beforehand saying 'take it or leave it'. The South African political atmosphere was still explosive, while the Johannesburg township of Alexandra was becoming a new and bloody

battlefield: and before the meeting the churchmen Tutu
and Naude, together with Allan Boesak, stepped up their
terms for the bankers: they now wanted not only the white
government's resignation, but the seizing of South Africa's
assets abroad, including aircraft and ships.

Leutwiler faced a nerve-racking meeting. The Americans wanted more than 5 percent up front, and many
bankers wanted better terms on the interest rate. Leutwiler
insisted that South Africa could not afford more: he would
walk out if the proposals were not accepted. He had
warned the South Africans that if they defied the banks
and tried to be self-sufficient 'there would be a lot of court
cases: South African aircraft would be attached, likewise
ships. The lawyers would be happy and extremely busy.'*
Eventually the bankers agreed to Leutwiler's plan. Pretoria would repay $500 million over the next year, while
the other 95 percent of the frozen debt would be 'rolled
over' pending a reassessment after twelve months – a
stipulation on which Leutwiler insisted, which was to hang
over Pretoria like a black cloud. Leutwiler issued a statement that the banks had reached a 'broad consensus', and
later sounded confident that the banks would keep up the
political pressure. 'Within these twelve months something
must happen,' he said on British television the following
Sunday. 'Promises must be delivered and implemented.'
And he warned Botha: 'If he does not deliver reforms, my
patience is limited and so I think is the bankers' patience.'†

The deal was agreed, but far from settled: American
banks quickly complained that there was no such 'broad
consensus', and that they had been steamrollered: they
dreaded the next round of annual meetings, where the
protesting shareholders, having tasted political blood,
would step up their attacks. The bankers, as the *Financial
Times* warned, now had to live with a new fact of life: 'This
reality is the unexpected emergence of the banking system

---

* TV Channel 4, London: Business Programme, February 23, 1986
† *Ibid.*

as a conduit for the US public's attitude towards the situation in South Africa. It has allowed shareholders, depositors and the public directly to impose an economic sanction without having to persuade their government to do so.'*

Leutwiler himself lay low, but he was soon further disillusioned by Botha and told him (it was rumoured) that he must get down to talking to the black leaders. In July 1986 a colleague announced that Leutwiler had given up his mandate because of his disappointment at the new state of emergency: Leutwiler promptly denied it but made it known that Botha had let him down by not pushing ahead with his promised reforms.† In the meantime South Africa's prospects of repaying her debts looked more doubtful with sanctions overhanging them; and confidence was not increased when the ambassador to London Denis Worrall warned that South Africa might renege on its debts if sanctions were imposed.

Even Barclays Bank in London – which half-owned Barclays National, the biggest bank in South Africa, and which had so long stonewalled against shareholders' complaints – was now rapidly changing ground. Its chairman Sir Timothy Bevan was cautious and conservative, but he was fed up with losing student accounts and personally outraged by Botha's policy. By the middle of 1985 he and his board, including his future successor as chairman John Quinton, were doubtful whether their South African business was worth the odium: they were longing to remove their name from the blue signs in South African branches, and were still more embarrassed when Barclays National advertised in Britain for computer specialists with the slogan: 'Fill in your passport to a lifestyle of your dreams.'‡

Barclays became bolder in their contacts with black

----

* *Financial Times*, February 19, 1986
† *Financial Times*, March 9, 1987
‡ See 'Barclays Shadow Report 1986', published by End Loans to South Africa, P.O. Box 686 London NW5

leaders, and after talking with Tambo were more reassured
about the prospects under a future black government. By
November 1985 Sir Timothy had become more open,
explaining that Barclays had talked to the ANC and attacking apartheid as 'repugnant, wrong, unchristian and unworkable'. Then in March 1986, just after Leutwiler's last
meeting, Sir Timothy produced his annual report with the
comment at the end:

> Our policy on further lendings to South Africa is quite
> simple: we shall commit no new money to that country
> nor shall we be party to any formal debt rescheduling
> until South Africa has demonstrated its ability to reduce
> its indebtedness and meet its obligations and until there
> are changes which confirm an end to the bankrupt policy
> of institutionalised racial discrimination.

> But the present moratorium does mean that the prob-
> ability of South Africa receiving the benefit of foreign
> capital inflow is virtually non-existent and without inflow
> it will be increasingly difficult for South Africa to pro-
> mote economic growth to employ the ever-growing non-
> white population.

It was the nearest any bank had come to spelling out the
total connection between politics and money, including
the terrible bankers' word '*bankrupt*'. They would not lend
a penny more unless the policy was changed; and without
new money, South Africa was facing catastrophe.

Would the blacks, then, come to see capitalism as on the
side of their freedom in South Africa? Certainly the world's
bankers had travelled far since the seventies, when they
had encouraged investment and repeatedly disowned political or moral responsibility. The long collaboration between international finance and apartheid, which had its
first roots in the diamond and gold fields a century earlier,
had now come to a very dead end. The financial world
appeared to have experienced a very sudden disillusion;

and President Reagan claimed in his speech in August 1986 that 'the market-place has been sending unmistakable signals of its own' about the wrongness of apartheid. South African businessmen, for their part, were appalled by what they depicted as the irresponsibility of the bankers. 'More by accident, it seems, than by design,' said Gavin Relly, the new chairman of Anglo-American, 'the international banking community may itself be in the process of bringing about the economic wasteland of South Africa.'* Many ironies remained after the bankers' turnabout: while Pretoria was accusing the ANC of being communists, the ANC was looking to the capitalists to exert pressure and avert a bloodbath; and as sanctions moved forward, President Botha began to sound even more hostile to Western capitalists than to Eastern communists.

It was another matter to persuade the young 'comrades' and schoolboys in the black townships that capitalism was on their side; and the market-place was never as consistent or as logical as Reagan suggested. As the South African crisis worsened through 1986 the markets made new twists. Within South Africa, the less confidence investors had in the future of industry, and the higher the inflation, the more they put money in the stock market which reached new peaks; while new doubts about the world economy – together with the fears about South Africa itself – helped to push up the price of gold, which in turn pushed up the currency and improved Pretoria's prospects of repaying her debts. Gold which had so suddenly created the country's wealth a century ago, and which still made up half its exports, still had some new surprises up its sleeve.

And behind many of the bankers' calculations there was, in truth, a fearful pessimism. They had pulled the plug and turned off the taps but they could not bring themselves to support any alternative solution or power; privately they talked only about chaos and bloodshed. Three months after Leutwiler's agreement, before a new state of emer-

* *Guardian*, October 7, 1985

gency, old Lex in the *Financial Times* uttered a devastating analysis of how the 'banking parlours will commemorate a decade in which the South African experiment well and truly fell to bits'. It concluded 'the numbers are suggesting that the financial community will sit on its hands, with its capital written off, until South Africa and half a continent slide away'.*

Had the South African experiment totally collapsed? Were the bankers now dealing with a nation, or only with an accidental combination of peoples and forces which had never really coalesced? Since its union in 1910, South Africa had always had an uncertain identity, like so many subsequent African states. Its three main components were always at odds. The English-speaking capitalists who first developed its gold and diamonds had little contact with either the Afrikaner settlers or with the black tribesmen whom they lured into their mines. The Afrikaners had remained a separate tribe, more separate than the Zulus or Xhosas; while the blacks who made up the vast majority were kept outside the democratic system, without votes or rights.

The generation of older leaders from these three components, whose lives had spanned most of their country's history, had little contact with each other. President Botha, whose father fought in the Boer War, had little in common with Harry Oppenheimer, whose father had emigrated from London to build up Anglo-American, the biggest corporation in the country. Oliver Tambo, who had run the ANC for the last quarter-century, had never met either Botha or Oppenheimer. Individuals from the different groups were more likely to see each other in New York or London than in their own country. It was like an atlas where the roads only met off the map. Each of these three men could look back on their own proud journey, but with no certainty that their paths would eventually meet.

* *Financial Times*, June 2, 1986

3

Capitalists against Nationalists

Nowhere in the world has there ever existed so concentrated a form of capitalism as that represented by the financial power of the mining houses in South Africa, and nowhere else does that power so completely realise and enforce the need of controlling politics.

J A Hobson, *The Evolution of Modern Capitalism*,
1930

Few existing multinational corporations can claim more extraordinary origins than the Anglo-American Corporation and its sister company De Beers which was founded twenty-two years before South Africa itself. Few businesses have been so dominated by single individuals – first by Cecil Rhodes, later by Ernest Oppenheimer and his son Harry. The Oppenheimers were chairmen of Anglo-American for sixty-five years. Today Harry Oppenheimer can look back on a country which is only two years older than himself, which has grown up in uneasy partnership with the corporation that controls a large slice of its wealth.

Among all the social transformations wrought by capital and industry in the nineteenth century, none was so abrupt, with such extremes of poverty and wealth, as the discovery of diamonds and gold in South Africa. Up till 1867 the white colonies and republics at the bottom of the continent

were predominantly rural communities, clustered round
the ports like Cape Town and Durban, with a few isolated
towns like Pretoria or Bloemfontein: only sixty-five miles
of railway ventured inland from the coast. The Republic
of the Transvaal had only a few thousand Afrikaners, who
had trekked up from the coast to escape British liberalism,
subduing black tribes on the way. Most of the black farmers
had never seen white men. The settlements of Southern
Africa were far less prosperous than the rich lands of
Australia and New Zealand; and the chief importance of
Cape Town, before the opening of the Suez Canal, was as
a coaling station on the way to India.

But the discovery of diamonds in 1867 in 'New Rush' –
soon to be renamed Kimberley – 500 miles inland from
Cape Town, brought a stampede of adventurers and international money which transformed the tiny settlement and
the surrounding black tribes. (It was two years after the
American civil war had ended, and a year after the Civil
Rights Bill for black Americans had passed through Congress.) The corrugated-iron diamond town became one of
the new wonders of the world. 'A city in the desert,' as
the geographer Morton described it in 1877, 'dropped, as
it were, from the clouds, so detached does it seem from
all the ordinary surroundings of civilised communities. A
city of tent-cloth and corrugated iron, and here and there
substantial brick.'[*]

It was an essentially white city. The diggers were determined to exclude blacks from the digging, complaining
that they stole the stones. They burnt their tents, flogged
them if they tried to dig and imposed a system of passes
to keep them out of the fields, against protests from the
Colonial Office in London. Soon blacks were only allowed
to work on the fields as labourers or servants, and the
colour bar was built into the diggers' society. But the
diggers still needed thousands of workers and began to

---

[*] Morton: *South African Diamond Fields*, Proceedings of the
American Geographical Society, 1877

lure blacks from surrounding tribes, who were encouraged
by their chiefs to work in Kimberley to earn money to buy
guns. The diamond fields soon gave European travellers a
very different glimpse of Africa from the pastoral accounts
of missionaries and explorers. When Anthony Trollope
visited Kimberley in 1878, he was fascinated by the transformation. 'This black man, whose body is only partially
and most grotesquely clad, and who is what we mean when
we speak of a Savage, earns more than the average rural
labourer in England.' He was struck by the capacity of the
blacks to work and to become part of a disciplined and
civilised society: unlike savages elsewhere in the British
Empire they were not 'perishing while we have been considering how we might best deal with them. Here, in South
Africa, a healthy nation remains and assures us by its
prolific tendency that when protected from self-destruction
by our fostering care it will spread and increase beneath
our hands.' But Trollope ridiculed the idea that blacks, or
'Kafirs', would soon become entitled to vote under the
liberal franchise of the Cape Colony. 'The suggestion
that the "Kafir" should have a vote,' wrote Trollope, 'is
received by Europeans in South Africa simply with a
smile.'*

It was this abrupt conjunction of peoples which provided
the origins of the first major international corporation in
Southern Africa, when in 1888 the rival miners and dealers
were amalgamated into a single diamond monopoly, De
Beers Consolidated Mines, which for the next century
would remain one of the most successful cartels in the
world. It was the creation of the most famous of all imperial
entrepreneurs, Cecil Rhodes, who saw it from the beginning as an instrument to extend British domination over
the whole continent. The character of Rhodes – with his
combination of shrewdness and adolescence, romanticism
and ruthlessness, imagination and vulgarity – has eluded

* Anthony Trollope, *South Africa*, London, Chapman and Hall 1878,
pp. 158–89

all his biographers. As Geoffrey Wheatcroft describes it: 'The looming gap between his deeds and his unfathomable personality remains.'* But the myth of Rhodes remained potent for both admirers and haters, and he came to personify the capitalist imperialism of the late nineteenth century. He was part of the intricate financial mechanism which channelled the surplus capital of the late Victorians to develop vast tracts of territory, and turned the savings of small investors into 'red on the map'. 'Every man has his foible,' said Lord Milner. 'Rhodes' foible was size.'

In purely financial terms De Beers was small compared to Rockefeller's Standard Oil Trust formed in 1882, six years before the De Beers monopoly. But De Beers was far richer and more powerful compared to the country which it helped to transform. Fifteen years after diamonds were discovered South Africa had 1,620 miles of railway connecting Kimberley to the ports of Cape Town and Port Elizabeth. Finance was closely interlocked with politics and military force: De Beers' original trust deed gave Rhodes the ability to invade the territories to the North which soon bore his name; while by 1890 he was also prime minister of the Cape Colony.

Kimberley itself set a pattern for total segregation which few visitors challenged. The whites had their own village called Kenilworth, which Rhodes had planned as his special hobby, planted with eucalyptus trees, shrubs and vines and equipped with a club-house, billiard-rooms and reading-rooms. The black workers lived in the compounds, specially devised to prevent diamond smuggling with the help of elaborate inspections. Lord Randolph Churchill who visited the diamond fields in 1891 described how 'stark naked, they then proceed to the searching room, where their mouths, their hair, their toes, their armpits, and every portion of their body are subject to an elaborate examination. White men would never submit to such a

* Geoffrey Wheatcroft, *The Randlords*, London, Weidenfeld & Nicolson, 1985, p. 283

process, but the native sustains the indignity with cheerful equanimity, considering only the high wages which he earns.'*

Ten years after the discovery of diamonds a prospector, George Harrison, had made a far more important discovery of gold on the Witwatersrand or 'ridge of the white waters' near Johannesburg, 250 miles from Kimberley. In the subsequent gold-rush prospectors and entrepreneurs raced to Johannesburg, buying up farms and staking out claims. Three years later, just when the gold seemed to be running out, the discovery of deep-level gold opened up limitless prospects. The gold-rush on the Witwatersrand (or 'The Rand') unlike Klondyke or Yukon, had come to stay; and gold, unlike diamonds, could be mined indefinitely without depressing the price. Johannesburg was at first largely financed from Kimberley, but the deep-level mining required a continuing flow of capital from the rest of the world. Two great finance houses straddled both diamonds and gold. Cecil Rhodes was chairman both of De Beers and of Consolidated Gold Fields which produced about a tenth of the gold. But the real gold giant was the partnership of the two Germans, Julius Wernher and Alfred Beit, with their Johannesburg partner Hermann Eckstein, working through their partnership Wernher, Beit, which became known as the 'Corner House'. Beit, who had already helped to put together De Beers, was the financial genius who foresaw the full prospects of the Rand, raised money through Rothschilds in Germany and France and put together the new company Rand Mines which boldly bought up land in anticipation of the deep levels. It was Beit who dealt Rhodes into his company, thus setting a pattern of interlocking ownerships ('Rhodes' brains are not to be despised,' he wrote, 'and if we had interests apart from theirs there would always be friction'). The Corner House and Rand Mines, which later merged into Central

* Lord Randolph Churchill, *Men, Mines, and Animals in South Africa*, London, Sampson Low, 1893, pp. 45ff

Mining, became the central engine of South African capital, with its own intelligence system, its political nominees, and its newspaper, the *Star*.*

The gold millionaires in Johannesburg acquired fortunes which, if not on the scale of Rockefeller or Vanderbilt, brought a new stimulus to European stockmarkets. Their London offices attracted the same kind of excitement as railway shares forty years earlier – with far less knowledge of the underlying conditions; the word *Kaffirs* was soon used to describe the shares rather than the people who worked behind them ('Tintos climbed to 12¼ and even Kaffirs raised their sickly head' 1889). The mine-owners brought an ostentatious new wealth to London as well as Johannesburg, acquiring Park Lane mansions, racehorses and country houses, and even penetrating the 'Marlborough House Circle' of the Prince of Wales which in the 1890s was 'galvanized by a spectacular infusion of new wealth from the gold and diamond mines of South Africa'.† In 1902 a popular new musical in London, *The Girl Kays*, featured a vulgar South African mine magnate called Hoggenheimer of Park Lane who was to take his own nasty place in Afrikaner mythology.‡

The mine-owners needed far more black workers on the Rand than in Kimberley, particularly in the deep-level mines. They naturally wanted to use the cheapest workers available and they had no interest in protecting the jobs of the more expensive white miners. When the white miners pressed for a colour bar the Chamber of Mines opposed it, but they could not prevent the Transvaal passing the first statutory colour bar in 1893.§ Thus from the beginning, the mine-owners were not necessarily in

* A P Cartwright, *The Corner House*, London, Macdonald, 1965, pp. 61–131
† Philip Magnus, *King Edward the Seventh*, London, John Murray, 1964, p. 245–6
‡ *Standard Encyclopaedia of Southern Africa*, Vol. V, pp. 559–60
§ Merle Lipton, *Capitalism and Apartheid*, London, Gower Temple Smith, 1985, p. 112

favour of discrimination, as Merle Lipton points out in her analysis of capitalism and apartheid. But they did impose rigid segregation through the compound system they had devised in Kimberley to accommodate migrant workers, which helped to conceal the 'native problem'. John Hays Hammond, Rhodes' American engineer, objected to the dependence on migrant workers: 'In order to ensure a permanent supply of efficient miners, I suggested to Rhodes we establish native villages near the mines, where boys could live with their wives and families.'* But the other mine-owners did not approve, and it was many years before they were to face the political consequences of the workforce they had created.

The mine magnates soon found that doing business in Johannesburg had one fundamental difference from Kimberley; they were not now in the British Cape Colony, but in the Transvaal Republic, ruled by 50,000 Afrikaners who had little connection or sympathy with the booming new industry. The British had briefly annexed the Transvaal in 1877 but after bitter fighting in the First Boer War they gave it back four years later to the Afrikaners, who were all the more determined to resist British influences. The rugged biblical figure of their leader Paul Kruger, with his top hat and wide beard, became a symbol of stubborn intransigence, a much more formidable tribal chief than any black leader. Kruger saw himself in the Old Testament, leading a chosen people who were facing ungodly invaders. To Barney Barnato, the most flamboyant of the mine-owners, the Transvaal government was 'an unlimited company of some 20,000 shareholders'.† To Kruger the mine-owners were representatives of the devil. 'Every ounce of gold taken from the bowels of our soil,' he said, 'will yet have to be weighed against rivers of tears.' Yet Kruger was quite content to exploit them, and well aware

* The autobiography of John Hays Hammond, New York, Farrar and Reinhart, 1936, Vol. 1, p. 304
    † Paul Emden, *Randlords*, Hodder & Stoughton, 1935, p. 142

of the importance of capital: in 1890 he encouraged the setting up of the National Bank in Pretoria to conduct the banking business of the Transvaal government: Kruger himself laid the foundation stone and was photographed surrounded by the early staff.*

The contrast between the foreigners or Uitlanders in Johannesburg – English, German, American, Jewish – and the Afrikaners in their capital in Pretoria thirty miles north was obvious to every visitor, as it has been ever since. The millionaires who had been largely unrestricted in Kimberley found it intolerable to be subject to taxes, monopolies, delays and obstruction from a backward foreign people; and most British visitors agreed with them. When Randolph Churchill arrived in Johannesburg he was fascinated by the manifestation of the power of money (all the more, no doubt, because he was a shareholder in gold mines): 'one is confirmed in the belief that there is nothing that money cannot do.' But he complained that 'if this country had been in the hands of the English or the Americans it would probably now be peopled by some millions of Europeans . . . but Providence has cursed it with the rule of 50,000 Boers, and for a time, but I expect only for a time, it is destined still to languish.'†

By the 1890s the tension between Pretoria and Johannesburg was reaching breaking point after Kruger had introduced a new law which required foreigners to wait fourteen years before getting the vote. In 1895 the mine-owners plotted – in the office of Rhodes' Consolidated Goldfields – to take the law into their own hands, with tacit encouragement from the Colonial Secretary in London, Joe Chamberlain. Rhodes, Beit and the other mine-owners financed an armed raid to capture Johannesburg, led by Dr Leander Jameson. The raid was foiled and the Afrikaners captured its leaders, imposing heavy fines and sending them to London for a spectacular trial, after which Rhodes

---

* Barclays International: A Banking Centenary, 1938
† Churchill, pp. 58–91

and his colleagues were briefly disgraced. The Jameson
Raid was seen by British liberals as an unforgivable blunder
– while later liberals speculated whether South Africa
might have had a more peaceful future if it had succeeded.

The Afrikaners were still more distrustful of the mine-
owners: they imported weapons from Germany and France
and built forts round Pretoria against a new threat. But the
mine-owners became still more impatient as the financial
importance of Johannesburg increased. By 1899 the Transvaal had overtaken Russia, Australia and America as the
greatest gold power in the world. Their new opportunity
came with the arrival in 1897 of the new British High
Commissioner, Sir Alfred Milner, who shared their interest
in a new showdown with the Afrikaners, as the prelude to
his vision of a united Southern Africa. Milner began to see
war as the only solution; and while Rhodes was wary,
Alfred Beit was prepared to sacrifice the short-term losses
of earnings from gold if war broke out. His firm eventually
guaranteed a loan of £50 million. As the historian of the
Boer War Thomas Pakenham has shown: 'the gold-bugs,
contrary to the accepted view of later historians, were thus
active partners with Milner in the making of the war.'*

Milner was determined that Britain would annex the
Transvaal and establish 'a self-governing White Community, supported by well-treated and justly governed
black labour from Cape Town to the Zambezi'. He
achieved his immediate object in 1899 when Kruger refused to give way, thus provoking the Boer War; but the
blacks soon proved the chief losers. When the British
captured Johannesburg they were cheered by blacks on
the pavements; but they soon enforced colour-bar laws
more strictly than the Afrikaners: 'The laws that made
Africans into the helots,' says Pakenham, 'were now to be
applied with an efficiency that the Boers had never been
able to muster.'† The young Oxford graduates from New

* Thomas Pakenham, *The Boer War*, London, Weidenfeld &
Nicolson, 1979, p. 89
    † Pakenham, *op. cit.*, p. 554

College whom Milner brought in as his 'kindergarten' to reconstruct South Africa had their own insulation and arrogance. Lionel Curtis, the 'prophet' of the kindergarten who became town clerk of Johannesburg (and who later wrote a memorandum which was the first step to the Union) described the situation in 1900:

> The very presence of black men in large numbers makes the white minority indolent and incompetent. The relative proportions of black and white are such that I am not hopeful of the ultimate future of the country. It would be a blessed thing for us if the negro like the Red Indian tended to die out before us, for he acts like decay among teeth. The tendency of Trade Unions to exclude coloured labour should be fostered by all patriotic men in Australia and America.*

It was a revealing and confused complaint, for much of the wealth of the country now depended on black workers without whom the deep-level gold-mines would be unworkable. As the historian de Kiewiet wrote: 'What an abundance of rain and grass was to New Zealand mutton, what a plenty of cheap grazing land was to Australian wool, what the fertile prairie acres were to Canadian wheat, cheap native labour was to South African mining and industrial enterprise.'† And the white workers with their unions were soon to cause more difficulties for the mine-owners than the blacks without unions.

The Boer War was won by the British at an expense of over £250 million, with 400,000 British soldiers in South Africa at one time. But the treaty at Vereeniging that ended the war soon proved a victory for the Afrikaners. The English-speaking whites had gained the franchise; but they soon lost their hope that a flow of British immigrants

* Lionel Curtis, *With Milner in South Africa*, Oxford, Basil Blackwell, 1951, p. 226

† C W de Kiewiet, *A History of South Africa*, Oxford University Press. 1941, p. 96

would outvote the Afrikaners who, as Pakenham puts it, 'had a secret weapon in the shape of the cradle' (President Kruger alone had 156 living children, grandchildren and great-grandchildren).* In South Africa, demographics were to make their own logic. The irony of the war was not lost on contemporaries: 'The British colonials know quite well,' said 'Indicus' visiting South Africa from India in 1903, 'that unless they can disenfranchise or in some way gerrymander the Dutch, power must pass . . . into Dutch hands.'† Four years after the end of the war the Afrikaner leader Louis Botha, leading his populist party Het Volk, won the election in the Transvaal.

The mine-owners could return to expansive conditions. Wernher and Beit, who controlled a third of South Africa's gold, were among the richest men in the world. When Beit died in 1906, even in the midst of a new slump, he left £8 million – the biggest will to be proved in Somerset House. But the gold millionaires could never connect their wealth with political power and many anyway loosened their links with South Africa. Wernher retired to Luton Hoo, his huge country seat north of London, which his son Harold took over, marrying Lady Zia, the daughter of a Russian grand-duke: two of their grandchildren married English Dukes (Westminster and Abercorn). Beit's nephew, Sir Alfred, still lives in the great Irish mansion Russborough; (his nephew and heir Theodore Bull married a Zambian princess and took part of the Beit fortune back to Africa).

The Boer War was soon seen by Marxists as a prime example of the power of international capitalism. 'The South African war, openly fomented by gold speculators for their private purposes,' wrote the Manchester economist J A Hobson in his famous book *Imperialism*‡ in 1902, 'will rank in history as a leading case of this usurpation of

* Pakenham, *op. cit.*, p. 259
† *'Indicus': Labour and Other Questions in South Africa*, London, 1903, p. 130.
‡ J A Hobson, *Imperialism*, London, Allen & Unwin (3rd edition), 1938, pp. 127, 346

nationalism.' But he also foresaw that 'a South African federation of self-governing states . . . will demand a political career of its own, and will insist upon its own brand of empire, not that of the British government, in the control of the lower races in South Africa.' Hobson in turn much influenced Lenin when he wrote his own book on Imperialism in 1916* in which he inaccurately described Cecil Rhodes as 'the man who was mainly responsible for the Anglo-Boer War' – while Lenin's theories in turn heavily influenced Third World governments after independence. Contemporary Marxists still see the Boer War, in the words of Jack and Ray Simons, as 'a classic example of imperialist aggression prompted by capitalist greed'.

Hobson and later Marxists had reason to suspect that the mine-owners had fomented the war; but were the war-mongers really acting in their own long-term interests? When Sir Norman Angell wrote his popular book *The Great Illusion* in 1910, arguing that aggression does not pay economically and that groups do not necessarily act in their own interests, he pointed out how the British government could not capture any of South Africa's wealth as a result of the war, and that 'the *political* control of the area containing one of the great sources of the world's gold is in process of passing out of the hands of Britain'.†

The real victory of the Afrikaners was to come in 1910 with the creation of the Union of South Africa, which united the two colonies, the Cape and Natal, with the two Afrikaner republics, the Transvaal and the Orange Free State, to form an independent state within the British Empire. It was to remain an uneasy combination of Afrikaner rulers, international capitalists and voteless blacks of whom little notice was taken. It was at the cost of any further black advancement, and the superseding of the old liberal Cape constitution which had allowed some blacks

---

* V Lenin: *Imperialism*, Moscow, Progress Publishers, 1978, p. 75
† Sir Norman Angell, *The Great Illusion, 1908–1914*, 1933 edition, London, Heinemann, pp. 194–5

the vote. For the blacks, the outcome of the Boer War was the opposite of the American civil war forty years earlier.

And the First World War hastened the development of South Africa's 'own brand of empire'. Facing perilous sea-lanes the mining companies had to become less dependent on Britain, and soon found they could extend to other industries, producing many manufactures more cheaply than imports; while the mines were becoming less dependent on foreign capital and the second-generation South Africans no longer saw themselves as expatriates. After the war, high tariffs continued to encourage local manufacturers, while Western corporations and banks were beginning to look to South African investments inside the tariff walls. Ford had arrived in 1923, and the next year General Motors set up a car-assembly plant in Port Elizabeth. In 1925 the National, Kruger's old bank, was bought out by Barclays in London.

Central Mining, the legacy of Wernher and Beit, remained the dominant group; Rhodes' old company Consolidated Goldfields rapidly acquired other industrial companies. But it was a new group founded by Ernest Oppenheimer in 1917, with the grand name of the Anglo-American Corporation, which was to become the cornerstone of the new South African capitalism and which developed into the biggest concentration of financial power in the continent.

Ernest Oppenheimer provided a bridge between the early diamond days and the new intricate gold-mining empires. The son of a German cigar merchant, he had become a clerk in the London diamond firm of Dunkelsbuhler and went out to Kimberley to represent it, mastering the finances of diamonds and becoming Mayor of Kimberley. The war was a setback for men with German-sounding names, and Oppenheimer retreated back to London; but he soon returned to Johannesburg to investigate the potential of very deep-level gold-mines which needed still larger investments to develop them. He was convinced of the prospects, but his company had the difficulty, in the middle of the First World War, of being one-third owned by German shareholders;* so Oppenheimer raised funds to form his own mining company which would be doubly unique: it would be based not in London but in Johannesburg; while it would raise most of its capital not in London – where the war restricted investment – but in New York. Oppenheimer made many American connections through his mining engineer William Honnold, including the 'great engineer' Herbert Hoover, the Newmont mining corporation, and the banker J P Morgan. He first wanted to call his company the African American Corporation, but Honnold cabled back: AFRICAN-AMERICAN WOULD SUGGEST ON THIS SIDE OUR DARK-SKINNED FELLOW COUNTRYMEN AND POSSIBLY RESULT IN RIDICULE . . .† And Oppenheimer eventually agreed to call it the Anglo-American Corporation of South Africa, thus embracing all three continents. The chief advantage of a South African base was the lower taxation; but Oppenheimer from the beginning stressed his company's patriotism, and he and his family were much more thoroughly committed to the country than the earlier mine-owners.

With himself as chairman and permanent director, Oppenheimer formed the Anglo-American Corporation in 1917, and soon used all his ingenuity to extend his interests in the new very deep-level gold-mines: already by 1918 his group controlled four of the eleven mining companies on the East Rand. He was already preparing a bold strategy to move into diamonds, and began stealthily to encircle De Beers by gaining control of the new diamond fields that had opened up independently of the Kimberley monopoly; first the fields in South West Africa which had

* Duncan Innes, *Anglo-American and the Rise of Modern South Africa*, Johannesburg, Ravan Press, 1984, p. 91
† Sir Theodore Gregory, *Ernest Oppenheimer and the Economic Development of Southern Africa*, Oxford University Press, 1962, p. 88

lost their German control after the war; then fields in
Lichtenburg and Namaqualand; then in West Africa. He
played his cards with extraordinary patience and skill –
until by 1929 De Beers were compelled to accept him
as chairman, as the only means to impose order. Soon
afterwards the depression provided the opportunity to
integrate the diamond business more thoroughly, and to
reinforce the De Beers monopoly. He was now king of
diamonds as well as gold. He was also moving into South
African manufacturing industry, and beginning his partnership with the British explosives and chemical combine ICI
(*see* page 124). And he could also use his financial and
technical base to develop resources elsewhere in Africa,
particularly in the British colony of Northern Rhodesia
(now Zambia) where he developed lucrative copper mines
in competition with the American group of Chester Beatty.
Anglo-American's expansion was increasingly self-
financing, and after the Second World War, when
Oppenheimer gained control of new goldfields near
Welkom in the Orange Free State, he was able to finance
their development largely with the profits from De
Beers.

Oppenheimer was soon the new personification of the
South African capitalist; an updated version of Cecil
Rhodes as hero and villain. He had none of the territorial
ambitions of Rhodes, and his style was low-key: but he
was more single-minded in his pursuit of financial power.
His admiring biographer, Sir Theodore Gregory, saw him
as an indispensable entrepreneur who could mobilise capital with a decisiveness and direction which dramatically
speeded up African development. The Afrikaner nationalists saw him as the reincarnation of Hoggenheimer, the
Jewish exploiter. The Marxists insisted that his own personality was largely irrelevant: Anglo-American, wrote its
chronicler Duncan Innes, 'was responding to the underlying tendencies of concentration and centralization of production and capital which characterize monopoly
capitalism . . . Oppenheimer's "genius" lay in the fact that

he correctly perceived the fundamental tendencies of the time.'*

Certainly Anglo-American, as it expanded and inter-locked with other groups, showed some signs of monopoly capitalism as described by Hobson and Lenin, with a concentration of money, power and technology which towered over the Pretoria government and employed the biggest black labour-force in the continent. But South Africa was hardly a perfect model of a Marxist state. The Afrikaner governments were less and less like 'the executive committee of the bourgeoisie'. The mine-owners were far from certain where their true interests lay as they confronted both black and white workers; while the sudden impact of capital and industry was soon countered by two successive nationalisms, Afrikaner and African, which increasingly challenged them for control of the wealth of the young nation.

One of Oppenheimer's last public acts was in 1957 when the slight, unobtrusive old man opened the splendid new offices of De Beers, at the end of London's 'diamond street' of Hatton Garden, now sharing the same building as Anglo-American, formally marrying diamonds to gold. It was a monument to South Africa's own capitalism: by the time of Oppenheimer's death six months later his company was producing not only all of South Africa's diamonds, but 30 percent of its gold, 44 percent of its coal, and more than half Northern Rhodesia's copper.† His political legacy in South Africa was less certain: he was astute in handling Afrikaners, but like the other mine-owners he remained insulated from the huge black work-force which he had helped to build up; and his official biography records no black individual. When in 1955 Sir Ernest read the bestselling book *Naught for your Comfort* by Father Trevor Huddleston, which described the full

---

* Innes, *op. cit.*, p. 111
† Edward Jessup, *Ernest Oppenheimer: A Study in Power*, London, Rex Collings, 1979, p. 317

miseries of black South Africans, he maintained (according to his son Harry) that it was biased and unfair; but he decided to look again at the conditions of blacks in Soweto, and soon afterwards he persuaded the mining houses to lend £3 million for black housing.*

Already in 1933 Ernest's son Harry was sitting in on his father's meetings, and over the next twenty-five years he was groomed as the successor. Harry had none of the rough schooling of a self-made entrepreneur: he was educated in England, at Charterhouse school and Christ Church, Oxford. He seemed overshadowed: he was shy and self-effacing with embarrassingly good manners, sidling sideways into a room, listening patiently to bores and seeing guests out to the front door. He admired the English tradition, was brought up an Anglican, married a very English South African, recruited many public-school men. Yet, like his father, he was as hard as a diamond in business deals. He was always aloof from English influences, contemptuous of the sleepy old boy network of the City of London; and he became a rare example of a son inheriting both a genius and a drive for business, and vastly extending his inheritance. 'When you are brought up in the purple,' he once said to me, 'the only thing worth doing is to be some kind of an artist. I found I couldn't be that; so there was nothing to do but business.' He became an artist in that.

He was intensely aware of his political vulnerability ever since, as MP for Kimberley, he had come up against the Afrikaner fanatics of the National Party clamouring to nationalise Anglo-American. He did not shirk political commitment: in the 'fifties he financed the 'Torch Commando' of war veterans who defended the constitution against the Nationalist government, and he went on to subsidise liberal politicians including his friend Helen Suzman. He considered his own political career a failure,

---

* Speech on March 11, 1958, unveiling his father's memorial tower (Gregory, p. 580)

though he was much more far-sighted and imaginative than other mine-owners or even his father.

But he faced far more testing political problems than his father after the coming to power of the Afrikaner nationalists in 1948. The very dominating success of Anglo-American – like the monopoly of IG Farben in Germany in the 'thirties – could be exploited by the state to make it more dependent. And the immediate need to conciliate Afrikaner nationalists could easily obscure the long-term need to come to terms with black nationalists who would provide a much more serious threat to the future of his corporation.

4

Afrikaners against Blacks

We are not a nation of jellyfish.

P W Botha, July, 1986

Pieter Willem Botha, who was born six years after the union of South Africa, could look back on a far more heroic and military version of history than that of the Oppenheimers and mine-owners. His father had been one of the 'bitter-enders' who fought to the end of the Boer War; his mother had been in a British concentration camp where she lost two of her children; and eighty years after that war Botha still continually reminded his audiences that his people 'nearly brought the British empire to its knees'. From his youth on his father's farm through his first career as a National Party organiser he was imbued with the belief that the future of South Africa depended on the unique qualities and endurance of the Afrikaners.

When South Africa became a nation in 1910 it was already dominated by Afrikaner leaders, with one war-hero Louis Botha as prime minister and another, Jan Smuts, as his minister of interior, mines and defence. The old dreams of a British South Africa as conceived by Rhodes or Milner were already modified, and Afrikaans had official equality with English. The first government was conciliatory towards the British, and many Afrikaners fought on their side in the First World War. But by 1914 another hero of the Boer War, General Hertzog, had already formed his more extreme National Party; and two years later a group of nationalists formed the Broederbond, the secret society which countered the Englishmen's power establishment with its own network dedicated to Afrikanerdom.

The Union was one of the most disparate and fragmented nations in the world. It was not only that the blacks were thoroughly segregated from the whites. The Indians in Natal never mixed with the blacks or the whites; the coloureds (of mixed blood) in the Cape were shunned by their white cousins, and looked down on the blacks; and the two dominant white groups – the English-speaking businessmen and the Afrikaner politicians – went their separate ways with a legacy of distrust. When the English talked about 'the racial question' they usually meant the Afrikaners, not the blacks. Afrikaner politicians were to remain obsessed by the injustices and sufferings of the Boer War, rightly proud of their wartime resistance: 'The first of the freedom fighters,' as they would depict themselves afterwards. Successive British governments on their side would treat Pretoria with a mixture of awe, guilt and contempt which made normal communication impossible, while English writers and publicists from John Buchan to Baden-Powell would invest rural Afrikaners with an enduring romanticism and their language would be infused with the vocabulary of treks, spoors, laagers and sjamboks.

But the Afrikaners were themselves becoming industrialised: as their many children left the farms for the cities they faced the full discipline of the gold-mines and factories, with scarcely better qualifications than the blacks; and there began a new kind of revolt. In the first years after the First World War, the mine-owners in Johannesburg had a brief honeymoon with the government under Smuts, who knew that profitable gold-mines were crucial to development. But a sudden fall in the gold price precipitated their first major clash with white workers in the 'red revolt' of 1922, a more brutal showdown between capital and labour than any in Europe or America. The Chamber of Mines insisted on using more black miners until the white miners' protest escalated into a general strike under the famous slogan: 'Workers of the World unite for a White South Africa.' It was more like a war than a strike, and Smuts eventually won it with troops and artillery: over 250 people were killed, and the leaders were hanged. (P W Botha would speak with some jealousy about Smuts, who was so ruthless at home yet preserved his high-minded reputation abroad.) The mine-owners pressed ahead with sacking whites and employing more blacks, and in 1924 they declared record profits. But it was a Pyrrhic victory; for in the same year Smuts was defeated by a coalition of nationalist Afrikaners and white labour unionists under General Hertzog, united in championing white labour. Hertzog's Afrikaner supporters were soon dominant, and determined to protect white workers, farmers and local manufacturers against international industry and finance: they established nationalised industries including the extravagant state-owned steelworks Iscor, to provide secure jobs. The young urban Afrikaners, with the help of the Dutch Reformed Church, resisted the integrating forces of industry and cities.

The Afrikaner nationalism amidst which P W Botha grew up was already semi-socialist, with bitter experiences of capitalism as well as imperialism. The mine-owners still had some clout: during the depression Hertzog tried but failed to prevent Ernest Oppenheimer from closing diamond mines; and he dared not embark on large-scale nationalisation.* But by the 'thirties the Afrikaners were already seriously limiting the profits and expansion of the capitalists, who blamed them for inhibiting economic progress. 'A basic cause of the low average income of the inhabitants of the Union,' Professor Herbert Frankel, who was also Oppenheimer's economic adviser, wrote in 1938,

* Lipton, *op. cit.*, p. 266

'is the lack of "economic mobility" of its workers – both black and white.'*

The depression forced Hertzog into a coalition with Smuts and English-speaking voters to produce a fused 'United Party', which still favoured farmers and manufacturers against the mine-owners. The more militant Afrikaner nationalists were still more implacable, augmented by the growing number of poor whites and the Afrikaner-based industries which felt damaged by the British connection. In 1934 they formed the new 'purified' Afrikaner National party under Dr Daniel Malan – which young P W Botha was to join as an organiser two years later – which would change the face of South Africa. It was pledged to establish a genuine Afrikaner state, supported by a powerful religious and patriotic lobby, and it had a strong nationalist socialist element, influenced by Nazi Germany. One of their most powerful intellectuals, Dr Nico Diedrichs who later became State President, studied Nazi politics and economics in Germany and back in South Africa was closely involved in setting up Afrikaner financial institutions including the bank Volkskas, the 'people's bank' which provided an important financial base. Many of the National Party leaders, including Albert Hertzog the son of the General, called for wholesale nationalisation of industry including the gold-mines. The combination of ethnic and economic appeal was irresistible; and in 1938, when the nationalists re-enacted their Great Trek into the interior a century earlier, the wave of nostalgic nationalism revealed the full force of the Afrikaner pride.

During the war, while Smuts again supported the British, many of the National Party leaders openly sided with Hitler and some attempted sabotage, through a new right-wing group the Ossewabrandwag: the future prime minister John Vorster was imprisoned together with his future intelligence chief Hendrik van den Bergh. When Hitler

* Sally Herbert Frankel, *Capital Investment in Africa*, Oxford University Press, 1938, p. 143

started losing, the future appeal of the National Party
seemed more doubtful, and Smuts emerged after the war
as an international statesman; but most English-speakers
had underestimated the power and organisation of Afrikaner nationalism. Then in 1948 the general election
brought Dr Malan into power with a new infusion of
National Party MPS, including P W Botha. 'For the first
time since Union,' said Malan in his triumph, 'South Africa
is our own, and may God grant that it will always remain
our own.' It was the beginning of a virtual Afrikaner
monopoly of power over the next four decades. The historian Arthur Keppel-Jones *had* predicted the nationalist
victory in a prophetic book published eighteen months
before the election called *When Smuts Goes*: it forecast
that the Nationalists would introduce authoritarian laws,
leave the Commonwealth, provoke a black revolt and go
to war with Britain in 1977, after which South Africa would
eventually revert to barbarism. Keppel-Jones' own moral
was 'that the salvation of the country can lie only in a
reversal of historic tendencies, a reversal so thorough as
to constitute a revolution'.* In the years after 1948 his
readers would anxiously watch his predictions coming true.

The National Party had conflicting economic ambitions.
Most of the dominant leaders wanted to take over the
existing industrial system, replacing English-speakers with
Afrikaners and building up nationalised bodies to counterbalance the Anglophone strongholds. They saw the Industrial Development Corporation, run by H J Van Eck,
partly as a 'bulwark against the Anglo-American Corporation'.† Others with trade union support still wanted to
nationalise much of the economy. But they were united
in their determination to build up Afrikanerdom and to
enforce the new policy called apartheid which the National
Party had been formulating over the previous years.

* Arthur Keppel-Jones, *When Smuts Goes*, Pietermaritzburg, Shuter
and Shooter, 1950, p. *xii*

† Andries Wassenaar, *The Assault on Private Enterprise*, Cape Town,
1977, p. 123

There was nothing fundamentally new about apartheid: thorough segregation had been advocated by the white Labour Party as well as Afrikaner Nationalists in the 'thirties, and Smuts himself sternly defended segregation. As P W Botha later explained with only some exaggeration: 'Apartheid as we understand it existed in South Africa from previous centuries under British rule . . . Colonial paternalism had a racial connotation and whites for some four hundred years had governed blacks all over the world. South Africa inherited colonial paternalism and this entailed the governing of blacks by whites.'* But the unique characteristic of apartheid was to institutionalise both segregation and racialism just when the Western world was repelled by it at the end of the war against Hitler, with a more ruthless division than anything that the British or Smuts had attempted. Within two years of 1948 the National government had passed the two bedrock laws which enforced discrimination: the Population Registration Act ensured the purity of the white race – with the help of a Board which could examine skin, hair and nails – while the Group Areas Act enforced separate residential areas. There followed a quick succession of laws to enforce segregation in schools, universities, local government and political systems. It was the total opposite to the trend in the United States. In the early 'fifties the conditions of many blacks in the Southern States could be compared to those in South Africa. But by 1954 the Supreme Court in Washington had dismissed the old doctrine of 'separate but equal' and declared that segregation in public schools must end – the year after the Bantu Education Act in South Africa had enforced separate education, with a built-in inequality.

The implementation of apartheid – particularly the inferior education – was also clearly damaging to long-term industrial expansion; for white workers were already in short supply. But the English-speaking opposition in the

* Interview with Bruce London, *The Times*, London, August 23, 1986

United Party, which represented most business interests, was reluctant to oppose the new apartheid laws, and felt vulnerable to attack for encouraging a black flood. 'It is not always useful,' as de Kiewiet put it in 1956, 'to distinguish between the English and the Afrikaner in racial matters.'* The British Labour government in London had few illusions about the racial dangers of apartheid, and the British High Commissioner, Sir Evelyn Baring, frequently compared the Nationalist government to the Nazis. In his farewell despatch (which impressed his Prime Minister, Attlee), he warned that 'to despise or ignore the strong and expanding force of South African Nationalism in 1951 would be as unwise as it was to decry in March 1933 the power of Hitler to do harm . . . Nationalist fanatics control a strong and important country.' But he also warned that 'it will be useless to attempt to draw a complete *cordon sanitaire* round South Africa and to cut ourselves and our African dependencies off from that country'.† The Labour government in London, anxious to secure uranium and to reach a new gold agreement, was easily bullied by Pretoria, and timid in challenging apartheid in the British protectorates on its frontiers which they feared South Africa would take over; when Seretse Khama, the chief of the Bamangwato tribe in Bechuanaland (later Botswana) married a white woman, Ruth Williams, in 1949, they refused to recognise him for five years.

But the early apartheid of Dr Malan and his successor, Hans Strijdom, was relatively modest compared to the ambitious 'grand apartheid' of the third nationalist prime minister, Dr Hendrik Verwoerd. A professor of both psychology and theology, with little interest in economics, he had been educated largely in Germany and acquired a total confidence in his Calvinist view of the world, which radiated from his innocent face and beatific smile. He was

* De Kiewiet, *op. cit.*, p. 32
† Charles Douglas-Home, *Evelyn Baring, The Last Proconsul*, London, Collins, 1978, p. 214

a religious leader as much as a political one: speaking, he clasped his hands and looked upwards as if for inspiration. He took apartheid much more literally than his predecessors, and was prepared to make genuine sacrifices. His fellow ministers including P W Botha were easily silenced by his confidence which took apartheid to its logical limits. As secretary for native affairs, Verwoerd had already been the architect of the new Bantu 'homelands' and Bantu education and had constructed a system which saw no role for the blacks, except as servants, in the white men's cities.

Verwoerd's theory of apartheid stressed above all that the blacks were not part of the South African nation, but a group of separate tribal nations – Zulu, Xhosa or Sotho – which would gain dignity and self-respect outside the white man's world. 'The Bantu is neither a backward black Englishman, nor a backward black Afrikaner,' as Schalk Pienaar, one of his most articulate intellectual supporters, put it in 1960. 'He is not even a backward black Bantu. He is a Zulu or a Xhosa or a Sotho or what you will. A nation in his own right.'* Pienaar and many other Afrikaners projected the blacks in their own image, as proud tribes that did not wish to be assimilated: 'We will not deny the Bantu what we have claimed for ourselves.' And as black Africa moved towards independence they saw a new justification: 'The black nations of South Africa can become free even as Ghana is today.' Much of the Afrikaner intellectual confidence was based on ignorance of urban black society; and while the Afrikaners were determined to preserve their tribe – even at the cost of economic and industrial development – most political blacks were determined to escape from tribalism, and to become a single nation.

But Afrikaner students could see Verwoerd's apartheid as much purer and more acceptable than the cruder version

* S Pienaar and Anthony Sampson, *South Africa, Two Views of Separate Development*, Oxford University Press, 1960, pp. 9–15 and 56

of Dr Malan. 'I remember the excitement, even thrill, some experienced when it was explained for the first time,' wrote the liberal Afrikaner politician Van Zyl Slabbert, recalling his time as a student at the Afrikaans university of Stellenbosch. 'Any aware young Afrikaner knew instinctively and with a pervading sense of doom that apartheid until then was a holding action, that a solution to living with the blacks still had to be found. Here, some sensed, was the beginning of one. It made logical sense and addressed very prickly moral issues. The beauty of it was the audacity of its most basic assumptions: "You don't have to find a solution to living with blacks, because there are no blacks, only ethnic groups who cannot really tolerate one another anyway . . ."'*

Western governments never recognised the supposed independence of the homelands; and the extravagant costs and suffering involved in the territorial separation were soon very apparent, with forced removals, shack villages and endless bus-journeys to carry workers to the white factories. But Afrikaner politicians including Botha could never abandon the idea, for it enabled them to think in terms of black minorities rather than a single black majority. And many multinationals as well as local companies at first propagated the idea that the homelands were beneficial to both blacks and industry. 'The South African government's policy is to encourage and assist the Bantu to develop their territories into self-governing national homelands,' reported Roy Hill, the local general manager of Colgate Palmolive in 1966. 'Decentralisation of white territories and the establishment of industries in border areas near the national homelands, calculated to ensure a more equitable distribution of wealth and contribute to the economic development of the homelands, are firm matters of government policy.'†

* Frederik Van Zyl Slabbert, *The Last White Parliament*, London, Sidgwick & Jackson, 1986, p. 76
† Jerome Blood (editor), *Management looks at Africa*, American Management Association, 1966

But the extremism of Verwoerd's grand apartheid was becoming an embarrassment to Britain, which was still by far the biggest foreign investor but also had growing interests in black Africa, which was moving rapidly towards independence. Verwoerd's fanaticism soon came face-to-face with British pragmatism. At the beginning of 1960 the Conservative prime minister Harold Macmillan made a historic tour of the continent, flying from newly-independent Ghana via Nigeria and Rhodesia to South Africa. He was preparing a major speech to the parliament which was celebrating its fifty-year jubilee. When he reached Cape Town he stayed with Dr and Mrs Verwoerd, where he was amazed by their Calvinist zeal: there were no black servants, only Afrikaners including a doddering butler. 'I began to realise to the full extent,' Macmillan wrote afterwards, 'the degree of obstinacy, amounting really to fanaticism, which Dr Verwoerd brought to the consideration of his policies.'* Macmillan was more worried by the dogmatism of apartheid than its economic consequences: 'If they didn't make an ideology of it they would almost certainly succeed in getting the results they seek with a minimum of concession,' he told his press secretary Harold Evans. 'Economic differences between black and white would alone be sufficient to achieve practical separation . . .'† But when he finally revised his speech (the British High Commissioner Sir John Maud complained privately), he left out some criticisms, including a reference to Lord Melbourne's dictum that: 'Nobody ever did anything very foolish except from some high principle.'

Macmillan's eventual speech brilliantly summed up the Afrikaner's predicament. He began with his own tactful historical analysis, stressing how South Africa had built up its strong economy with much help from British capital. But he continued with a warning about the growth of

* Harold Macmillan, *Pointing the Way*, London, Macmillan, 1972, pp. 150–60
† Sir Harold Evans, *Downing Street Diary*, London, Hodder & Stoughton, 1981, p. 102

African Nationalism: 'The wind of change is blowing through this continent, and, whether we like it or not, this growth of national consciousness is a political fact.' He went on 'to soften the impact' (as he explained afterwards):

Of course you understand this better than anyone. You are sprung from Europe, the home of nationalism, and here in Africa you have yourselves created a new nation. Indeed in the history of our times, yours will be recorded as the first of the African nationalisms . . .

But his concluding message was unambiguous. However much Britain wanted to give support and encouragement to another Commonwealth member, 'there are some aspects of your policies which make it impossible for us to do this without being false to our own deep convictions about the political destinies of free men to which in our own territories we are trying to give effect.'

The speech was received in parliament (where I watched it from the press gallery) with a slow double-take: the members were so dazed by its range and eloquence that they took some time to realise, after reading British comments, that Macmillan was beginning to back black Africa at the expense of white. 'We have our last chance of contact with Europe – which is drifting away,' the then editor of *Die Burger*, Piet Cillie, said to me before the speech. 'Isolation leads to insanity.' But the speech made South Africans much more aware, as the *Cape Times* put it, that 'our isolation is practically total'.

Three months later, after the Belgian Congo had collapsed into independence and chaos, the 'Wind of Change' already looked more menacing: Macmillan had to explain that it was 'not the same thing as a howling tempest which would blow away the whole of the new developing civilisation'.* Inside South Africa the Sharpeville massacre

* Anthony Sampson, *Macmillan*, London, Allen Lane, The Penguin Press, 1967, p. 190

(*see* next chapter) led to a sudden wave of protest and reprisals which further antagonised world opinion. Verwoerd was determined to turn South Africa into a republic, for which he won a referendum by a narrow margin in October 1960: but he still wanted South Africa to remain within the Commonwealth, to which South Africa had to re-apply at the conference of prime ministers in March 1961. Macmillan also hoped to keep the Republic inside the Commonwealth, while the Treasury was fearful about its gold leaving the Sterling Area. But Verwoerd, said Macmillan, 'seemed to have no understanding that anyone could consider the political and social position of the vast majority of the population of South Africa was not a purely "domestic" question'. Verwoerd refused any concession to the non-white members of the Commonwealth, and insisted that any black diplomats visiting South Africa would have to stay in a separate non-white hotel. It was a comic irony that this social aversion should be the breaking-point – when only a few years later Pretoria would be welcoming black diplomats from neighbouring states to multi-racial hotels. On March 13 Macmillan formally told parliament that 'the Commonwealth ties with South Africa, which have endured for fifty years, are shortly to be severed . . .' Diplomats continued to argue whether Britain might have better influenced the Republic if it had remained inside the Commonwealth, while many black politicians insisted that *their* people had never left it.

As a republic the Afrikaner government had finally achieved their longed-for independence from the British and they were soon rewarded with striking economic success. While the Labour government in London after 1964 would hurl more words against apartheid, the Afrikaners knew that British companies were becoming still more eager to invest and trade; and by the time P W Botha became minister of defence in 1966 he was well able to channel European investment and technology into his expanding military machine. But Botha and his colleagues who had so triumphantly established their own nationalism were now coming up more sharply against another nationalism which they had helped to provoke, as the British had provoked theirs. And however much they hoped to divide and control the black tribes by separating them into smaller units, the facts of industrialisation and cities were now pushing the blacks harder into the opposite direction, towards a single nation.

5

Blacks against Apartheid

*The truest optimism in South Africa is in the crowded,
disease-ridden and crime-infested urban locations. They
represent the black man's acceptance of the new life of
the western world, his willingness to endure a harsh
schooling and an equal apprenticeship in its ways.*

C W de Kiewiet, *The Anatomy of South African
Misery*,
Oxford University Press, 1956, p. 37

The leaders of the African National Congress, Oliver
Tambo and his jailed colleague Nelson Mandela, could
look back in January 1986 on seventy-five years of their
organisation's history: the ANC was two years older than
Botha's National Party and only two years younger than
South Africa. From the beginning the blacks had associated the Union with diminishing rights, with a political
system from which they were shut out, and with white
leaders they never met. But they insisted that they were
South African patriots, loyal to the new nation rather than
the tribe. 'Under apartheid one of us must be the foreigners
in South Africa,' said Tambo: 'It will not be us.'

And they saw themselves as an integral part of the
industrial society that had been created long before the
nation. Already when De Beers was established in Kimberley in the 1880s an urban black population was developing

outside the compounds: about 20,000 blacks were working in four 'locations' as servants or employees of traders and contractors. A few were the 'educated natives', mostly Xhosas or Mfengu, who came from mission schools, particularly from Lovedale in the Eastern Cape, for whom the sudden Kimberley boom provided some modest openings for young blacks. The post office could not persuade whites to deliver telegrams, so it took on black school-leavers who were content to take lowly jobs. 'We are just emerging from barbarism,' wrote the black writer John Knox Bokwe in 1894, 'and have to find our way, and by degrees gain their (whites') confidence.'* Among the black telegraph-boys was the young Sol Plaatje who later became secretary of the African National Congress. And among the 'savages' described by Trollope in the diamond mines was Peter Matthews, a Christian from the Barolong tribe who worked in the mines until his leg was run over by a mining-truck, when he opened a small tea-and-buns café in a township. Matthews instilled into his six children that education, as much as guns, had been the weapon with which the white men had conquered his people. Four of them became teachers: one of them was to become Professor Z K Matthews, a prominent leader of the ANC in the 'fifties and the first ambassador of Botswana to the United Nations.†

It was the Union in 1910 which directly precipitated the founding of the Congress in 1912. The blacks had already seen clearly that Afrikaner dominance would reduce their hopes, and after the Boer War they had set up black 'vigilance associations' to protect their rights and land. In 1909 a delegation of blacks sailed for London to protest against the 'colour-bar clause' in the proposed union which threatened to disenfranchise the blacks and (said the black

* Brian Willan, *Sol Plaatje: South African Nationalist*, London, Heinemann, 1984, p. 30

† Z K Matthews, *Freedom for My People*, Cape Town, David Philip, 1983, pp. 8–14. *See also* Anthony Sampson, *The Treason Cage*, London, Heinemann, 1958, pp. 118–20

educationalist D D T Jabavu) 'struck the death-knell of
Native confidence in what used to be called British fair
play. The cow of Great Britain had gone dry, they said,
and they must look to themselves for salvation.'*

In the same year as the Union, an ambitious young Zulu
lawyer returned to South Africa from London. Dr Pixley
ka Izaka Seme (named after an American pastor) was one
of the much-mocked 'School Kaffirs'; but he had a strong
sense of black dignity: a contemporary photograph shows
him in a top hat, morning coat and spats and he was related
to the Zulu royal family (one of his nephews was to become
Chief Buthelezi, the present Zulu leader). Seme was appalled to see his people in the Transvaal being pushed off
pavements, dodging cars, kicked and knocked and herded
into cattle-trucks. He was determined to unify the black
tribes into a common nation which could defend itself
against the new white state. He collected three black
lawyer friends from different tribes – Mangena, Montsioa
and Msimang – and wrote a manifesto: 'We are one people:
these divisions, these jealousies, are the cause of all our
woes and of all our backwardness and ignorance today.'
His agitations led to a conference of black leaders at
Bloemfontein two years after the union. 'It was a gathering
of tribes that had never met before except on the battle
fields,' Seme's follower Richard Selope-Thema later described it.† Seme addressed them eloquently:

> Chiefs of royal blood and gentlemen of our race, we
> have gathered together to consider and discuss a scheme
> which my colleagues and I have decided to place before
> you. We have discovered that in the land of their birth,
> Africans are treated as hewers of wood and drawers of
> water. The white people of this country have formed
> what is known as the Union of South Africa – a union
> in which we have no voice in the making of the laws and
> no part in the administration.

* D D T Jabavu, *The Black Problem*, Lovedale, 1920
† *How Congress Began*, *Drum* magazine, Johannesburg, July 1953

They agreed to form a 'South African Native National Congress' – vaguely modelled on the American Congress, on the British parliament and chiefly on traditions – with an upper house of chiefs who sat behind the office-bearers and pronounced verdicts separately from the elected lower house. A sergeant of arms presided in a strange regalia, with a military tunic, breeches and gaiters, a skin shield, knobkerry and axe. Its first leaders all came from the small black professional class or aristocracy, including Dr Seme as treasurer and Sol Plaatje as secretary, with the Zulu teacher Dr John Dube as president. It was the first occasion where blacks had dropped tribal loyalties – anywhere in the continent – to accept a common nation. It was not nationalist in the sense of being anti-white, militant or revolutionary: it was heavily influenced by Christian teaching, not at all by socialism, and pathetically hopeful of white allies. But it marked the birth of African nationalism in the sense of giving loyalty to the nation rather than the tribe.

The next year Congress saw its worst fears borne out, when the new Union government passed the Native Land Act which forbade the black three-quarters of the population to own land anywhere outside the 'reserves' which covered only one-thirteenth of the country. 'The South African Native found himself not actually a slave,' wrote Plaatje, 'but a pariah in the land of his birth.'* After the First World War, when blacks loyally supported British troops as non-combatants, Congress sent a delegation to London, who saw the British prime minister David Lloyd George. He was visibly moved and later wrote forcefully to Smuts advising him to talk to the Congress leaders. 'You have in Africa men who can speak for native opinion and make themselves felt . . . if they do suffer under disabilities and if they have no effective mode of expression it is obvious that sooner or later serious results must ensue.'

* Sol. T Plaatje, *Native Life in South Africa*, London, P S King, 1916, p. 17

Smuts responded that Congress was not representative and that Pretoria was working on 'improved machinery for voicing the needs of and interests of the Natives'.* It was the beginning of a long non-dialogue.

There were some political stirrings from the harsher new world of black factories and urban slums; and in the twenties a brilliant black demagogue, Clements Kadalie, set up a high-sounding 'Industrial and Commercial Workers' Union' (ICU). But Kadalie was deflected from his militancy by white patrons, and his movement split, crumbled into corruption and left a trail of bitterness.

The emerging black intellectuals were too fascinated by Western culture to look far back into their own cultural roots. They were steeped in the Bible and in English literature. 'I discovered that Shakespeare had things to say not only to his England or to the Western men who have read him since, but also to me, a twentieth century African,' said the young Z K Matthews, the son of the Kimberley mineworker, who in 1924 became the first black to take a South African degree. 'I was a new specimen in the zoo of South African mankind,' he wrote afterwards. 'In the public service there was not a single post anywhere as yet provided for such a one as I.'†

The First World War and the Russian revolution had helped to make blacks more politically conscious, which worried some white employers. In January 1918, in Kimberley, Sol Plaatje had asked De Beers to donate an old tram shed as an assembly hall for the blacks (which he had already suggested to Ernest Oppenheimer). De Beers agreed, conscious of the wave of black unrest and realising (as their director Sir David Harris explained) that the gift might enhance 'their loyalty to De Beers as a generous employer of labour'.‡ It was the only recorded case of De Beers subsidising Congress. When the Communist Party

* Willan, p. 244
† Matthews, *op. cit.*, pp. 54, 82, 130ff
‡ Willan, *op. cit.*, p. 220

of South Africa was set up in 1921 it held little promise for blacks. All its delegates and executives were white, and the Rand Revolt the next year brought out all the racialism of white workers: the white martyrs who sang the Red Flag on the scaffold after the mine strike had little interest in their black brothers. But by the mid-'twenties the communists turned more emphatically to the blacks, trying to build up trades unions in factories and townships, and a small band of white communists spread their political education among blacks through night-schools and meetings: for the next thirty years the SACP would be the only interracial political party. But the communists faced bitter quarrels as they tried vainly to reconcile white and black workers, and in 1927 the Comintern in Moscow adopted a new policy of a 'native republic' for South Africa which antagonised many white communists and black leaders.

The black chiefs and professional men in Congress were fearful of the idea of equality. In 1927 Congress elected a radical new president James Gumede who was fêted in the Soviet Union (he said) as if he were the prime minister. Congress briefly swung to the left: and the communists began a national pass-burning campaign. But the government stamped it out and the black communists antagonised the conservatives in Congress. 'The Tsar was a great man in his country,' said one chief, 'of royal blood like us chiefs, and where is he now?'* By 1930 Congress turned back to its staid co-founder Dr Seme who was autocratic in his dealings with blacks and sycophantic towards the government.

The lowest ebb of Congress came in 1935, the jubilee of union, when the coalition of Hertzog and Smuts gained the necessary two-thirds majority to deprive all blacks of their remaining votes. The ANC attended a convention of five hundred who appointed a delegation to see Hertzog; but they were divided and placated by being allowed to

* Roux, *op. cit.*, p. 219

elect their own 'native representatives' and 'native representative council' which soon proved to be a 'toy telephone'. The persistent hopes of Congress leaders in front of so many slamming doors continued to exasperate their critics, including the communists. Certainly the ANC was less ready for martyrdom than the Indian Congress or other liberation movements in Asia. But black South Africans were both less confident of their own roots, and faced a far more formidable power structure and industrial system.

The Second World War gave far more serious grounds for hope. Hitler's racialism, while it was supported by the Afrikaner extremists, generated a strong anti-racialism among many whites; while the need for black support – particularly when the Japanese might invade – induced the government to promise better conditions, even the abolition of the pass laws. The blacks identified themselves with the fight against tyranny, and the President for nine years from 1940, Dr Alfred Xuma, was a pillar of black respectability who had married a black American. The end of the war produced a surge of optimism, as the idealism of the UN and the Atlantic Charter swept into South Africa with returning troops; and Congress drafted its own Bill of Rights based on the Charter, which they took very literally. But the first hopes were soon shattered when 70,000 black miners went on strike in the gold-mines in 1946. Smuts and the mining companies were united: police with bayonets charged into the compounds to force them back into the mines, and after five days nine blacks were killed and hundreds wounded.

But the most permanent change from the war was in the character of the cities. It brought a new surge of blacks escaping from drought and starvation to work in the booming new industries. By 1943 manufactures had overtaken mining in their share of the gross national product, calling for more sophisticated and settled black workers, including women: the government even briefly suspended influx control. The migration produced the same kind of chaos and squalor as existed round the edges of São Paulo or Mexico City, but further out of sight, and out of mind. The cluster of townships to the south-west of Johannesburg which came to be called 'Soweto' was already one of the biggest cities in Africa; but few white Johannesburgers had ever been inside it, and the maps did not even show it. On the wrong side of the mine-dumps, where the wind blew the gold-dust, Soweto was made up of tens of thousands of tiny box houses without electricity, dominated by the police stations, with only hoardings breaking the skyline. It looked uniformly proletarian; but it pressed together black teachers, small businessmen, clerks, gangsters and layabouts, who all piled every day into the packed trains or buses which shuttled them to work in the white city. By the 'fifties many Sowetans were the third or fourth generation of town-dwellers – grandchildren or great-grandchildren of the first miners and other migrants to the gold and diamond mines – who had never seen a homeland. In the evenings the townships came to life with a vigour and confidence, vibrating with jazz, jive and American slang, which defied any notion of temporariness or tribal-ism, or any lingering white hopes that the blacks like Red Indians would destroy themselves with drink and despair. As de Kiewiet wrote: 'The great Bantu race refused to follow what one Australian governor called the "natural progress of the aboriginal race towards extinction".'*

In fact they were beginning to establish a more urban culture than the Afrikaners who were so determined to keep them tribalised. '. . . It was only when our labour was needed that a deliberate drive was made to haul us from our tribal havens to come out to work,' as the black writer Can Themba reflected in 1957. 'And when tribalism did not help to demonstrate the dignity of labour, tribalism had to be smashed. They were so bloody successful that now they fear they have drawn too many of us into the fields of urban industry and have sired themselves a prob-

* De Kiewiet *op. cit.*, p. 179

lem.'* Or as Ezekiel Mphahlele described the predicament
of the urban black in 1962:

> He drifts to the towns to seek work so that he may pay
> his taxes and levies and feed his dependants who remain
> scratching for a living on poor soil in the reserves. He
> must understand his employer's instructions in English
> or Afrikaans, read names of streets and shops. He feels
> utterly inadequate in this respect, and he begins to
> realize how vital education is to the needs of his kind.
> 'You must go to college, my son, and come and look
> after me and your brother and sister. They must also go
> to school.' So said my mother when I went to high
> school. This kind of 'pep talk' has launched thousands
> of Africans into the uncharted seas of an insecure edu-
> cation in an insecure life.†

It was this intensely urbanised world which was the background to the new generation of more militant black politicians, who included Nelson Mandela and Oliver Tambo
who had been fellow-students at Fort Hare, the black
university college. They both came from the rural background of the Transkei: Mandela came from a royal family,
with a tall commanding presence, while Tambo was a
peasant's son – still with his ritual tribal scars on his
cheeks – who was quieter and more introverted and taught
mathematics before becoming a lawyer. They were both
founder-members of the Youth League that was set up
inside the ANC in 1944, inspired by an austere Zulu Catholic,
Anton Lembede, who was appalled by the moral degra-
dation of the urban black slums. Lembede mocked the
fatuous petitions of the 'Old Guard' and their preoccupation with Western culture: 'A pair of boots,' he said, 'is

* Can Themba, 'The Bottom of the Bottle', from *The Will to Die*,
Heinemann, London, 1972
† Ezekiel Mphahlele, *The African Image*, London, Faber & Faber,
1962, p. 56

better than all the plays of Shakespeare.'* The Youth
Leaguers saw themselves as pure black nationalists who
could appeal to the industrialised blacks; and they called
for boycotts, mass organisation, mass education. The most
influential was Walter Sisulu, a self-taught former plough-
boy and miner who by 1949 was the ANC's secretary-general
– its only full-time official. It was he who found a job in a
law office for Nelson Mandela. The Youth Leaguers were
at first fiercely anti-communist, and wanted to expel communists from Congress. But the Suppression of Communism Act in 1950 ironically helped to bring communists
closer to the ANC leaders, to whom they could offer an
opening into a wider world: only the Communist Party was
committed to one man, one vote. As Mandela later said:
'For many decades the communists were the only political
group in South Africa who were prepared to treat Africans
as human beings and their equals; who were prepared to
eat with us; talk with us, live with us, and work with us.'†
The law firm of Mandela and Tambo was a hive of left-wing
multi-racial activity in the early 'fifties, in an old building
near the centre of Johannesburg; but it had no links with
the white business world or the great stone fortress of
Anglo-American round the corner.

After the victory of the Afrikaner nationalists in 1948
the Congress leaders still followed a cautious path for a
time. Dr Xuma was ousted from the presidency, but replaced by Dr James Moroka who was scarcely more militant: a landowner and doctor with a ponderous style. But
the Youth League and the threat of apartheid soon gave
Congress a sharper edge; and at its conference in Bloemfontein in 1951 the ANC took the boldest step in its history.
It was still little known: when I arrived to report it the
only other whites were two bored local journalists, the
communist journalist Ruth First and a small clergyman

---

* Profile in *Drum* magazine, Johannesburg, January 1954; and Lodge
op. cit., pp. 21–2
† Statement to the court, Pretoria, April 20, 1964

with a wispy beard, Arthur Blaxall. Many delegates had never been photographed before, and some objected. The meeting began three hours late and rambled on for three days under hot corrugated iron, sounding more like a prayer-meeting than a political conference. But behind the scenes the Youth Leaguers including Sisulu and Mandela had been pushing forward their 'programme of action' against apartheid; and later in the meeting a joint planning council including the Indian Congress produced a report calling for the repeal of 'six unjust laws' – failing which they proposed a defiance campaign to challenge the laws. It was the first step on the road to total confrontation

In June 1952 the Congress launched the defiance campaign with a discipline and control which took whites by surprise: a small group of Africans and Indians entered a location at Boksburg, near Johannesburg, without permits and were arrested and sentenced to short terms of imprisonment. In the bleak dusty township this challenge to the state seemed eerily calm and anti-climactic. But over six months more than eight thousand went to jail. They owed something to Gandhi, who had first experimented with passive resistance forty-five years before in South Africa, and whose son Manilal still lived on his father's old ashram in Natal. But the ANC was more pragmatic and less spiritual than the Gandhis: and they knew they were dealing with a much more determined government, and a more industrialised society. It was the Eastern Cape which produced 71 percent of the volunteers, centring on Port Elizabeth which had been rapidly industrialised in the 'forties, with car and tyre factories including Ford, Volkswagen and General Motors. The workers had wretched conditions and were nearly all from one tribe, the Xhosa, with a long Christian tradition. It was a forewarning that the factories of the Eastern Cape would provide the most fertile seed-bed for future revolt.*

* Tom Lodge, *Black Politics in South Africa since 1945*, London, Longman, 1983, pp. 45–60, analyses the causes of militancy in the Eastern Cape

The ANC could not maintain the momentum of defiance, and the apartheid government soon showed itself far tougher than the British in India. After riots and the murder of a white nun they passed two drastic laws – supported by the white opposition – which made it an offence to encourage blacks to resist the law. They arrested twenty leaders, including Dr Moroka, and charged them under the Suppression of Communism Act: the judge convicted them all of 'statutory communism' – which he explained had nothing to do with communism as usually recognised – and gave them suspended sentences. The campaign fizzled out with recriminations: Dr Moroka disowned his own role and the young 'kingmakers' of Congress, including Sisulu, Mandela and Tambo, replaced Moroka with another traditional leader, the Zulu chief Albert Luthuli. But Luthuli was a much more courageous leader: he had just been sacked from his chieftaincy for taking part in the campaign, and after his election he eloquently summed up the disillusion of his generation: 'Who will deny that thirty years of my life have been spent knocking in vain, patiently, moderately and modestly, at a closed and barred door?'

Professor Matthews, one of the most conservative Congress leaders, first proposed the next step: a 'Congress of the People' to point the way to a new society for all South Africans. It was held on a football field outside Johannesburg eighteen months later in 1955, where the ANC proclaimed its new bill of rights, the 'Freedom Charter' which had been painfully agreed in the previous months. It was the nearest they ever got to a serious manifesto. Sounding more like a psalm than a policy, full of deliberate vagueness, it included two contentious sentences which resounded across future decades: 'South Africa belongs to all who live in it, black and white,' and 'the mineral wealth beneath the soil, the banks and monopoly industry shall be transferred to the ownership of the people as a whole.' The Freedom Charter was soon to be pickled in history, endlessly reinterpreted after its authors were jailed and the organisations banned. It would often be depicted as Marxist, though it was hardly more radical than the contemporary Labour Party manifesto in Britain which likewise called for nationalising all the means of production; and it was actually less socialist than the wartime programme of Malan's National Party. Nelson Mandela wrote that the Charter 'strikes a fatal blow at the financial and gold-mining monopolies and farming interests', but went on to explain optimistically that breaking them up 'will open up fresh fields for the development of a non-European bourgeois class'.*

The police were soon raiding and searching the houses of anyone involved with the Freedom Charter and in December 1956 they arrested and charged 156 of them with 'high treason' – including Luthuli, Matthews, Mandela and Tambo as well as Indians, whites and coloureds. In the subsequent 'Treason Trial' the prosecutor argued that the Charter was a prelude to revolution which aimed to set up a communist state: it would drag on for five years before the last accused, including Mandela, were acquitted in March 1961. Like subsequent trials it had achieved its main object: to put any effective black leadership out of action.

But the Freedom Charter had itself precipitated a serious breakaway from Congress by 'Africanists' who rejected its idea of a multi-racial society, and who soon briefly proved a greater threat to the government. They were led by a thirty-three-year-old university lecturer, Robert Sobukwe, who left the ANC in 1959 to set up the new Pan Africanist Congress (PAC) which identified strongly with the newly-independent states to the North. The concept of Africa as a single entity was now rapidly impinging on both black and white South Africans. The Mau Mau rebellion in Kenya and the transformation of the colonial Gold Coast into independent Ghana had reverberated through the

* *Liberation* (Johannesburg) June 1956 quoted in Lodge, *op. cit.*, p. 73

townships, and small boys called themselves Jomo or
Kwame. The map of Africa was looking different as air-
routes took over from sea-routes, opening up new links
between countries. The independent black states further
alarmed the whites in the South, and added to the frustration of the blacks who thought they were much more
westernised than the 'peasants' to the North. In fact South
Africa remained a totally separate case; not only because
it had far more whites, but because its dynamic industrial
machine was pressing whites and blacks alike into a new
mould.

Sobukwe called for a purer black nationalism, as had
the Youth League ten years earlier. 'In a country where
everyone says white is beautiful we *have* to say that black
is beautiful,' he once said to me. 'The government doesn't
want us to be proud of being black: that would make them
worried.' He and his followers – including many young
intellectuals – were courageous and impatient; and they
planned to defy the pass-laws in March 1960 with remarkable optimism and lack of planning. The atmosphere
seemed full of revolution: Macmillan had proclaimed the
wind of change two months before, and the Congo was
suddenly independent. The ANC were planning their own
anti-pass campaign, but it was the PAC who got in first.
Sobukwe himself led his followers to a police station in
Soweto and was promptly arrested – never to be a free
man again. But it was the black township of Sharpeville,
fifty miles south of Johannesburg near the state steel mills
of Iscor, which brought the situation to a flashpoint, with
its background of unemployment, rent increases and rigid
influx control. Thousands of blacks gathered outside the
police station. The police panicked, shot sixty-seven blacks
dead, and prepared the way for a revolt which soon seemed
close to revolution. After more shootings in Langa outside
Cape Town a twenty-three-year-old disciple of Sobukwe,
Philip Kgosana, led a procession of 20,000 blacks towards
Parliament Square. The police stopped them and their
commander promised Kgosana that the minister of justice

would see him if he dispersed the crowd. Kgosana, determined to remain non-violent, told the huge procession to go home quietly – which they did. When Kgosana returned to see the minister, he was arrested.* With this strange anti-climax the revolt collapsed, and with it most black confidence in non-violent protest. The police cordoned off Langa and moved in with armoured cars, batons, crowbars and guns, arresting 1,500 people and forcing the rest back to work.

Would South African history have been different had Kgosana not dismissed the crowd? Recriminations continued. Certainly for a few weeks after Sharpeville many blacks believed they could be on the verge of liberation like the movements in the north. The ANC in Johannesburg had already made its own plans to defy the pass laws: it organised a successful one-day strike and a pass-burning campaign; Chief Luthuli himself burnt his pass. International protests were inhibiting the government, and the police were ordered not to arrest blacks without passes. The expectations were enhanced by the attempted assassination of Dr Verwoerd by an eccentric English-speaking farmer, David Pratt. The blacks wondered if their white masters might be driving each other mad. The acting Prime Minister Paul Sauer promised that: 'The old book of South African history was closed at Sharpeville.'

When I visited Soweto at that time there was heady talk, expecting a real revolution: 'This is *it*.' 'We never dreamt it could come so soon,' said a Congress leader. 'The police are so polite, *it hurts*,' said a messenger boy. 'Jeez a cop even called me *meneer*.' I found Mandela touchy about the PAC's initiative, but cautiously confident about the prospects of the ANC: 'We've got to have the machinery, the organisation.' His colleague Duma Nokwe reckoned that 6,000 people had already burnt their passes: 'We'll

---

* For the account by Kgosana, now in Sri Lanka, *see* Joseph Lelyveld, *Move Your Shadow*, London, Michael Joseph, 1985. New York, Times Books, 1985, pp. 315–27

have them roasted . . . This country is in a pre-rev . . .'
(he stopped himself). No one then would have imagined
that another sixteen years would follow before the next
serious confrontation with government.

But it was a short honeymoon. In April 1960 parliament
voted by 128 to sixteen to declare both the ANC and the
PAC 'unlawful organisations': and after forty-eight years,
Congress ceased to have an official existence inside South
Africa. Immediately hundreds were detained. A month
after Sharpeville the government had totally regained control. Saracen tanks patrolled the townships, protesters and
strikers were beaten into submission. The pass-laws were
reimposed still more strictly. Verwoerd recovered and Paul
Sauer soon disappeared from political view. 'This isn't *It*,'
said the black writer Can Themba, gazing into a brandy
glass. 'They seemed to think that *It* was just round the
corner. It never seemed to occur to them that the wind
might be only a breeze.' 'The 'mopping up' continued
for months afterwards, with hundreds of ANC and PAC
supporters tried under the Suppression of Communism
Act.

The banned leaders knew that they were coming to the
end of the road of peaceful protest, and prepared for
violence. The PAC was the most ruthless, contemptuous of
the ANC's restraint: 'They think sabotage will frighten the
white men. But you couldn't frighten Hitler,' Zeph Motho-
peng who was its acting leader told me in 1962. 'Essentially
the struggle is here: the world won't help: it backs the
winning horse.' The PAC formed its own underground
terrorist movement called Poqo (meaning 'pure') which
was dedicated to a black revolution with reckless terrorism.
By 1964 202 Poqo members had been convicted of murder.* But the PAC leadership had become increasingly
disorganised and vulnerable to infiltration by South African spies. It moved from Lesotho to Tanzania, and later to
Zambia, but increasingly riven by dissidents and deserters;

* Lodge, *op. cit.*, p. 241

and after Poqo was crushed it produced no very effective action inside South Africa.

The ANC was now led underground by Nelson Mandela, who first tried secretly to organise a three-day stay-at-home strike which was suppressed by the army, and was then convinced that only more violent tactics could influence white opinion. By June 1961 a handful of ANC leaders had decided, as Mandela said, that 'it would be unrealistic and wrong for African leaders to continue preaching peace and non-violence at a time when the government met our peaceful demands with force'. Already in 1961 the first recruits had been sent abroad for guerrilla training. But Mandela still hoped to confine the attacks to sabotage, which 'did not involve loss of life, and offered the best hope for future race relations'. Their targets for sabotage were chosen carefully with an eye on international opinion: 'We believed that South Africa depended to a large extent on foreign capital and foreign trade,' Mandela explained. 'We felt that planned destruction of power plants, and interference with rail and telephone communications, would tend to scare away capital from the country.'* It would be another quarter-century before the internal violence began to have that effect – in a far less disciplined context than Mandela had planned.

The armed struggle was entrusted to a military wing, called Umkhonto we Sizwe, 'the Spear of the Nation', with Mandela as its commander-in-chief, and a high command and structure copied from the Jewish Irgun organisation set up in Palestine in 1944. It soon announced itself with remarkable haste. On two days in December 1961 a succession of explosions hit public buildings and installations in Durban, Johannesburg and especially Port Elizabeth, while Umkhonto leaflets optimistically explained: 'We hope we will bring the government and its supporters to

---

* Nelson Mandela, statement to court at the Rivonia Trial, April 20, 1964. Republished in *The Struggle is My Life*, London, International Defence and Aid Fund, 1978

their senses before it is too late . . .' Mandela was
smuggled out of South Africa early in 1962 to visit African
states: he then realised, he said, that nearly every black
movement before independence had received aid from
socialist countries, and he later urged the ANC to send a
mission to the East. But he also looked to Britain, where he
talked with Labour Party leaders including Hugh Gaitskell
and Denis Healey, and the Liberal leader Jo Grimond.

Mandela was already a minor legend. Back in South
Africa as the 'black pimpernel' he was hunted by the
police while he and other revolutionaries with aliases and
disguises were preparing a new wave of sabotage on a
farm at Rivonia, outside Johannesburg. It was a foolhardy
venture: the police had been infiltrating Umkhonto and
breaking its secrets with the help of torture and informers.
Mandela was caught in Natal in August 1962 (with the
help of CIA information, it was later revealed) and was tried
two months later, charged with incitement to strike and
sentenced to five years. But the police in the meantime
were tracking down the other conspirators and in July 1963
they swooped on Rivonia and arrested several of them,
together with piles of documents.

Three months later the conspirators, including Mandela,
were charged with sabotage and seeking to overthrow the
government by violent revolution. It was a tense and
dramatic trial, bristling with police (watching it one day,
when I gave a signal of recognition to Mandela I was
immediately taken out for questioning). The state prosecutor Percy Yutar had an easy task in proving sabotage
and revolutionary intent. In his long final speech, carefully
prepared with the help of his fellow-prisoners and lawyers,
Mandela recounted his political development, how he had
turned to sabotage and guerrillas but cherished the ideal of
a democratic and free society. 'If needs be, it is an ideal
for which I am prepared to die.' He and seven others were
sentenced to life imprisonment and were sent to Robben
Island, South Africa's Alcatraz, off the coast of Cape
Town.

But the state could not prove the most serious charge, that they were part of an international communist conspiracy. It had produced documents in Mandela's handwriting including one which began with the incriminating words: 'We communist party members are the most advanced revolutionaries in modern history,' and continued '. . . the enemy must be completely crushed and wiped out from the face of the earth before a communist world can be realised.' Twenty years later President Botha was to quote it as evidence that Mandela was a dangerous communist. But as Mandela explained to the court he had copied it out (he copied out many very contrasting documents) from a Chinese pamphlet by Liu Shao-chi called 'How to be a good communist'.*

Mandela's relationship with communism would stir up constant argument a quarter-century later. In his final speech he insisted that 'The ANC has never at any period of its history advocated a revolutionary change in the economic structure of the country, nor has it, to the best of my recollection, ever condemned capitalist society.' He explained that: 'The communist party sought to emphasise class distinctions whilst the ANC seeks to harmonise them.' He admitted that he had been influenced by Marxist thought, like Gandhi or Nasser, but explained that, unlike Marxists, he admired the Western parliamentary system, the impartiality of British judges and the American separation of powers. He compared the ANC's co-operation with communists with the Western wartime alliance with Stalin:

It is perhaps difficult for white South Africans, with an ingrained prejudice against communism, to understand why experienced African politicians so readily accept communists as their friends. But to us the reason is obvious. Theoretical differences amongst those fighting against oppression is a luxury we cannot afford at this stage.

* See the transcript provided by the CIA to Senator Jesse Helms in the Senate debate on sanctions, Washington, August 14, 1986

With Mandela and his colleagues on Robben Island, and the Poqo terrorists convicted, the black opposition was crushed. Many went into exile. Mandela's friend and colleague Oliver Tambo had already been designated by Luthuli to lead the ANC in exile, and after Sharpeville had slipped out of the country. He first based himself in London, and toured the United States and Western Europe, vainly seeking financial support and boycotts of South African goods. Then the ANC established its headquarters first in Tanzania, later in Zambia, where it gradually built up its military and diplomatic force. Tambo looked for friends where he could; Mandela had already forged a link with the FLN army in Algeria, which helped to train Umkhonto and provided some financial help, and Tambo later travelled with an Algerian passport. The Organisation of African Unity (OAU) which was formed in 1963, gave some help, but never enough; while in western Europe only the Scandinavians and Dutch gave money. But when Tambo went in 1963 to the Soviet Union he was promised a supply of weapons free of charge.* And the ANC thereafter looked increasingly to Russia and East Germany, not only for weapons, but for funds, training and jobs.

To most white South Africans the ANC now appeared finally broken. The police became more brutal in their use of torture, and more sophisticated in their intelligence and control with the help of training in Europe and computers from IBM or ICL. The sporadic sabotage was ineffective and provided pretexts for further reprisals. Mandela was out of sight and out of mind. And the way was clear for the biggest boom in South Africa's history since the first gold-rush.

* Evidence to the Foreign Affairs Committee of the House of Commons, October 29, 1985

6

The Apartheid Boom

I have seen the wicked in great power,
And spreading himself like a green bay tree.

Psalm 37, verse 35

Each trade agreement, each bank loan, each new investment is
another brick in the wall of our continued existence.

John Vorster, 1972

When the Afrikaners came to power in 1948 they had been determined permanently to separate the races just when industrial pressures were moving in an opposite direction. 'The perverse economics of apartheid,' as de Kiewiet put it, 'sees alien invaders instead of needed immigrants, and over-population where there is really under-population.'* By 1951 manufacturing industry already accounted for 22 percent of South Africa's national income, while gold-mining contributed only eleven percent; and factories called for a more stable and skilled black workforce than the migrants in the mines. The numbers of blacks employed in private manufacturing had doubled in ten years to over 300,000 in 1947–8 – increasing much faster than white employees. The very visible surge of blacks into the towns blatantly contradicted the apartheid theory that they had

* De Kiewiet, *op. cit.*, p. 67

no permanent place in the white man's world. Many observers insisted that these economic pressures were bound to prevail over the dogma of apartheid. 'It is the irresistible force of economic integration which wins and must win,' wrote Basil Davidson of the *New Statesman* in 1952, 'however hatefully the majority of whites may resist its pressure.'*

But businessmen remained ambivalent. They wanted stable and more skilled black labour, but they shared many of the Afrikaner government's fears about the black flood, and some of their racial prejudices. They wanted both to have their blacks and contain them. Much of the segregation within corporations – whether in canteens, toilets or sports grounds – turned out, on investigation, to be customary rather than statutory. Hardly any white businessmen, whether South African or expatriate, had any social contact with black people except as servants or as a labour-force: they were totally cut off from the black politicians and intellectuals who were already shaping the character of the opposition. Only a very few Western businessmen asserted themselves to promote black workers against the pressures of apartheid. One of them was Wayne Fredericks, a young executive who had come out in 1948 to set up a cornflakes plant near Johannesburg for the Kellogg company of Battle Creek, Michigan. 'I always believed there was a measure of sovereignty behind the factory gates,' he said afterwards; and he later maintained his opposition to apartheid in the State Department and the Ford Company. But most American expatriates reckoned that if they wanted to be promoted when they returned home they should not rock the boat.

The South African industrialists were still overwhelmingly English-speaking and their lives in the suburbs had little contact with the Afrikaner suburbs. The contrast under Kruger was now more complete, between the Afri-

* Basil Davidson, *Report on Southern Africa*, London, Jonathan Cape, 1952, pp. 109–14

kaners who controlled politics in Pretoria and the English and other later immigrants who controlled the wealth in Johannesburg. The Anglophones were now decisively in a minority, as they had never been in Australia, New Zealand or Canada, and they were bitter about their exclusion from power. But there was a tacit assumption which suited many: they were left to make money, while the Afrikaners made politics. And as politics became rougher the bargain had its advantages: the Anglophone businessman could blame the brutality of apartheid and Afrikaner police, while offering no real alternative. To white immigrants, particularly to Englishmen escaping from winter, austerity and rationing, the opportunities and luxury of South Africa seemed magical. Apartheid might in the end be damaging for business, but it also meant no unions, low taxes and cheap and obedient servants.

Was capitalism fundamentally on the side of apartheid? Many Marxists, seeing the Afrikaners in the image of Nazi Germany, could now argue their case with added moral conviction, branding capitalists as racists. In fact the crude charge could not be upheld: as Merle Lipton wrote in her study of capitalism and apartheid, the Afrikaners' policies clearly showed that they were acting against the interests of urban capitalists, and in 1948 they precipitated a flight of capital and of skilled and professional whites out of the country.* But there were more sophisticated arguments which will recur: that business interests, including American and British, were far too easily seduced by the apartheid government into conniving with their system, much as Hitler manipulated German industrialists after 1933; and that businessmen never seriously tried to dissociate themselves from apartheid or to identify with black aspirations until violent opposition compelled them, too late. It is an argument which cannot be purely economic; for the question is not only whether businessmen were condoning apartheid, but whether they were seen to do so by the

* Lipton, *op. cit.*, p. 284

emerging black political class. And in a country of almost unique financial concentration the answer lay with individuals as much as economic forces.

The argument became more virulent after Sharpeville, when the repression of the black opposition was more ruthless and evident. For a few months after Sharpeville Western investors appeared to have voted with their wallets, making their own decisive judgment about South Africa's future under apartheid. South African shares plummeted and £48 million left the country almost immediately. International capitalism appeared to be decisively dissociating itself from apartheid. The flight of capital ran down the foreign exchange reserves to only £77 million by May 1961, while economic growth was down to zero. The government quickly had to impose controls on imports, foreign exchange and hire-purchase to stem the flow.

But the capital flight proved short-lived and less fundamental than it looked. Most of it came from foreign investors selling their shares, and as the crisis subsided shrewd investors – including Anglo-American and the British financier Isaac Wolfson – began buying at the bottom of the market. The direct investment by British multinationals remained committed, and even in 1961 £9 million flowed into the country. Anglo-American took the lead in restoring confidence, both by buying up shares and by obtaining a record loan of $30 million in 1961, guaranteed by Barclays in London after heavy pressure from Oppenheimer in person. But South Africa also received welcome endorsement from one of the high-priests of international capital, David Rockefeller, the chairman of the Chase Manhattan Bank. After visiting Africa two years before – to open an office of the bank in Johannesburg – the Chase led a loan to South Africa. Now, after Sharpeville, Rockefeller realised that by supporting Pretoria in a time of trouble he could be on the inside track; and the Chase lent $10 million to South Africa and joined a new consortium to lend $150 million. Churchmen and others protested against this stamp of approval, but the Chase replied: 'We believe it would endanger the free world if every large American bank deprived developing countries of the opportunity for economic growth. If one hopes for changes in the Republic of South Africa or elsewhere, it would do little good to withdraw economic support.' Four years later the Chase involved itself much more deeply in the Republic by buying a 15 percent share of the Standard Bank, its second-biggest bank which was also now spreading round the world – discreetly omitting the words 'of South Africa' from its name.

By 1964, with the black leaders in jail or in exile and the government clearly in control, the way was open for the great boom, a wonder-decade in which South Africa's economic growth was outstripping nearly all Western countries, averaging 6 percent a year during the 'sixties. The first recovery after Sharpeville had been achieved without much help from foreign investors who were wary of the political risk; but by 1965 they were piling in faster than before Sharpeville, contributing heavily to the high growth-rate and bringing in new technology which added to future growth. By 1970 foreign investment totalled $7.9 billion compared to $3.6 billion in 1960, and the annual net inflow of capital was $343 million – six times what it was before Sharpeville.*

Multinational corporations could not resist the prospects of rapid expansion and a return on investment averaging 15 percent by 1967 – far higher than in Europe.† The Pretoria government wanted to become less dependent on Britain – particularly since leaving the Commonwealth – and successfully encouraged corporations from the rest of Europe and the United States: by 1970 the big three American car-makers (Chrysler, Ford and General Motors) had invested over $75 million in ten years, and six out of ten of the cars and trucks made in South Africa

* Johnson, *op. cit.*, pp 28, 30. *Also* Jim Hoagland, *South Africa, Civilizations in Conflict*, London, Allen & Unwin, 1973, p. 338
† UKSATA, London, Purpose and Progress 1965–7

were now made by American companies.* France acquired
a special importance as the provider of arms, particularly
Mirage fighters. But the most dynamic and confident new
partner was West Germany, which increased its investment
from R70 million in 1965 to over R1000 in 1970 and which
by 1974 was providing more imports into South Africa
than Britain. The names of Hoechst, Siemens or Mercedes
sprung up on the hoardings and BMW established its only
foreign plant in South Africa, from which they began
exporting cars to the Middle East. And the 'Bonn–Pretoria
Axis' was soon to have a special importance in providing
military technology.†

Britain remained by far the biggest investor. By 1968
South Africa had moved from fourth to third place among
Britain's investment territories (excluding oil, banking and
insurance), overtaking the United States. 'Considering
the relative size and growth prospects of these two countries,' wrote John Stopford and Louis Turner, 'one must
conclude that the lure of easy profits remained, for many
firms, more important than building for the future.'‡ And
while South Africa accounted for only about 1 percent of
America's total investment overseas in 1970, it made up
10 percent of Britain's.§ Most British multinationals were
still increasing their stake, often in close partnership with
South African state corporations; while the Afrikaner
government was strengthening its hold on the economy,
and trying to ensure that expanding industry would support
the system of apartheid.¶ Industry was usually happy to
oblige. Courtaulds not only made fabrics, stockings and
paper in South Africa, but invested heavily in a wood-pulp

    * Hoagland, *op. cit.*, p. 338
    † R W Johnson, *How Long will South Africa Survive?* London,
Macmillan, 1977, p. 35
    ‡ John M Stopford and Louis Turner, *Britain and the Multinationals*,
Chichester, UK, 1985, p. 81
    § Ruth First, Jonathan Steele and Christabel Gurney, *The South
African Connection*, London, Temple Smith, 1972, p. 31
    ¶ Lipton, *op. cit.*, p. 303

company, Saiccor, which exported to its rayon factories elsewhere (the state industrial development corporation had a one-third stake in Saiccor, and appointed the chairman). Rio Tinto-Zinc bought 39 percent of the huge Palabora copper mine (the American Newmont mining company owned another 30 percent). The mine employed 2,000 blacks close to a homeland in the Northern Transvaal, and brought RTZ – as they explained – into a 'very, very close understanding with the government'.*

Some multinationals with big interests in black Africa were worried about investing more in apartheid. 'It would be undesirable to appear to be expanding our interests in South Africa,' said the Special Committee which ruled Unilever in 1964, 'in view of the attitude to South Africa of other African States.' But when this policy was questioned the chairman Lord Cole explained revealingly that:

> in principle there was no objection to risking more money in South Africa provided this was not done in such a way as to provoke repercussions in other African states and that any new projects were sufficiently remunerative short term for us to see the possibility of getting our money back in five to six years.

In fact many profits were high enough to offer such returns; and only a few months later Unilever bought the Robin Cheese company in South Africa. Unilever saw itself as firmly at odds with Pretoria: 'Unilever's commercial interests put it in the anti-apartheid camp in South Africa,' wrote a historian of the company, 'as surely as his desire to sell more soap to the English working-class had buttressed William Lever's enthusiasm for social reform in Britain half a century earlier.' But it continued to pay its black workers a quarter the wages of the whites, and like most British companies it was reluctant to interfere with the

---

* House of Commons Expenditure Committee, 1973: Wages & Conditions of African Workers, Evidence, Vol. 1, pp. 88, 251

apartheid patterns. The Special Committee stressed that they had to 'proceed slowly in the replacement of Europeans by Africans . . . we had to take care not to upset the white community.'*

The flow of investment and trade was hardly affected by political changes in Britain, and after 1964 the Labour government actively encouraged it. In 1967 John Davies, the director-general of the Confederation of British Industry, went out to South Africa armed with a supporting letter from Anthony Crosland, the President of the Board of Trade, which stressed that a third of South Africa's exports still went to Britain and said: 'Our concern to see this valuable trade develop and to avoid any economic confrontation with South Africa has been repeatedly made clear in parliament and the UN.' And the British trade department issued *Hints to Businessmen* which pointed out that the two main political parties in South Africa 'do not disagree about the principle of separate treatment for those of European and non-European descent'. In a craven sentence it recommended: 'When engaged in business dealings visitors would be well advised not to become involved in controversy on political and social matters that arouse deep feeling in South Africa.' †

Many industrialists suggested that they were discreetly persuading Pretoria to modify its policies; but there was no real evidence of it, and the trade lobbies almost imperceptibly turned into lobbies to defend apartheid. In 1966 British businessmen set up the UK-South African Trade Association, or UKSATA, as an offshoot of the CBI, which soon became a zealous apologist for Pretoria, working closely with its sister-body in South Africa, SABRITA. UKSATA's vocal chairman William Luke – who was also chairman of Lindustries which had much business in South Africa – went frequently to Pretoria, where he always saw cabinet ministers. 'Since I know them, lunch with them and

* David Fieldhouse, *Unilever Overseas: The Story of a Multinational, 1895-1961*, pp. 133, 139, 140–2

† First *et al.*, *op. cit.*, pp. 214–16

sometimes joke with them,' he said in 1973, he believed he could 'quietly influence them . . .' UKSATA's president Sir Nicholas Cayzer, the very wealthy chairman of British and Commonwealth Shipping, who was a major contributor to the Tory party, usually saw the prime minister when he went to Pretoria.* What right had Britain or any other nation, he asked, 'to create moralistic barriers to the natural process of evolution in South Africa?'†

British and American businessmen also worked closely with a well-funded new lobby, the South African Foundation, which had been formed just before Sharpeville to improve the country's image abroad: 'It was the desperate need of the times that shaped its aims.'‡ It was supported by leading South African industrialists including Harry Oppenheimer and Anton Rupert; and its first president was Sir Francis de Guingand, formerly Chief of Staff to Lord Montgomery, who had emigrated to Johannesburg. Charles Engelhard (*see* below) was one of the original committee; most major American companies, including General Motors, Mobil, Chrysler, Union Carbide and Caterpillar, subscribed to it; and in Britain both Luke and Cayzer were among its trustees. Throughout the 'sixties the Foundation was very effective in inviting British and other grandees, including Field Marshal Montgomery, to visit and praise white South Africa. By its tenth anniversary it could claim that it had helped to 'stem the tide of ignorance, criticism and misrepresentation against the Republic'.

Businessmen were still more buoyant after 1966, when Verwoerd was assassinated and Balthazar John Vorster took over as prime minister. He was hardly a liberal: he had been imprisoned as a supporter of Hitler during the Second World War – together with Van den Bergh who became head of his secret service, Boss – and as

---

* House of Commons Expenditure Committee, November 1983 Vol. 1, p. 9

† First *et al.*, *op. cit.*, p. 220

‡ Johannesburg *Sunday Times*, May 14, 1967

Verwoerd's Minister of Justice he had been relentless in stamping out black opposition. But he had visibly mellowed, enjoyed golf and drinking, and was welcomed to the Rand Club, the traditional stronghold of English finance. He was not a theological fanatic like Verwoerd, and he faced up to the need to do business with South Africa's black neighbours, by launching a policy of *detente* with alternate bullying and friendship. The old fears of physical contact with blacks – which had precipitated the ejection from the Commonwealth – now dissolved in the face of diplomatic necessities, as black leaders were received in style. Many businessmen looked to Vorster to open up wider markets to the north, while maintaining order in the south; yet he was never really interested in the views of industrialists. He took the view, as Gavin Relly of Anglo-American later complained, 'that the politics of our country was none of our business. I think he was scared of businessmen, but in any event he found it offensive if they ever voiced a view about the political situation in the country.'*

South Africa was certainly acquiring a special dynamism and an exciting sense of the future – at least the short term – encouraged by entrepreneurs who were well able to compete internationally. Much of the pace was set by a remarkable group of descendants of Jewish immigrants who had nearly all been refugees from the same region of Lithuania on the edge of Russia in the late nineteenth century: many first arrived as pedlars, but quickly built up fast-growing businesses. Joffe Marks who arrived in 1884 began importing flour and bought up the small Premier milling company which was inherited by his nephew Harry Jaffe and by *his* nephew Joe Bloom, whose son Tony Bloom is now chairman of the present wide-ranging Premier Group. Heris Hersowitz who also arrived in 1884 had a son, Bob, who became a mining engineer and went into partnership with Simeon 'Slip' Menell, the son of a London

* Interview with Hugh Murray, *Leadership* magazine, 1985

furrier, to form a new gold-mining company Anglo-Vaal – which is still run by the founders' sons, Basil Hersov and Clive Menell. Meyer Ackerman arrived in 1883 and began dealing in ostrich feathers: his son Gus, financed by another Lithuanian, Morris Mauerberger, built up a chain of Ackerman's stores, which were then bought by another ex-Lithuanian group; while Gus Ackerman's son set up his own successful group of Pick 'n Pay supermarkets. One of the last Lithuanian immigrants was Nathan Gordon who arrived in 1918 and became credit manager for Advance Laundries: his son Donald, an accountant, raised money to set up his own Liberty Life assurance company, now the third biggest in the country, interlocked by the Standard Bank and South African Breweries.* These and other immigrant families were able to mobilise South African savings and capital to transform local industries, services and life-styles, with a speed of innovation and enterprise which surprised American as well as European business rivals.

The economic euphoria of South Africa in the 'sixties was promoted in *The Economist* in 1968 by their star writer Norman Macrae, in a survey called 'The Green Bay Tree' which encouraged both businessmen and diplomats in the West (*see* page 156). Macrae insisted that it was 'almost certainly to everybody's advantage' that the Republic should continue to get richer. The business community was visibly to the left of government, and in South Africa 'richer and securer generally means lefter'. It was true that apartheid was wickedly unequal and full of unnecessary cruelties; but the notion of a 'revenging black tide' sweeping down from the north was 'good-hearted balderdash' in the light of the disasters in black Africa, while the urban blacks in the Republic were benefiting from the industrial advance. Moreover South Africa had the benefit of a new generation of bubbling entrepreneurs including Afrikaners

---

* For a full account of Jewish immigrant families see Mendel Kaplan, *Jewish Roots in the South African Economy*, Cape Town, C Struik, 1986

such as Jan Marais of Trust Bank and Anton Rupert of Rembrandt tobacco, together with civil servants with a 'wickedly admirable detachment'; while the Reserve Bank, within the limits of its appalling social system, was 'the very best sort of central bank' run by crisp and efficient Dutch bankers; and since black trade unions were prohibited 'the country has the real economic good fortune of not generally suffering from a trade-union-generated cost-push inflation'. The military seemed to have a complete grip on any black revolt, which was visibly incompetent and fifth-class. 'This white nationalist government of South Africa,' Macrae concluded, 'is meeting a tryst with the twentieth century in its continent, even though so many of its social attitudes belong deplorably to pre-nineteenth century days.'*

At the heart of this business optimism was Harry Oppenheimer, the chairman of the Anglo-American Corporation which was now riding high on the boom. He still seemed diffident and self-effacing, talked softly, listened carefully. He still liked to hire and promote Oxford graduates (to the annoyance of some Afrikaners including Wim de Villiers who thought they 'never got to grips with problems on the shop-floor'). But in action he was now far more confident, like his father but more proudly South African. He was also extending Anglo's interests to the north: his group was by far the biggest investor in the continent, with its income dwarfing most emerging black states. His personal sensitivity made him a patient diplomat, as he became the object of anti-imperialist rhetoric in Tanzania or Zambia: he became friendly with President Kaunda, even though he took control of Anglo's copper mines. But South Africa remained all-important, and Anglo was soon dominating the gold-mines still further.

Oppenheimer acquired an important new partner when in 1958 Anglo bought control of Central Mining (the old Wernher-Beit 'Corner House'), with the help of the bulky

* *The Economist*, 'The Green Bay Tree', June 29, 1968

and grunting American tycoon Charlie Engelhard, who was suspected of being the original of Ian Fleming's character Goldfinger. He was the son of a German emigrant to America who had set up the Engelhard Metals and Minerals Corporation in 1890; but Charlie made his own bigger fortune, and became the 'Platinum King'. He joined the board of Anglo – thus making it more genuinely Anglo-American – and bought a mansion in Johannesburg. Unlike Oppenheimer he loved flaunting his wealth, gambling, over-eating and flying in his private plane, the Platinum Plover, complete with two butlers. After Sharpeville he did much, together with Oppenheimer, to attract new investment and loans from America. As a friend of Presidents Kennedy and Johnson, he could make South Africa more acceptable to Americans. When Vorster took over he explained that his policy was 'as much in the interest of South Africa as anything I can think of . . .'* But he never challenged colour bar customs: after the black singer Miriam Makeba had sung to his white guests in his Johannesburg home she was taken to the kitchen for supper.

Anglo-American soon extended its intricate web. The Oppenheimer–Engelhard interests merged Central Mining to form the conglomerate Charter Consolidated based in London; and in 1960 Anglo was able to buy Johannesburg Consolidated Investments (Johnnies), Barney Barnato's old company, forestalling Afrikaner interests. Four years later and more far-sightedly Oppenheimer deliberately allowed the Afrikaner group Federale Mynbou to gain control of another group of gold-mines, General Mining, with Anglo as a minority shareholder. For the first time in eighty years an Afrikaner group owned a major stake (9 percent) in the country's gold industry. By the end of the 'sixties, Anglo also had minority interests in two other gold-mining groups, Gold Fields of South Africa and Union Corporation, all of them interlocked with director-

* First *et al.*, *op. cit.*, p. 132

ships. Only the smallest of the six groups, Anglo-Vaal, now remained separate from the Oppenheimer network: the group which was still controlled by its two founding families, the Menells and the Hersovs.*

As his gold-mines needed less capital during the 'sixties Oppenheimer seized every chance to expand into manufacture, finance and property, frequently in partnership with foreign companies who brought in advanced technology, though he found that the companies which ran themselves performed better.† With ICI Anglo built up the chemical-and-explosives company AE&CI to become South Africa's biggest industrial company, making plastics, ammonia and textiles as well as ammunition and explosives; and also SA Nylon Spinners, the country's biggest producer of synthetic fibres. The twin giants faced little competition: Courtaulds complained that AE&CI had told them: 'your chemicals go up by 10 percent from this evening. If you do not accept, you get no chemicals': though ICI angrily denied it.‡ In steel, Anglo used Newmont from America and Davy from Britain to establish its biggest single project Highveld Steel and Vanadium, to produce high-grade steel, which became the country's fourth biggest manufacturer; and with the help of General Steel Industries and the Abex Corporation in America it built up Scaw metals to make steel parts and grinding balls. With Bowater from Britain it formed the Mondi Valley Paper Company. Anglo's newspaper empire, however, came to it by accident, when it bought JCI in 1960, bringing with it effective control (40 percent) over the Argus Group which included the influential Johannesburg *Star*: eventually in 1971 the Argus gained control of South African Associated Newspapers (SAAN) which included the liberal Rand *Daily Mail*, thus giving Anglo indirect control over

* See above, p. 91
† Innes, p. 193
‡ Expenditure Committee Vol 1, pp. 87, 298

seventeen out of twenty English-speaking papers – but no Afrikaans.*

Behind all these companies lay a growing financial network. Already in 1955 Sir Ernest had formed Anglo's own merchant bank called Union Acceptances, with the help of Lazards and Barclays in London, which soon produced its own offspring the Discount House of SA. By 1968 UAL was the seventh biggest bank in South Africa, and the biggest merchant bank. Anglo also built up its own property subsidiary called Amaprop, run by Oppenheimer's ex-son-in-law, a hearty rugby footballer and son of a Glasgow stockbroker, Gordon Waddell. Its chief monument is the Carlton Centre in Johannesburg, the biggest hotel complex in Africa and one of the first multiracial hotels.

Oppenheimer dominated the country's economy in many ways more pervasively than Rhodes sixty years earlier; but like Rhodes he remained in awkward tandem with the Afrikaner political monopoly. Anglo was as consistently English-speaking as Pretoria was Afrikaans-speaking; and the government had plenty of leverage over Anglo, through contracts, taxes and military links: in some ways a semi-monopoly was much easier to control. Oppenheimer financed a spectrum of political groups, like Gianni Agnelli in Italy whose Fiat empire had similar ramifications, including both the Progressive Party formed in 1959 with its courageous and solitary MP Helen Suzman, and the South African Foundation which helped to whitewash the country abroad. Later Anglo helped Chief Buthelezi in KwaZulu, and even offered some support to the Black Consciousness Movement. Within South Africa Oppenheimer appeared emphatically liberal, always advocating reforms in his speeches; but abroad he felt compelled to defend his government, and discourage foreign pressure.

* Innes, p. 205

Inside Anglo's spacious womb the white executives could easily believe that their benign expansion was resolving the racial problems, like booming companies in the American Deep South – a confidence which radiated from the lush house magazine *Optima*. Anglo estates and Anglo factories spread out across the virgin veld, built on Anglo land financed by the Anglo bank. It seemed almost a state within a state – like De Beers in Kimberley half a century earlier – with its own diplomats, intelligence and mine police. From inside its rational, self-enclosed world, with smiling black chauffeurs and clerks, the compounds and slum houses of Soweto seemed a world away. Oppenheimer was a masterly financial and industrial manager, and he knew how to pick British and other executives and give them motivation and drive. The 'Anglo boys' in Johannesburg became a distinctive and confident breed, riding at the Inanda Club, swimming at the Country Club, flying in private Anglo planes. Developing Africa was rewarding psychologically as well as financially: it was their wives who were often left to try to mitigate the insoluble social problems of black families in the wake of their industrial progress.

White businessmen and overseas visitors could be reassured by what was known as the 'Oppenheimer Thesis': that economic growth would make apartheid wither away, as blacks were drawn into skilled jobs and middle class life. It was supported by a much-quoted historical analysis, written in 1964 by an Anglo executive Michael O'Dowd, which insisted that South Africa's political and social development was not abnormal for a country just emerging from the first stage of industrialisation – like contemporary Mexico or like Britain in the 1850s – where a minority government ruled harshly. Social injustice, he argued, was not merely normal in a developing economy but 'it is absolutely universal and if not inevitable it has certainly never yet been avoided'. He explained that 'a watershed is reached when the supply of unskilled labour ceases to appear inexhaustible and the ruling minority starts to find that it actually needs the rest of the population'. He predicted (with some accuracy) a period of major reform in about 1980 but his analysis did not accept that South Africa's development posed any special racial problem; and like most businessmen he showed little interest in the black political attitudes that might be forged in the meantime.*

Black nationalists as well as communists began to see Anglo as the living model of monopoly capitalism. This is how the ANC secretary-general Alfred Nzo depicted it in the Congress magazine *Sechaba* in 1970:

> South African companies like the Anglo-American Corporation under Harry Oppenheimer and many others have all got interlocking interests and directorships with British and US companies. Economically therefore, the South African racists who cling to apartheid are an integral and key part of the sinister plot of exploitation by the imperialists on an international scale. The merger of White S.A. capital with international finance has been a specific feature of S.A. penetration in the economies in many countries in Africa and elsewhere. There is no other country in the world in which the imperialists have been prepared to relegate their differences to the background and unite their efforts economically, technically and militarily as they have done in South Africa.†

The debate about capitalism and apartheid would continue over the next two decades. Certainly many foreign investors welcomed features of the apartheid regime, after the black political leaders were out of sight: and Pretoria made the most of its appeal to the union-ridden industrialists abroad. And viewed from the black side of the curtain there was little evidence that economic growth was in

* From Adrian Leftwich (editor), *South Africa: Economic Growth and Political Change*, London (Allison and Busby) 1974, pp. 34–42
† *Sechaba*, February 1970

itself liberalising apartheid. 'South Africa's most dramatic period of economic advance between 1967 and 1976,' said Joe Slovo, the later Chairman of the South African Communist Party, 'was also a period during which more was done than at any time during our history to implement the worst features of apartheid.'* A new school of young Marxist South African writers emerged during the 'sixties who maintained that apartheid was really an extension of capitalism; and neo-Marxist historians and sociologists were to acquire a dominating position in many South African universities.

But many Marxists had an oversimplified view of the capitalists, who themselves had increasingly divergent interests, particularly as manufacturing and retailing rivalled mining. The old colour bar in jobs which had been entrenched in the gold-mines long before the apartheid government was getting in the way of more sophisticated industries. Mechanised factories called for more skilled black workers, living in stable conditions: there were not enough white workers to fill the jobs, and their rapid turnover became absurdly rapid and inefficient; while it was becoming obvious that black workers could do the same jobs for much lower wages. The sheer cost of Verwoerdian apartheid, including decentralising industry to the borders of the homelands, was increasingly evident. And both manufacturers and shopkeepers were looking enviously towards the black middle class to provide a market for their goods. By 1970, according to the Bureau of Market Research at the University of South Africa, the blacks accounted for 22.5 percent of total personal income; by 1975 25.4 percent.†

The gold-mine owners were also having doubts as to whether the colour bar and the use of cheap migrant labour were in their interests, or even in the interests of the white workers. It was true that they had kept down black wages

---

* Speech to SACP, July 1986: *see* Chapter 17
† See Financial Mail, Johannesburg, September 14, 1979

with extraordinary success. Between 1889 and 1969 (according to Francis Wilson in his pioneering study) the real wages of black miners seemed actually to have fallen. But Wilson also showed that the colour bar added to the cost of producing gold, restricting both output and total employment, including the employment of skilled whites. 'Is it possible,' he asked, 'that the existence of the colour bar is actually against the interests of white workers?'* The mine-owners were reluctant to challenge the government on which much of their profits depended. But by the late 'sixties most major industrialists were beginning to press for a relaxation of job bars: though this did not mean (as Merle Lipton points out), that they necessarily rejected all aspects of apartheid.†

The Afrikaner government in the meantime was gradually becoming more influenced by economic arguments. In the first years of apartheid under Malan and Verwoerd, the Afrikaners' tribal pride and fierce racial doctrine seemed almost immune: while they were able both to get richer and to extend the apartheid system. But by the late 'sixties the tribal unity was beginning to crack, while apartheid was not so obviously acting in all their interests. The Afrikaners were also more keen to extend their own share of the free-enterprise system, encouraged by their own emerging business leaders. The most remarkable of them was Anton Rupert, the scientist who had built up the Rembrandt tobacco company with the help of German capital from the small Voorbrand tobacco company. He had always had Afrikaner backing and links with the Broederbond: 'we were asked to smoke and cough for Volk and Vaderland' as one Broeder complained.‡ But he was intellectually adventurous, sounding often more like a don than a businessman, and sometimes in trouble with

* Francis Wilson, *Labour in the South African Gold Mines 1911–1969*, Cambridge University Press, pp. 141, 118–19

† Lipton, p. 146

‡ Ivor Wilkins and Hans Strydom, *The Broederbond*, New York, Paddington Press, p. 428

the Broeders. When I met him in his house in Stellenbosch in February 1960, just after Macmillan's wind-of-change speech, he said it was just what he would have written himself, and insisted that 'the coloureds must be admitted into the white world – even with the vote'. He built up his global tobacco empire, including Rothmans in Britain, into what he claimed was 'the world's first truly multinational group'. He depicted Afrikaners as the much-needed cata- lysts for developing a continent full of incompetents: 'The more disillusioned men there are in the chancelleries of the West, the more we shall be needed.'* He became more critical of the harsher aspects of apartheid, yet in the end he was always loyal to his Volk, and never wanted to be accused of damaging their interests. He continued to see his own people, like the Jews, as having a special destiny and leadership after surviving the ordeals of Africa. 'As fourteenth-generation Africans – and indeed the first free- dom fighters in Africa – we are in a position to take the lead . . . Since the early 'thirties, when one of every three Afrikaners was indigent, we have fought for and won a place in the economy of the country through study, dili- gence, daring, audacity and perseverance.' He preferred to discuss blacks – like his fellow-Afrikaner Laurens van der Post, in terms of flora and fauna, or catalysts and chemicals, rather than as ordinary people or a practical political problem.†

But most of the new Afrikaner businessmen were not so much entrepreneurs as managers of the state-owned industries and nationalised services – including the state steel company Iscor, the state electricity Escom, the airline SAA, the railways SAR, the radio (and later TV) SABC, and the state oil and gas company Sasol; while the new develop- ment corporations for the homelands, like the Bantu In- vestment Corporation or the Xhosa Development

* Anton Rupert, *Progress through Partnership*, Cape Town, Nasion- ale Boekhandel, 1967, p. 157

† Anton Rupert, *Priorities for Co-existence*, Cape Town, Tafelberg, 1981, p. 26

Corporation, gave new jobs to Afrikaners as well as blacks. The Industrial Development Corporation, which Hertzog had set up in 1927, had now become an industrial conglomerate which (as Andries Wassenaar of the insurance group Sanlam described it) 'tended to enter into direct competition with the private sector instead of assisting it'. Many English-speaking businessmen would complain that South Africa had become (as Gavin Relly of Anglo-American put it later) 'one of the most socialist countries in the world, because the Afrikaners, like any strong tribal group, have built it up to distribute the wealth among themselves'.* Even Afrikaners were worrying about the incompetence of this bureaucratic state network and Wassenaar later wrote an explosive book which infuriated politicians by complaining about 'the natural inclination of Afrikaners towards socialism' and the Jekyll-and-Hyde attitude of South Africa: 'It is obsessed with anti-communist legislation, but it follows economic policies which appear to move in the opposite direction.' He blamed gold for many of his country's problems and asked: 'Would this psychosis have come about had it not been the need, so it was thought, for Afrikanerdom to fight the power of money? It is difficult not to see behind all this the shadow of Gold.'†

At the iron heart of this Afrikaner state sector was the fast-growing arms industry; and it was here that the multinational corporations were most vulnerable to attack for supporting apartheid. For much of the new business in the long South African boom was interlocked directly or indirectly with the military and police machinery, with its cogs and levers for the control of the black population. It had become far more dominant after Sharpeville: between 1960 and 1969 the defence budget had risen from £22 million to £136 million a year, amounting to 17 percent of the total budget and 2.4 percent of the country's GNP. But

* Interview with author, May 1986
† Andries Wassenaar, pp. 123–51

the formal statistics understated much of the increasing penetration of defence and police contracts into apparently civilian activities. The defence forces took a huge leap under the new minister of defence P W Botha in 1967, who in one year doubled the numbers in military training in the Citizen Force and Command Units, to 32,500.*

Most of the new spending went into the home-grown arms industry. During the 'fifties, South Africa had imported most of its arms, including tanks, submarines and destroyers, from Britain: when the new Buccaneer strike aircraft was produced in 1955 for the Royal Navy its only other customer was South Africa which ordered sixteen. But after Sharpeville, where British Saracen tanks rolled in to control the crowds, it became harder to distinguish between external defence and internal repression, and arms sales to Pretoria were fiercely attacked. By 1964 the United Nations, pressed by its new black members, had called for a total embargo on the sale of arms, ammunition and arms-making equipment to South Africa. The British Conservative government had abstained, but the Labour government joined a full embargo of arms. It was never as full as it looked: it let through existing orders, including the Buccaneers, while Marconi (a subsidiary of the British General Electric) still equipped the underground radar base at Devon in the Transvaal. Both the British and the Americans did restrict their arms exports, but their purpose was soon frustrated by the French who became the chief arms suppliers to Pretoria: over the next decade they provided sixty-four Mirage fighters and seventy-five helicopters to South Africa which became their third biggest arms customer; while they were also supplying weapons, with their customary impartiality, to black clients further north. The Germans also became important suppliers of technology, particularly to the Simonstown military communications centre.

* Foltz & Bienen, *Arms & The African*, Yale University Press, 1985, p. 127

Pretoria still importuned the British and Americans for weapons, and in 1967 the Labour government nearly relented, pressed by the Minister of Defence Denis Healey who was desperate to increase exports, before the prime minister Harold Wilson turned the tables. (After losing office in 1970 Healey quickly went out to South Africa to rebuild his bridges with blacks, delivering an attack on apartheid in Durban and visiting Mandela on Robben Island. When an ANC journalist asked him about selling arms he admitted 'I now think I was wrong even to support the matter being considered.'*) Pretoria still pressed, warning foreign companies that they would suffer unless the embargo was lifted. British businessmen responded obediently, and tried to lobby their government. The trade association Uksata protested against the 'adolescent action' of the arms embargo, and the President of the CBI Sir Stephen Brown complained about the 'irresponsible obstacles' to trade.† One of the most powerful lobbyists was the managing director of Shell, Sir Frank (later Lord) McFadzean, who was friendly with the prime minister Vorster, and warned his government that the arms embargo would 'have repercussions in other commercial fields'.‡

Pretoria tried again when the conservatives returned to power in 1970 under Ted Heath, pledged to resume arms sales. There was an open split in the cabinet, led by Jim Prior; but eventually Pretoria only asked for a few Navy helicopters – which were never supplied. As Harold Wilson pointed out, what Pretoria now wanted was not so much the weapons as a 'certificate of respectability', or 'to get pregnant' (as the Pentagon elegantly put it) by the Western powers, to commit them to their support. For South Africa was now becoming more self-sufficient in arms. Already in 1962 ICI had helped Pretoria (through AECI) to build

* *Sechaba*, January 19, 1971, p. 15
† *Cape Times*, December 21, 1967
‡ Bingham Report, p. 258

three armaments factories to produce ammunition, tear
gas and rockets; by the next year Pretoria claimed to be
producing all the ammunition they needed. After the UN
embargo Pretoria embarked on extravagant new arms-
making programmes, discreetly helped by American and
European companies. By 1967 Vorster had opened the
first aircraft factory to make Impala planes based on British
and Italian technology;* and the next year the defence
minister P W Botha established the new state-owned
Armaments Development and Production Corporation
(Armscor) which became the centrepiece of the military-
industrial complex. Armscor was protected by strict
secrecy – no newspaper could publish details of any defence
deal – and the full collaboration with Western industrialists
may never emerge. But it commanded great patronage
and leverage and Pretoria's grand design was to commit
companies deeply to the military expansion and 'strategic
investment'. It was becoming harder to distinguish, not
just between external and internal security, but between
civil and military purposes. The issuing of pass books, the
surveillance of townships, the tapping of telephones and
the monitoring of car rentals all used computerised technology which appeared peaceful but could easily be
adapted to a sophisticated police state.

By the time the UN voted for mandatory sanctions in
1977, thus cutting off most of the French arms connection,
South Africa was already very well equipped. Many opponents of sanctions would argue that the arms embargo
had been counter-productive, by helping Pretoria to become self-sufficient in weapons, and thus to pursue military
policies unrestrained by the West. In fact Pretoria was
never as self-sufficient, or as successful in exporting
weapons, as the government propaganda made out: the
more sophisticated weapons required hundreds of
components, many of which still had to come from abroad,

* UN Special Committee on Apartheid: Note on Military and Police
Build-up, February 21, 1968

with the help of intricate evasions; and the ageing French
Mirages, and still older British Buccaneer strike aircraft –
which were frequently used for deadly cross-border raids
– had to be replaced with a South African version of the
Mirage which still needed components smuggled in from
France and Israel. The black opposition claimed that Pretoria's arms programme was itself dependent on general
Western investment. 'This enormous expenditure on arms
and other weapons of war,' said Tambo at the time of the
ANC's sixtieth anniversary in 1972, 'is only possible because
of the thousands of millions of imperialist investment in
the South African economy. Without this support, without
the backing of the imperialist countries, South Africa
would long have gone bankrupt even while we were fighting, literally, with our bare hands.'*

By the early 'seventies the long South African boom was
petering out, and in 1971 the growth-rate was down to 3.3
percent compared to 7.1 percent three years earlier. The
economy was partially saved by the sudden revival of its
old staple, gold – which still accounted for 60 percent of
the world's supply. For forty years the gold-price had been
fixed at $35 an ounce, which had become increasingly
unprofitable: by the late 'sixties Consolidated Goldfields
was considering moving out altogether. But the crisis of
the dollar in 1971 produced a new demand; the market
price was unfixed; and Pretoria discreetly restricted production to force the price up. By June 1972 the gold price
in the free market was above $60; by the beginning of 1974
it was $130; by the end of 1974 it was $198. The gold-mines
once again became the key source of profits, and Anglo-
American made more mergers and deals with weaker
industrial rivals. In finance Anglo merged their own bank
UAL with Syfret's Trust and the Dutch bank Nedbank
to form a powerful financial group called Nedsual, and
increased their stake in Barclays National. In cars they
emerged with a threequarter stake in a new Sigma motor

* *Sechaba*, April, 1972

corporation, with the other quarter owned by American Chrysler. The biggest merger was in reverse: the engineering group Thomas Barlow took over Rand Mines to form Barlow Rand, which could use gold to underpin its industrial business. But Anglo, through its subsidiaries, could control nearly 25 percent of the shares of Barlow Rand. By 1976, according to Duncan Innes, 'Anglo group companies held top positions in every one of South Africa's economic sectors except agriculture'.*

But the gold boom could not solve the fundamental problems of manufacturers, who found too small a market: much of Africa was closed to them, while their products could not compete outside the continent. The cheapness of black labour was often illusory, as factories needed to mechanise with skilled and stable workers. And as markets turned down and inflation turned up, the black workers who had been brought in by the boom were beginning to show the first signs of giving serious trouble.

* Innes, pp. 212–18

7

The Roots of Revolt

No other workforce in the history of industrialisation has been so excluded for so long from the system it made possible.

Heribert Adam and Kogila Moodley, *South Africa without Apartheid*, Berkeley, University of California Press, 1986, p. 22

Whatever the failures of apartheid, for a long time it succeeded brilliantly in sweeping the black opposition under the carpet. During the election campaign of 1970, when I was back in South Africa, the white voters saw scarcely a sign of black unrest or protest. The Vorster government was preoccupied by the threat from the right, from the breakaway Herstigte (reconstituted) National Party led by Jaap Marais, a passionate advocate of ethnic purity. 'No other will ever love us,' he said. 'That is a law of international politics.' But Vorster was returned in triumph, with much business support, and there was little serious concern about a black revolt. 'The government can't lose so long as they've achieved the basic fact of apartheid,' said the editor of the *Johannesburg Sunday Times*, Joel Mervis: 'putting the African danger out of sight.' Western diplomats in Pretoria seemed to accept that apartheid had come to stay, and could only hope that it would become more liberal. 'Diplomats are always looking for glimmers of hope: they have to find a reason for doing nothing,' said the Afrikaner commentator Stanley Uys, 'so Pretoria has a special department to supply glimmers.'

Yet some Afrikaner intellectuals, having built up their great wall of apartheid, were already beginning to see its shortcomings and contradictions. Pretoria went ahead with establishing the 'independent' homelands, beginning with the Transkei in 1963, which they hoped would divert black ambitions away from urban revolts, back towards their own tribal roots. But the Transkei under its prime minister Kaiser Matanzima – a nephew of Nelson Mandela – was already under a permanent state of emergency and its parliament had no real autonomy, while no Western nation would recognise the homelands as independent nations. And the blacks were still surging into the white cities, where industry depended on them more than ever. When I talked in 1970 to the Afrikaner editor Schalk Pienaar, who had confidently argued the case for Verwoerdian apartheid with me ten years earlier, he began by saying: 'I no longer think that the blacks can be denied a permanent place in the white cities.'

Behind the great wall there were rumblings of trouble to come. The churchmen were more perceptive than the businessmen. 'Nowadays when visitors want to talk to African priests it's hard to get anyone to meet them,' said the dissenting Afrikaner pastor Beyers Naude in 1970: 'Of course the Africans are becoming more interested in Black Power . . . some of the government are realising that they unleashed a social-political force which they can't control.' The membership of black separatist churches had doubled in five years, and blacks were abandoning the conventional Christian churches. 'When I ask them why they're leaving the Anglican Church they talk about Black Power,' said Father Leo Rakale, a more conservative black theologian. 'But when I ask them about it they don't come again.' Western culture, led by the Bible and Shakespeare, still held its attractions, but partly because of its revolutionary implications. (When the former headmaster of Eton Sir Robert Birley went to teach in Soweto he was surprised to find that his black pupils took the side of Bolingbroke against King Richard II, and that they understood the conspirators' scenes in Julius Caesar better than he did.)

I found it much harder now to talk politics with the blacks in Soweto. 'You know I don't dare tell my own brother what I'm thinking,' said one young black politician. 'So you've come to pick up the old threads?' said a veteran campaigner. 'Well, they're broken.' Informers were everywhere, and the young tsotsis or gangsters were paid to give any news of saboteurs or guerrillas. Some blacks were even complaining that it was guerrillas who got people tortured and killed in detention; but cases of sabotage were now rare. What would happen if a guerrilla did appear in Soweto? I asked blacks in a shebeen: 'Someone would give him away just for a quiet life.' A few were beginning to talk about total terrorism: only real massacres, they said, would interest the outside world, and only when blacks feared their own people more than the police would the informer network be broken (a forewarning of necklaces to come). The government's policy of harassing urban blacks, separating them from families and herding back to reserves, was taking its toll. But blacks were still refusing to behave like American Indians (as one of their banned leaders put it) – losing their sense of identity, or being decimated by drink and despair.

The ANC and the PAC remained banned. No word by Mandela or Sobukwe could be published; to be seen with a Congress document was to go to jail. 'By the end of the 1960s,' wrote Thomas Karis, the American historian of black politics, 'the ANC seemed to be little more than a shadowy presence in South Africa.'* Mandela's wife Winnie was soon being pressed into politics herself: in 1969 she and twenty-one others were arrested and charged with

---

* Thomas Karis, 'Black Politics in South Africa', *Foreign Affairs*, Winter 1983–4

supporting the banned ANC; the evidence showed how frail their own communications were and how deeply informers had penetrated. But after two trials, acquittals and re-arrests, and after 491 days in solitary confinement, Winnie Mandela emerged a far more determined political figure who was (she said) not afraid of anyone.

Sobukwe of the PAC was under house arrest in Kimberley, writing a novel about his childhood, and under constant surveillance. (When I visited him in 1970, we drove in a hired car as we talked, but a police car was following us after a few minutes.) He still carried authority, with his strong eyes and huge laugh, though he suffered from paranoia after his long isolation and he was convinced the police had inserted a listening device into his body. He sounded much more moderate than the young blacks of Soweto: he deplored the growing signs of black vengeance, but was not surprised. He despised John Vorster and thought the split among Afrikaners would widen. Not a word of his moderation could be published.

Oliver Tambo, the president of the ANC in exile in Zambia, faced an unpromising prospect. Western governments and the UN were condemning apartheid, but with no visible influence on Pretoria. Only the sports boycott, preventing South African teams from competing at international games, had visibly dented apartheid thinking. The armed struggle was having its own problems: in 1965 some of the ANC's guerillas in their army Umkhonto were in Rhodesia on their way back to South Africa, but they suffered humiliating setbacks, causing discontent in the training camps. Tambo himself remained a devout Christian, close to radical priests including the Anglicans Father Huddleston and John Collins, the Canon of St Paul's. But he had to reconcile very different strands, including Christians, communists and straightforward black nationalists; and since Congress had little help from the West the communist influence inevitably increased. ANC members were invited to Moscow or East Germany and weapons were supplied from the Soviet Union. The com-

munist influence among exiles worried some former Western supporters of the ANC; but in the meantime within
South Africa a new black generation was taking a different
direction.

The first serious signs of renewed resistance came from
the factories, where the rising inflation and recession of
the early 'seventies quickly had their impact on black
workers, who were demanding not so much political rights,
as higher wages. By the beginning of 1973 black workers
were striking illegally in Durban, and later in East London
and on the Rand, revealing an unexpected new militancy
and organisation, with no formal leaders who could be
picked off or victimised. Afrikaners noted with relish that
English-speaking Natal was the focus; it was 'the irony of
the year', said the pro-government paper *Rapport*, that 'it
should be Durban that shows the country how scandalously
some industrialists treat their non-white workers'. Several
strikes originated in the factories of a single large company,
the Frame textile group whose wages were notoriously
low. The chairman Philip Frame, a nationalist member of
Vorster's economic advisory council, complained he was
a scapegoat 'for the total system of wage differentiation
for which every white citizen in this country shares responsibility'.* The employers could not easily replace these
semi-skilled workers who thus gained wage-increases,
which encouraged trades unionism; but the workers were
politically cautious, linking themselves to the white-led
unions of TUCSA which the ANC condemned for being preoccupied with white living standards. But the ANC nevertheless looked forward with some prescience to 'the most
turbulent period of industrial and political unrest in South
Africa's history. Coupled with the power the workers have
shown they can exert, is the growth of a new and dynamic
concept among the youth in particular and the people at
large: the concept of black consciousness, of black unity
against white racism.'†

* *Sechaba*, March 1973
† *Sechaba*, May 1973

Black consciousness provided the ideological impetus to black revolt, personified by the articulate young leader Steve Biko who in his short life helped to 'conscientise' a new generation of blacks. Tall and quick-witted, he made his first impact as a black student in the Eastern Cape, when in 1969 he rejected the white leadership of the partly multi-racial students' union NUSAS to form the new all-black South African Students' Organisation (SASO) – which in turn became the 'nursery' for the Black People's Convention (BPC). But both movements were deliberately not competing with the existing political bodies, the ANC and the PAC, and not trying to be an alternative force.*
Biko always denied that SASO was anti-white, but his break from white liberal leadership undoubtedly helped to give blacks a new confidence. His movement was part of a new insistence, influenced by African writers including the Algerian Frantz Fanon, that blacks had their own values and traditions; and the word 'black' was now being proudly adopted as part of a new pride and spirit, in Africa as in America. Many ANC supporters inside South Africa were worried that the new movement might get in the way of their own plans; but Winnie Mandela, banned from active politics, welcomed the young vigour and Steve Biko first visited her in Soweto in 1969, with his lieutenant Barney Pityana (now a vicar in Birmingham, England). As Pityana later recollected:

> We knew that the younger generation wanted to get on with things, with a broader base. Winnie had no ifs and buts, and opened her heart to us. Steve always went to see her when he was in Johannesburg.†

Like most African leaders Biko resented the influence of both superpowers: 'We have no illusions about the African

* Sam Nolutshungu, *Changing South Africa*, Manchester University Press, 1982, p. 149
† Interview with author and others, November 1986

policies of either the US or the USSR,' he told a Canadian
interviewer in 1977. But he warned the West that 'many
persons within the liberation struggles look upon the Marxist analysis of repression as the proper diagnosis of their
situation. And on top of all this there is the overwhelming
evidence of America's involvement in the Third World for
the sake of its own economic self-interest. Russia has no
investments to protect in Johannesburg. America does.'
Biko opposed all foreign investment in South Africa as
'nothing but an exploitation of the blacks' (as he said at a
trial in 1976). 'Harold Wilson stands up to criticise the
system here,' he complained, 'and several of his firms come
to invest in this country, among other reasons, precisely
because there exists in the country cheap labour from the
blacks.' But he remained pragmatic and tactical, and he
saw 'this whole foreign investment question as a vehicle
for generating pressure to sympathise with our point of
view'. He also attacked foreign investors for not using their
strength: 'when these people have got a point of leverage,
because they are not South Africans, because they are
subject back home, probably, to more liberal attitudes,
they don't make use of this.'*

By 1973 Biko was sufficiently effective to attract the
interest of the police: he was banned from leaving his home
district in the Eastern Cape, and he remained restricted,
at a time when the black political temper was rising again
all over South Africa. The growing pride in blackness and
the clamour for freedom were fired by the sudden collapse
of white rule in the Portuguese colonies of Angola
and Mozambique which had long provided a buffer
between South Africa and independent black Africa.
When Mozambique became independent under the
black government of Frelimo in June 1975, followed by
Angola under the MPLA five months later, they appeared
to black South Africans to mark at last a break in the

* Donald Woods, *Biko*, New York, Paddington Press, 1978, pp. 95–
103, 134–6

white wall. The South African army, under its minister of defence P W Botha, had been humiliated in Angola by the counter-offensive helped by Cuban and Russian support; while Mozambique now provided a base for black troops to invade Rhodesia, the last remaining white bastion apart from South Africa. The crumbling of the white buffers brought premature hopes to the South African blacks: and young blacks shouted 'Viva Frelimo!'

But it was the growth of Soweto with over a million intensely urbanised blacks which showed up all the contradictions between apartheid theories and the facts of industrial integration. In the industrial heart of South Africa, Soweto was a greater threat to Pretoria than any border state. Many young Sowetans were inspired by the new pride in black consciousness and became more militant with the recession on top of the repression. It was appropriate that the language teaching should be the cause of their explosion; but it was not because the blacks – like most nationalist movements – wanted to be taught in their traditional language. They wanted to learn in English which they saw as the language of Western culture and opportunity, while Afrikaans was the oppressor's language. English-speaking industrialists, who now desperately needed articulate black employees, should have shared their crusade but they did not. The issue of language went to the heart of the disunity behind the union of 1910 which had promised equality to Afrikaans. 'It is ironical,' wrote two students of Afrikaner politics in 1978, 'that the Broederbond, born out of the frustration caused by Lord Milner's policy of anglicising Afrikaners, should blunder a few decades later by trying to force its own language on blacks.'* The Broederbond was pressing for blacks to speak Afrikaans as their second language, while preserving their own Bantu language at home, and in 1974 the director of education in the Johannesburg region instructed black

* Wilkins and Strydom, *op. cit.*, p. 217

schools, against strong protests, to teach mathematics, history and geography in Afrikaans.

In January 1976 the new minister in charge of black education, Andreas Treurnicht, insisted on further teaching in Afrikaans. The Soweto schoolboys, and many teachers, were enraged; and in May students began striking in protest. The Institute of Race Relations in Johannesburg warned the minister of a serious crisis; students stoned buildings and a black Afrikaans teacher was stabbed. A Soweto councillor, Leonard Mosela, warned the police that enforcing Afrikaans teaching could lead to another Sharpeville. Few revolts had been so accurately predicted; and two days later on June 16 Soweto exploded. Ten thousand black students marched peacefully to the school where the strike had begun, where they were confronted with police with tear gas. The children threw stones, the police fired back and killed a child: the children ran riot and killed two whites, including Dr Edelstein who had devoted his life to black welfare. The first day's deaths were estimated at twenty-five; but rioting, arson and strikes spread through Soweto, which became a battlefield complete with armoured cars and helicopters.

The schoolchildren soon achieved their immediate object, the relaxing of rules about Afrikaans; but the rioting and striking continued, spreading to Cape Town and Port Elizabeth and revealing all the pent-up fury behind the previous surface of calm. The students turned to organising major strikes, with unexpected success, while white vigilantes and Zulu tribesmen fought back at the students and the police began mass arrests.* By the end of the year the death-roll was estimated at between 500 and 1,000.

The Soweto fury was more deeply-rooted and long-lasting than the anger in Sharpeville sixteen years earlier, for it was led by the children who were in fundamental

* For a thorough analysis of the revolt *see* John Kane-Berman, *Soweto*, Johannesburg, Ravan Press, 1978. *See also* R W Johnson, *op. cit.*, pp. 189–201

revolt against their schooling and indoctrination. The leader of the first protest march, the nineteen-year-old Tsietsi Mashinini, explained afterwards how 'the black student in South Africa is being fed the type of education that will domesticate him to become a better tool for the white man . . .' And many parents, in spite of the cost in lives, admired their show of strength. 'The buildings in Soweto and all over still went down despite the guns, you know,' said Mrs Phakathi, the national president of the YWCA.*

The government had denied that language was the main cause of the riots, and had tried desperately to defuse the anger by belatedly meeting black leaders. But they were determined to reimpose order in the townships, particularly Soweto; and the Broederbond promised its members that 'the routines and methods which their own police will use among their own people will sometimes be different from those of a white community'.† The promise was hardly necessary: twenty-six blacks had been tortured to death in two years. When a year after Soweto three former black students who had trained abroad killed two whites in Johannesburg the government had a further pretext for a new purge of potential terrorists.

The most famous victim was Steve Biko. Not directly involved in the Soweto uprising, he saw it as vindicating his principles. When asked in July 1977 for evidence that younger blacks were supporting his Black People's Convention he answered: 'In one word, Soweto! The boldness, dedication, sense of purpose, and clarity of analysis of the situation – all of these things are a direct result of black consciousness ideas among the young in Soweto and elsewhere.'‡ 'The real contribution of black consciousness to the revolt,' wrote Sam Nolutshungu, 'was in the demon it had roused: the defiant attitude among the youth in the

    * *This Week*, 'South Africa – there is no crisis', London, September 2, 1976

    † Wilkins and Strydom, *op. cit.*, p. 236

    ‡ Interview with Bernard Zylstra; Woods, *op. cit.*, p. 98

face of police violence, and the solidarity which emerged among blacks in the year and a half of the revolt.'* After Soweto Biko was inevitably a marked man. A year after it, in August 1977, he was stopped in his car near Grahamstown by the police, imprisoned for the fourth time without trial and interrogated. A month later the police announced that he had died in jail. The Minister of Justice, James Kruger, later told the delegates to the Afrikaner Nationalist Party, in a much-repeated phrase, 'Dit laat my koud' – 'it leaves me cold'. In the inquest the police interrogators, cross-examined by the family's lawyer Sydney Kentridge, described how Biko had been kept naked in his cell for two days, in handcuffs and leg-irons; and how when he collapsed he was driven 1,200 kilometres, naked in the back of a land-rover, to Pretoria prison hospital where he died on a mat on a stone floor. The torture to death of this intellectual who had never advocated violence probably did more than any single act to discredit apartheid among Americans and Europeans – and also among many South Africans. But it did not deter Vorster's government. A month after Biko's murder it cracked down on any further potential black leaders, many of them known for their moderation. It banned the black consciousness movements and the Christian · Institute, detained forty-seven black leaders including Dr Nthato Motlana in Soweto, and closed down the influential black newspaper *The World*, edited by Percy Qoboza.

The official report on the Soweto riots by Judge Cillie blamed the ANC, the PAC and the communists for encouraging the riots; but in truth the revolt came largely from schoolboys who were little influenced by Congress. 'We didn't deserve so much credit for Soweto,' Winnie Mandela told me afterwards, 'but we don't mind at all.' The ANC's prospects were fundamentally changed by the Soweto revolt, or 'the South African Uprising' as they preferred to call it. When police reprisals drove thousands of young

* Nolutshungu, *op. cit.*, p. 185

Soweto rebels over the frontiers, many eventually joined the ANC or its military wing Umkhonto. By mid 1978 Pretoria claimed that 4,000 refugees were being trained in Angola, Libya and Tanzania. The ANC's national executive in Lusaka had carefully not opposed the theories of black consciousness even though they cut across their own multi-racialism, and claimed to have helped to establish the new militancy;* while Tambo explained in 1977 that it was a stage of development:

> In a way we started from the point of black consciousness too. We formed the ANC from just Africans – because the British had delivered themselves of a constitution which cut us out of power. They transferred power to the white settlers and we had to organise ourselves to defend our rights. But we have not stayed there. We have developed to the position where we expect all the people in South Africa to form part of the movement for the transformation of the social, political and economic situation. Black consciousness, looked at from this point of view, is thus a phase in the struggle . . .†

The ANC still faced problems with dissenters who objected to collaborating with other races and with the communist party. In 1975 a breakaway group of 'ANC African national-ists', led by Tennyson Makiwane and including Luthuli's son-in-law Pascal Ngakane, had publicly attacked the com-munists' influence. The secretary-general of the ANC Alfred Nzo denounced the 'treacherous faction and conspiracy', and expelled them; Makiwane later worked for the Trans-kei government and was killed in 1980 – some suspected by ANC agents. The ANC also had a more serious new rival in the Azanian People's Organisation (AZAPO) which was formed in 1978 with its roots in black consciousness. It

---

* *See* interview with Tebello Motapanyane, the secretary-general of SASM, *Sechaba*, second quarter, 1977

† Interview with *Sechaba*, fourth quarter, 1977

was a more dogmatically socialist movement which saw capitalism as the enemy, more than apartheid; and its documents advocated much more specific policies than the ANC's, including the nationalisation of heavy industry and land, confiscation of emigrants' property, and disallowing most inherited property.

As for the PAC, whose thinking had helped to inspire black consciousness, it had been facing growing disputes in exile. It turned to communist China for funds, and made a splash at the UN with the help of its exuberant ambassador plenipotentiary David Sibeko, who had once plotted to assassinate Dr Verwoerd. But after the death of its founder Sobukwe in 1978 the PAC was more confused, and its acting leader Potlako Leballo had betrayed or alienated many of its supporters. In May 1979 he was succeeded by a three-man council led by Sibeko; but the following month Sibeko was assassinated by three men from a rival faction; and the movement never recovered its original unity and purpose.

Inside South Africa the ANC was beginning to face its most formidable challenge in the shape of the Zulu leader Gatsha Buthelezi. He had a traditional background: he came from the Zulu royal family and briefly worked as a clerk in the government's native administration. But he had also been through the same stable as many other black nationalists; he was at Fort Hare college with Sobukwe, before being expelled, and then joined the Congress Youth League. At twenty-nine he was installed as chief, while the ANC leaders were on trial for treason; but for years he appeared to resist Pretoria's pressure for a Zulu homeland. When Pretoria established KwaZulu in 1970 he was elected its chief executive; but he denounced apartheid from his new political base, explaining privately how he could buck the system, and still kept in touch with ANC friends in exile. It was the ANC who encouraged him in 1975 to set up his own movement, Inkatha, a revival of an earlier Zulu cultural organisation. The ANC (they later explained) wanted Buthelezi to 'use the legal opportunities provided by the Bantustan programme to participate in the mass mobilisation of our people . . .'* And Buthelezi always stressed his early friendship with ANC leaders: 'I cajoled Western governments for not supporting the mission-in-exile' (as he always studiously called the ANC leadership). But the ANC had seriously miscalculated, as they later candidly admitted:

> Unfortunately, we failed to mobilise our own people to take on the task of resurrecting Inkatha as the kind of organisation we wanted, owing to the understandable antipathy of many of our comrades towards what they considered as working within the Bantustan system. The task of reconstituting Inkatha therefore fell on Gatsha Buthelezi himself, who then built Inkatha as a personal power base far removed from the kind of organisation we had visualised, as an instrument for the mobilisation of our people in the countryside into an active and conscious force for revolutionary change. In the first instance, Gatsha dressed Inkatha in the clothes of the ANC, exactly because he knew that the masses to whom he was appealing were loyal to the ANC and had for six decades adhered to our movement as their representative and their leader. Later, when he thought he had sufficient of a base, he also used coercive methods against the people to force them to support Inkatha.

Buthelezi was undoubtedly a force among Zulus. His tactics were necessarily devious, since he was both benefiting from the apartheid system and denouncing it. Vorster saw him as a tool of the English-speaking press; but he sometimes liked to compare Zulus to Afrikaners. 'The Afrikaner himself did not ascend to power only through bloodshed,' he told a rally in Soweto in 1975. 'My daily prayer for him is that God should give him the grace he

---

* ANC NEC Political Report, *Sechaba*, December 1985

gave the English to bow to the inevitable while there is still time.'* To Steve Biko and other black consciousness leaders Buthelezi appeared as the stooge of Pretoria, and when he appeared at Sobukwe's funeral in 1978 he was shouted down and attacked. The ANC was soon painting him in the colours of Tshombe in the Congo or Muzorewa in Rhodesia: a puppet of the capitalists. But to white businessmen he appeared to be a welcome alternative to the revolutionaries of the ANC as he talked the language of negotiation and power-broking without violence while supporting free enterprise and safeguards for the whites.

Yet the ANC remained the chief beneficiary of Soweto, in spite of its sixteen years underground and in exile. The schoolchildren chanted the names of Mandela and Tambo at funerals and the slogans and flags began coming into the open again. The ANC retained its historic position as the oldest and broadest liberation movement; and its martyrs and prisoners had all the greater glory in their absence. The Soweto children had also rediscovered the fearful truth which the ANC had painfully reached in 1961: that when all political expression is suppressed, their only effective communication is violence. And the violence was now beginning to make some impact on the business community.

The schoolchildren of Soweto, on top of a depression and troubles in Angola, had provoked a crisis in many ways more serious than Sharpeville. On the morning of June 16, 1976 the gold-mines index in the *Financial Times* fell by 8 percent, and by another 3 percent the next day. There was less outflow of capital than after Sharpeville since exchange control was in force; but the London stock-brokers Williams de Broe reported that the situation was 'sufficiently serious to advise against new investment in South Africa until calm is clearly shown to be re-established in the area'; and Graham Hatton in the *Financial Times* warned that 'South Africa will need upwards of R1 billion

* Ben Temkin, *Buthelezi*, Durnall, 1977, p. 152

of new capital every year if it is to achieve a rate of economic growth that is high enough to prevent black unemployment from rising.'* Land values fell rapidly, bankrupting some property companies and threatening the banks, and several European and American companies began selling off their South African subsidiaries. Pretoria had to impose import controls and strict measures to save fuel.

And the Soweto riots shocked most South African businessmen into realising how much the young blacks hated their system. A week of violence had achieved more than decades of petitions. At Anglo-American, Oppenheimer was now much more worried: he felt the responsibility to improve black conditions, but recession made it harder to reassure white trades unionists. He conceded that Western pressure could be helpful, but the West must not expect Afrikaners to commit political suicide.† Basil Hersov of Anglo-Vaal told his shareholders in 1976 that 'private enterprise must re-examine its role in society' and that 'businesses will be weighing short-term expenditures against the longer-term rewards of helping to ensure greater possibilities of stability and growth in our society'. The Transvaal Chamber of Industries sent a memorandum to the prime minister explaining that 'the rising generation is no longer prepared to accept the limitations which its parents accepted as a penalty of having been born without a white skin'. But the average businessman's reaction, said the well-informed *Financial Mail* in Johannesburg, was to be comforted by the muted reaction overseas and to be convinced that Vorster still held a tight rein: 'whether he believes the next fifteen years will be as profitable as the last fifteen is another matter. His time horizon simply does not stretch that far.'‡

Soon after Soweto Harry Oppenheimer persuaded

---

* *Financial Times*, June 19 and 23, 1976
† Interview with author, May 3, 1978
‡ Kane-Berman, *op. cit.*, p. 160

Anton Rupert and other business leaders to set up the 'Urban Foundation', which aimed to improve conditions for Soweto and other townships with the help of new housing, electrification, sewage or building societies. It was described as a non-political fund, which could thus raise foreign loans, but it tacitly accepted that businessmen now accepted a wider social responsibility. 'There were still many people in government who clung to Verwoerdian ideas,' said Anton Rupert later, 'in the belief that you could think away the problems of Soweto if you tried hard enough. But of course we in business know that is not possible.'* The Urban Foundation and other business groups were now anxious to build up a black middle class as a bulwark against revolutionary elements, and to provide a stable community with solid materialist values – a strategy which also suited Pretoria. But they were tactless in spelling out their motives, which soon aroused resistance from radicals; and when they tried to meet black leaders many businessmen became rapidly aware of how few they could talk to – even fewer after the arrests of October 1977. When they did talk to them their message was not reassuring: Dr Motlana, the elder statesman of Soweto who kept in contact with the young rebels, told Oppenheimer that change was now more likely to come through chaos than through prosperity. Motlana was much criticised by the young – including his son – for even talking to whites; and he was now pessimistic of any help from the West. 'Why do the West hide their stick behind their back when they talk to South Africa?' he asked me in Soweto in 1978. 'The Africans like to see that stick out front. I wish the Russians would show more interest in South Africa – to compel the West to intervene.'

The business leaders were coming up against a deeper alienation than most of them realised. As the Johannesburg market-researcher Eric Mafuna put it: 'In the early 'seventies most blacks were aspiring to be part of the first

* HFO: some personal perspectives *Ibid.*

world. But after 1976 many of them felt they did not want to be part of an artificially enriched world: they preferred to be in the third world.'* And the anger of the Soweto children continued to seethe below the surface, passing down the school generations.

* Interview with author, June 19, 1986

8

Western Revulsion

What the hell would you do if you found out that God was black?

Bobby Kennedy, to a meeting of Afrikaner students
at Stellenbosch, 1966*

Through the boom years the Western protest against apartheid and repression had been frequently passionate, but largely ineffective. It had been the British with their long involvement with South Africa who were most vocal, spurred on by South African exiles; and it was one of them, Peter Hain, who achieved the most damaging blow against apartheid, the sports boycott. The Americans were slower to become interested, with less historical involvement and investment and far more interest in Latin America than Africa. Yet it was the Americans who were eventually to mount the more effective pressure, not so much through diplomatic leverage as by mobilising the machinery of capitalism itself.

In the years after Sharpeville American policy towards Africa was given low priority compared to Vietnam, Latin America and Europe. President Kennedy was genuinely revolted by apartheid and supported the UN arms embargo,

---

* Arthur Schlesinger Jr, *Robert Kennedy and his Times*, London, André Deutsch, 1978, p. 746

while the State Department reduced its support for Pretoria. In July 1963 the American embassy in Pretoria – far ahead of the British – invited blacks to a reception for the first time. Bobby Kennedy made a much-publicised visit to South Africa in 1966: as his plane took off back to Washington he said: 'If I lived in this country I would gather up everything I have and get out now.'* Lyndon Johnson as President maintained the Kennedys' hostility to apartheid, but he knew little about Africa and (as Anthony Lake wrote) 'as the rhetoric of American policy toward Africa took on a more elevated tone, the gap between word and deed became more noticeable'.† American blacks were largely preoccupied with their own civil rights campaign. The chief lobby for black South Africans was the American Committee on Africa (ACOA), set up by a dedicated Methodist minister George Hauser after the defiance campaign in 1952: but it gained only limited support from black Americans.

Washington was still much influenced by British policies and it was not until the arrival in 1969 of Nixon and Kissinger that American policies became more distinctive. Kissinger was bored by South Africa and Rhodesia – he did not refer to either in the first two volumes of his memoirs – but he was instinctively in favour of the *status quo* of the existing white regimes. Both the Pentagon and the National Security Council argued that economic growth supported by American businessmen could play a liberalising role, and officials were impressed by *The Economist*'s arguments that 'richer means lefter'.‡ Kissinger, exasperated by the State Department's influence, ordered a secret policy review by the NSC which was thoroughly sceptical about external pressure on Pretoria, and maintained that:

---

* Schlesinger, *op. cit.*, p. 748
† Anthony Lake, *The 'Tar Baby' Option*, New York, Columbia University Press, 1976, p. 74
‡ Lake, *op. cit.*, p. 127

For the foreseeable future South Africa will be able to maintain internal stability and effectively counter insurgent activity . . . The Whites are here to stay and the only way that constructive change can come about is through them. There is no hope for the Blacks to gain the political rights they seek through violence, which will only lead to chaos and increased opportunities for the communists.

It was an analysis which took little interest in black attitudes, and the ANC called it an 'infamous document'. Kissinger was presented with five options and chose number two, which proposed relaxation of American measures against South Africa – including easing the arms embargo – while giving more aid to black Africa, particularly Botswana. The National Security Council discussed it with some ignorance (Vice-President Spiro Agnew praised the South Africans for having achieved independence with a declaration modelled on America's, until Nixon suggested, 'Ted, you mean Rhodesia, don't you?'). The State Department, dismayed by the choice of option two, quoted the story of Brer Fox who made a Tar Baby to catch Brer Rabbit: each time Brer Rabbit hit the Tar Baby, he got more stuck to it. They called it the Tar Baby Option: the name stuck and so did the policy.*

The theory behind the policy, as David Newsom at the State Department described it, was that 'isolation can breed resistance to change. Open doors can accelerate it.' But who or what would come in through those open doors? Soon after the policy-shift the American ambassador to South Africa, John Hurd, went pheasant-shooting with government leaders on Robben Island, while the head of the defence forces in Pretoria, Admiral Biermann, was welcomed at the Pentagon. In the event, the Nixon–Kissinger policy effectively condoned Pretoria's apartheid

* Lake, *op. cit.*, p. 129

system, and left it to corporations and banks to try to liberalise it.

But by early 1969 Americans outside Washington were showing one of those mysterious surges of concern with a distant part of the world. Students and church leaders became suddenly aware of the evils of apartheid, and their interest merged with the eagerness of the disciples of Ralph Nader to challenge the social responsibilities of American corporations. European protesters were determined to use capitalism as an instrument of change rather than to attack it wholesale; and their patient application of pressure from shareholders was to prove the most effective leverage of all.

The first stirrings had already begun in the mid 'sixties. After his visit to the Republic, Bobby Kennedy had begun writing to American businessmen, asking them to define their responsibilities to their workers in South Africa. And black organisations, civil rights campaigners and churches launched a campaign against ten US banks which were lending to South Africa, picketed annual stockholders' meetings, asked awkward questions of chairmen, wrote letters to shareholders, leafleted depositors and sent delegations to the banks' headquarters. A chief target was the Chase Manhattan, which already featured large in student demonology. At its annual meeting in 1967 they held signs which adapted the bank's current slogan to say: APARTHEID HAS A FRIEND AT CHASE MANHATTAN. The chairman, David Rockefeller, declared: 'None of us holds any brief for apartheid. In fact we regard it as a dangerous and shocking policy'; but he went on to explain that 'the black people of South Africa are far better off economically than the black people anywhere else in the African continent'; and he insisted that the bank could 'exert a constructive influence on racial conditions in South Africa'. The Chase view of South Africa during the 'sixties was later described in suitably cold-blooded prose by Joel Stern, the President of the Chase Financial Policy in 1976: 'It was a period of exceptional growth in a highly industrialised and exceptionally productive and efficient society in the utilisation of physical and human resources.'*

But in 1969, when Kissinger was leaving it to corporations to liberalise apartheid, the limitations of that policy were revealed, when the Council for Economic Priorities in New York commissioned a study of how American companies actually behaved in South Africa. One young researcher, Tim Smith of the Council for Christian Social Action, went out to interview executives in twenty businesses in South Africa, armed with letters of introduction from parent companies. He elicited some candid replies. When R J Scott, the chief executive of Ford in South Africa, was asked if he had any non-white friends he replied: 'No, I don't mix with them here, and if I went back to the States, I wouldn't mix with them there either.' What did International Harvester think about the Bantustan policy? 'I agree with it 100 percent,' said their South African managing director James Hatos. 'It is economically and politically sound. I am sympathetic with what the South African government is trying to do. I don't want hundreds of Africans running around in front of my house.' Esso South Africa had provided a memorandum for their visiting executives, prepared by a young South African economist, David Knowles, which faithfully echoed Pretoria propaganda and explained that there would soon be total literacy among Bantu children. The chief executive of Goodyear, John Purcell, explained that American companies must inevitably be 'counter-revolutionary' in their concern to avoid radical political change. Many of the white managers who were interviewed talked confidently about black culture and problems, but none had any black friends. All of them were opposed to Washington's condemnations of apartheid. 'Individually, American businessmen generally support the racial policies of the South African government or a slightly modified form,'

* Senate Foreign Relations Committee: Subcommittee on African Affairs. Hearings on South Africa, September 6, 1976

said Smith, and he concluded that 'it seems clear that one of the costs of doing business in South Africa is the establishment of a friendly working relationship with the government'.

Few executives were actively trying to mitigate the effects of apartheid. A survey in 1969 of American and Canadian businessmen had shown that 31 percent of them would vote for the government policy if they had the vote. The multinational corporations stressed the importance of following local law: the first of the eight 'Principles of Caltex' was 'to comply in letter and spirit with laws and regulations, and to co-operate with government officials'.* But many executives seemed unaware of how much of the segregation – as in elevators or canteens – was dictated by custom, not law; and few exercised any 'sovereignty behind the factory gates'. And these impressions were corroborated by the *Washington Post* correspondent Jim Hoagland who concluded in 1972 that 'American investment has not had a liberalising effect on race relations in South Africa and in fact has probably strengthened the apartheid government's logistical and financial position'.†

Already some American shareholders were beginning to call for their companies to disinvest; and some South African industrialists became worried that the sports boycott could overspill into a business boycott.‡ The protesters' chief target was the biggest company, General Motors, which now had 5,000 employees (40 percent white) in its plant near Port Elizabeth, and which announced in 1970 that it would soon launch the first South-African-built car, the Ranger. General Motors was already under fire for its attitudes to black Americans, and had elected a black director, the Reverend Leon Sullivan, to join the board, who soon became closely involved in South Africa. He was a tall and resonant preacher from a popular

* Timothy H Smith, *The American Corporation in South Africa: An Analysis*, New York, United Church of Christ, 815 Second Avenue, 1970
† Hoagland, *op. cit.*, pp. 348, 350
‡ *Financial Mail*, September 11, 1970

Baptist church in Philadelphia, who was influenced by
the Moral Rearmament movement: and he knew how to
mobilise black and liberal opinion. When the Episcopal
Church which owned shares in GM asked it to withdraw
from South Africa, it was supported by Sullivan, causing
an unprecedented and much-publicised split on the board.
Only 1 percent of the stockholders backed up the protesters, but they now had a beachhead.* After visiting
South Africa Sullivan modified his demands (*see* page
170) but he still retained his weapon of demanding their
withdrawal.

A highly publicised American protest came from inside
the booming camera company Polaroid, whose inventive
president Edwin Land was also a trustee of the Ford
Foundation. In late 1970 two black employees began
picketing Polaroid to stop selling cameras or film to South
Africa where they were used for the hated pass-books.
South Africa provided only 1 percent of Polaroid's
revenues; but the company eventually sent four employees out to investigate, who came back proclaiming
that 'South Africa alone articulates a policy contrary to
everything we stand for'. Polaroid then gave a third of its
South African profits for black education, and their agent's
black wages went up by 22 percent, but the campaigners
were not satisfied and asked for total disengagement.
Polaroid claimed they had shown others what could be
done. But the South African Institute of Race Relations
concluded that the Polaroid experiment had failed to improve the wages and working condition of blacks in general
and reckoned that thirteen out of seventeen companies
which had revealed their wage-rates were paying wages
below the poverty line – including Unilever, AE & CI,
African Oxygen and NASA.†

The American protesters had produced some results.

* Hoagland, *op. cit.*, p. 352. *Also* Corporate Information Centre,
National Council of Churches, New York
† First *et al.*, *op. cit.*, p. 200

They had begun to learn how to use the engines of capitalism to challenge the apartheid system, with shrewd deployment of shareholders' resolutions. American companies put money into educational funds and wage increases: by April 1973 the State Department had issued its own guidelines, recommending wages of at least R100 a month. But the first hopes that American companies could challenge the whole apartheid system soon fizzled out. 'American executives running South African companies began to realise that they must make more sympathetic public statements to improve their public relations in the US,' said Tim Smith afterwards, 'but their co-operation with the South African government remained the same.'* The movement lacked staying power without major support from black Americans. 'If the anti-apartheid movement really is to get anywhere in the US,' Hoagland had concluded in 1972, 'it must rapidly develop truly concerned, articulate and informed black leadership.'†

South Africa continued to lure new American investment with its dazzling opportunities. As John Blashill, *Time*'s bureau chief in Africa, wrote in *Fortune* magazine in July 1972:

> The Republic of South Africa has always been regarded by foreign investors as a gold mine, one of those rare and refreshing places where profits are great and problems small. Capital is not threatened by political instability or nationalization. Labor is cheap, the market booming, the currency hard and convertible. Such are the market's attractions that 292 American corporations and subsidiaries have established subsidiaries or affiliates there. Their combined direct investment is close to $900 million, and their returns on that investment have been romping home at something like 19 percent a year, after taxes.‡

* Interview with author, June 1986
† Hoagland, *op. cit.*, p. 359
‡ John Blashill, 'The Proper Role of US Corporations in South Africa', *Fortune*, July 1972, p. 49

The American agitation moved to Britain which had four times as much investment in South Africa. A young reporter on the *Guardian*, Adam Raphael, who was in Washington during the Polaroid furore, toured South Africa (where he had family connections) looking into the wages paid by British companies. He found that most of them were paying less than the Poverty Datum Line (PDL) as reckoned by South African bodies including the Institute of Race Relations.* In March 1973 Raphael produced articles in the *Guardian* revealing that out of a hundred British companies investigated only three – Shell, ICI and Unilever – were paying all their employees above the poverty line. Among the worst offenders were the Illovo sugar estates owned by Tate & Lyle, Wilson Rowntree owned by the Quaker group Rowntree Mackintosh and the cement works at Lichtenberg controlled by Associated Portland Cement. 'The whole apparatus of apartheid,' said Raphael, 'has created a labour market where the only discipline is the employer's conscience.'† The articles soon led to hearings by members of parliament on the Trade and Industry sub-committee of the Expenditure Committee chaired by William Rodgers, who invited chairmen to give evidence. They provided a unique insight into the workings of British companies, many of which had been evidently paying blacks as little as they could get away with. 'We were horrified by what we read,' said Jim Slater after he had seen the *Guardian*'s revelations about the subsidiaries of his own group Slater Walker: 'We had tended to look at our investments in South Africa as an investment and we had not really looked into the problem in great detail.'‡

Rio Tinto-Zinc which controlled the huge Palabora copper mine were paying more than half their workers below the poverty line until they put up wages by 50 percent after Raphael's revelations: yet their chairman Sir Val Duncan

* *Guardian*, March 12–14, 1973
† Expenditure Committee, Vol. 1, p. 354
‡ *Ibid.*, p. 395

(when asked about reinvestment) explained that 'Palabora is in the position of being so profitable that the question of African wages is, in that context, irrelevant'.* ICI had to admit that 57 percent of the labour-force in AECI (joint-owned with Anglo-American), was paid just below or just above the minimum.† British Leyland and others still paid many of their workers below the line. Courtaulds quickly doubled wages for some workers and their chairman Lord Kearton explained that 'The tide of publicity has helped us to accelerate along the path on which we were already going . . . we try to push things along, not because we are saints, but because we think we owe it to ourselves.'‡

The trade association, UKSATA, through its chairman William Luke, explained that 'it would be unwise to have a black African union', that blacks lacked the 'mental capacity' to do many industrial jobs, and that 'there is a tendency for the black African, if you pay him more money, to put in less time'§ (which Unilever firmly contradicted).¶ 'The tribal Africans have really only been in contact with the Europeans perhaps during this century,' said Donald McCall of Consolidated Goldfields. 'Let us not try and jump too far in seventy or eighty years what has taken us, say, a thousand years to achieve.'‖

'British companies may wish to behave well and many believe they are doing so,' said Adam Raphael in his own evidence, 'but in many cases the wish has yet to be put into practice.' And he ended by quoting Byron's *Don Juan*:

> Alas! How deeply painful is all payment,
> They hate the murderer much less than a claimant.
> Kill a man's family and he may brook it,

* *Ibid.*, p. 244
† *Ibid.*, p. 308
‡ *Ibid.*, p. 88
§ *Ibid.*, pp. 1–10
¶ *Ibid.*, p. 167
‖ *Ibid.*, p. 222

But keep your hand out of his breeches pocket.*

To which the committee's chairman William Rodgers replied by quoting from T S Eliot's *Murder in the Cathedral*:

> The last temptation is the greatest treason
> To do the right deed for the wrong reason.

The industrialists played down any relationship between their high earnings in South Africa and the low wages, which were made possible by the lack of unions and the constraints of apartheid; but as the conservative *Economist* wrote when discussing the high British profits: 'It is impossible to pretend that this above-average rate does not come to a large extent from the very low wages paid in South Africa.'† The connection was reassuring to Marxists: 'Apartheid, far from being a doctrine peculiar to Afrikaner needs,' wrote the authors of *The South African Connection* in 1972, who included the communist ex-editor Ruth First, 'is an economic instrument, organically connected with the various sources of capital control in South Africa, and with the operation of international capital in the country.' But it was significant that Courtaulds admitted that they needed prodding by publicity into doing what might well be in their long-term interests anyway. They *were* doing 'the right thing for the wrong reason'; and Lord Kearton of Courtaulds said he had many letters from shareholders 'who would prefer to see lower profits if that would mean better conditions in South Africa'. Unilever emphasised that higher overall black wages would increase the market for their goods; but none seemed anxious to start the process themselves. What was striking about much of the evidence was the short-term view of the companies involved, which was sometimes explained by their expectation that they might not be able to stay there much longer anyway.

* *Ibid.*, pp. 359–60
† *The Economist*, June 5, 1971

The anti-apartheid campaigners, on their side, had taken a surprisingly long time to focus on the wretched wages which were a larger component of black misery. Many of them had been preoccupied with condemning the fundamental system, or demanding total disinvestment, while some did not want to suggest that capitalism could ever be made tolerable. In fact the threat of disinvestment proved the most effective pressure to get companies to improve wages and conditions, by pressing them to justify their presence; while these material improvements did not appear to diminish the black anger against apartheid.

In the United States, the combination of Soweto and Jimmy Carter, who became President six months later, heralded a major change in Washington's policy. Carter himself was committed to fighting apartheid, though he had been slow to support black Americans in the South. At the State Department Cyrus Vance was determined to stiffen the line, supported by a wiry Southerner Richard Moose as assistant secretary for African affairs. Even Walter Mondale, the cautious vice-president, warned Pretoria that they should not 'rely on any illusions that the United States will, in the end, intervene to save South Africa'.

Carter's boldest step was to appoint the thirty-nine-year-old black Congressman and preacher Andrew Young as ambassador to the United Nations, with a special brief on Southern Africa. Young soon identified with black South Africans: he visited Soweto, where he advocated an economic boycott as in the South, and agreed that the Pretoria government was 'illegitimate'. He was convinced that neither politicians nor businessmen in South Africa would change their policies unless they were constantly pushed from outside: 'you always have to keep up the pressure to achieve anything,' he told me. 'I learnt that with civil rights in the South.' But his policies were never as extreme as they sounded – particularly towards business involvement. Like other black Americans he could compare South Africa too readily to the South, and put too much faith in the 'Oppenheimer thesis' – that prosperity would in itself undermine apartheid. He looked to enlightened capitalists as allies, impressed that they were to the left of the government; and he stayed with Harry Oppenheimer in Johannesburg. 'You are meeting one of the most dedicated and brilliant minds', he told the Foreign Policy Association in New York when he introduced Oppenheimer in October 1977, 'one of the most sensitive and humane businessmen anywhere in the world.' Oppenheimer himself thought Young was too impressed by the influence of American companies and Atlanta banks on the Southern whites, and not sufficiently aware of the total difference of South African law and history.* Many blacks were more critical. 'Carter uses Andrew Young's colour as a special passport to the Third World,' said Steve Biko in July 1977. 'But Young has no programme except the furtherance of the American system. That's why he plays tennis in Soweto. Carter is doing more skilfully what Nixon and Ford did: to make the American system work more efficiently.'†

The Carter administration took some important steps away from Pretoria: after the murder of Biko, through the insistence of Andrew Young they voted for the mandatory arms embargo at the UN in 1977; they stopped sales of military equipment in the 'gray areas' and withdrew their naval attaché. Pretoria soon reckoned that their relations with the US were at an all-time low – reaching a new nadir when Donald McHenry, Andrew Young's black deputy, interrupted his negotiations over Namibia in Pretoria to attend Biko's funeral. But Carter also (as the Ford Foundation's Study Commission put it) 'emphasised the positive side of economic relations and enlightened capitalism as a positive force for change within South African society'. But the administration often seemed unaware of how easily capitalists identified themselves with apartheid. Just after

* Interview with author, May 3, 1978
† Woods, *op cit.*, p. 100

Pretoria's ruthless mass arrests in October 1977 the US Chamber of Commerce cheerfully opened a branch in Johannesburg, and the head of its international division boasted that 'commerce could disagree with the wishes of politicians and trade with whomsoever it chose'.*

But Soweto also provoked a new wave of American indignation against corporations conniving with apartheid, and in September 1976 the Senate sub-committee on African affairs held hearings to investigate them, chaired by Senator Dick Clark of Iowa who was becoming passionately concerned with South Africa, and who soon afterwards flew to South Africa to see Biko to give him American support. General Motors were the Senators' chief target, and their manager of overseas operations, Alex Cunningham, explained how they had constantly tried, within South African law, to modify apartheid provisions at their plant in Port Elizabeth; while the chairman Thomas Murphy had personally asked John Vorster to legislate for equal opportunities. The company believed they would 'continue to be a positive influence for improvement of economic conditions and social well-being of all races there'. But, Clark replied: 'I never met anyone who studied German society, economic politics in the 1930s and 1940s from the time Hitler came into power, who didn't say that the German people were a good deal better off under that system . . . but there is the political aspect, the human aspect . . .' 'We feel we can influence change from within with progressive policies,' said Cunningham, 'whereas, if we are not there, we could do nothing.' But Clark replied that none of the investments had 'brought us closer to what we would all agree is a more just society. Indeed, it seems that during the time of investment it has really gotten worse . . .'†

Clark was still more sceptical about IBM. It did not make

---

* *South Africa: Time Running Out*; report of the Study Commission on US policy towards Southern Africa, University of California Press, 1981, pp. 360, 362

† Hearings before the Subcommittee on African Affairs, September 22, 1976 p. 445

computers in South Africa, and had only 1,460 employees there (out of 289,000 world-wide); but contracts with the Pretoria government provided a third of its business in South Africa. IBM's vice-chairman Gilbert Jones had toured Africa earlier that year with his chairman Frank Cary, and Jones told the senators that his company opposed apartheid as 'a concept completely incompatible with the most fundamental principle of IBM – respect for the individual'. But IBM also 'recognised many years ago that our products could be used in ways possibly inimical to individuals and society . . . I must point out that once our equipment has been provided, we do not always know when a customer may change his applications to perform entirely different tasks.' Jones agreed that IBM had once bid to provide computers for the hated black pass-books, and did provide computers for the 'book of life' carried by non-Africans. 'How is that compatible,' asked Clark, 'with the principle that you have laid down for IBM – respect for the individual?' Jones explained that IBM had to deal with the government if it wanted to stay and 'there is no way that we can apply moral judgment to the South African government or to any other government'.*

Eighteen months later Senator Clark published a critical report on American corporations in South Africa, written by William Raiford, which condemned their 'abysmal performance' in the past and explained that the American economic interest 'has been pivotal in directly assisting the South African government during its worst economic difficulties in the past, and, if permitted, could do so in the future'. He recommended the US government actively to discourage American investment; to stop promoting the flow of capital and credit; and 'to deny tax credits to American corporations that invest or lend to South African government projects, or to companies which did not enforce fair labour practices'.†

* Hearings, pp. 656–701
† US Corporate Interests in South Africa. Report to the Committee on Foreign Relations, US Senate, Washington, 1978

American shareholders were also on the warpath again after Soweto: 'There is hardly a shareholders' meeting,' said *Fortune* in June 1978, 'at which the chairman doesn't have to face cross-examination and criticism, mainly from church and university groups, pressing them to explain why they are still in South Africa.' Americans still accounted for only 16 percent of total foreign investment compared to 57 percent from the European Community, but they were much more vocal. Leon Sullivan, the black director of General Motors, had by 1977 persuaded a group of twelve American companies – later much enlarged – to sign the six 'Sullivan Principles' which included a commitment to improving black living conditions, training and promotion, and more specifically promised non-segregation in cafeterias, washrooms and workplace; equal and fair employment practices; and equal pay for comparable work. They were not revolutionary, and were soon approved by Pretoria. Many companies were worried that their white employees would resent them; and General Motors themselves did not follow them closely: they removed the signs in their lavatories saying 'EUROPEANS' and 'NON-EUROPEANS' but replaced them with blue doors for whites and orange for non-whites.* But the principles did something to counterbalance the local pressures towards social apartheid; and the monitoring of the Sullivan rules was much more effective than the similar rules agreed by the European Community, which were widely disregarded.

Soweto also reactivated the campaign against American banks, forcing many of them to declare themselves more openly against apartheid and to admit some connection between banking and morality. The Chase under Rockefeller were criticised not only by shareholders and depositors, but by some senior executives and directors including Father Theodore Hesburgh, the President of Notre Dame University. In 1977 Rockefeller felt obliged to proclaim a new 'Code of Ethics' which specifically

* *Fortune*, June 1968

excluded any loans that 'tend to support the apartheid policies of the South African government or reinforce discriminatory business practices'. The Bank of America under Tom Clausen resisted any moral commitment, but eventually in 1979 announced in bankers' neutral prose that 'the consequences of apartheid policy create social unrest that adversely affects the country-risk rating of that nation. Hence the Corporation's lending activities in South Africa are restrained and will continue to be so.' Morgan's were under fire from august bodies including Harvard and Yale which both sold off their Morgan bonds. But the bank was non-committal, insisting that credit did not imply political approval, and that withholding loans could lead to hardship for blacks. The Chemical Bank in New York were vulnerable as bankers to the UN down the street: eventually their chairman, Donald Platten, pronounced that his bank was 'strongly opposed to apartheid, and consequently has a policy of prohibiting any loan transactions with the government of South Africa'.

Citibank was responsible for nearly a quarter of the American bank loans to South Africa and its combative chairman Walter Wriston became the target for protesters who wore buttons 'saying CITIBANK FINANCES APARTHEID. But Wriston was unrepentant and George Vojta, a Citibank vice-president, told the Senate that 'the rule for all multinational corporations round the world must be "hands off!"' Vojta also claimed that Citibank's presence in South Africa benefited all its people, and contributed to 'a more pluralistic social system'.* He was quickly contradicted by Tim Smith, now Director of the Interfaith Center, who argued that American firms were promoting the pro-white position, while the gap widened between black and white wages. 'US bank loans subsidise South Africa's military capability,' said Smith, 'and thus are a direct resourcing of machinery of oppression for the black majority.'† Eventually shareholders forced even Citibank

* Hearings, pp. 530–42
† *Ibid.*, pp. 542–6

to announce that they were no longer lending to the South African government or to state corporations: 'We regard apartheid as having a negative effect on South Africa's economic viability.' But it refused to promise that it would not resume lending to the government if its 'economic viability' improved.

In London Barclays Bank also came under greater fire, and tried to distance themselves with some embarrassment from their South African subsidiary. Soon after Soweto their chief executive in Johannesburg, Bob Aldworth, remarked on the difficulties of raising loans and was sharply rebuked by Pretoria: he made amends by buying fifteen million pounds' worth of Defence Bonds which the government had recently launched without much success, and explained that the bank was showing its social responsibility and supporting their staff: 'We do have a large number of our boys called up continually. We stand behind them.' The commitment to the army – from an old Quaker bank – outraged some British shareholders and an uproar broke out at the next annual meeting. The chairman, Sir Anthony Tuke, insisted that the British tax inspectors would not allow him to give instructions to the subsidiary (which was only part-owned), but when pressed he explained: 'I have suggested to the South African board that these bonds will be . . . er . . . should be sold as soon as it is permitted to do so.' Barclays were now increasingly caught between their banking in South Africa and in other black African states, which were protesting that Barclays cease lending to South Africa altogether. Nigeria, thanks to its oil, had become a more important trading partner to Britain than South Africa; and had a network of Barclays branches, 40 percent owned by the London parent. The Nigerian government, under President Obasanjo, warned 'double dealers' that they would have to choose, and by March 1978 they were insisting that Barclays should withdraw from South Africa: when Tuke refused they withdrew their deposits.

The coldest-blooded lenders were the International

Monetary Fund in Washington. Just before Soweto, Pretoria had asked them in January 1976 for a loan of ninety-three million dollars and a stand-by agreement to tide over its economic crisis which (as an IMF study reported) had been precipitated by military spending. The representative of black states, Antoine Yameogo, insisted that Pretoria's falling exports were due to their treatment of black workers. But the British representative, Peter Bull, explained that the stand-by arrangement would give Pretoria 'some feeling of international support, which they deserve'; and the loan was agreed. Five months after Soweto, when the gold price was falling further, South Africa asked the IMF for a new loan of $186 million which was granted by the IMF executive board without discussing arms spending or Soweto. During 1976 and 1977 the IMF had lent South Africa a total of $571 million, more than to all the rest of Africa and more than to any single country except Britain and Mexico. And the IMF loans almost exactly corresponded to the increase in South Africa's arms spending.*

But in commercial banking, if not in the IMF, moral objections were already having some effect in restricting loans to South Africa. Bankers would continue to insist that they were concerned only with profitability and credit-worthiness; and they took a short-term view that the Pretoria government could suppress political revolt for some years to come. But they were also concerned – at least in America – not to lose important customers, who were offended by their complacency towards apartheid. It was ironic that the bankers needed these 'moralising critics' as they like to call them, to tell them where in fact their own long-term commercial interests lay – in disengaging themselves from a dangerous commitment.

* James Morrell and David Gisselquist, *How the IMF slipped $464 millions to South Africa*, Washington, Center for International Policy, January 1978.

9

Botha's Businessmen

If ever a historical tide of change was determined by necessity, it is the move towards full political participation by blacks here in South Africa . . . The notion that the West's economic interests in South Africa give us a stake in the status quo is therefore old fashioned and dangerously misleading.

Edward Heath, Johannesburg, 1981

The arrival of P W Botha as prime minister in September 1978 came as an immediate relief to businessmen both in South Africa and abroad. It had been preceded by the spectacular 'Muldergate' scandal, in which the cabinet minister Connie Mulder had conspired with the head of the secret service, General van den Bergh, and the information director, Eschel Rhoodie, secretly to buy media and influence and spread propaganda round the world, leaving a web of corruption and blunders. The prime minister John Vorster was disgraced, and Botha emerged as the clean candidate in contrast to his tainted rival Mulder.

But as a reformer Botha seemed in many ways less promising than his predecessor. Like Vorster he had been steeped in Afrikaner nationalism from his childhood. He had been brought up on his father's farm in the Orange Free State, still in the shadow of the Boer War. After studying law he became an organiser for the National party, an accomplished heckler and the leader of gangs to break up the pro-British United Party. For part of the Second World War, like Vorster, he joined the pro-Nazi Ossewa Brandwag. When the nationalists won in 1948 he became an MP, and loyally supported every step in the steady build-up of apartheid laws and repression. He was never much involved in the business world, and his roots were rural. Dr Verwoerd made him a cabinet minister, and by 1966 he had reached the key post of minister of defence, where he stayed for twelve years, building up the military machine and founding the state armaments company Armscor which made South Africa more self-sufficient. Defence gave him a secure power-base and the friendship of the generals including Magnus Malan who later became his defence minister. As minister of defence he was fortified against most international criticism, and he developed his populist rhetoric – with constant finger-wagging, swaying and leering – which was unappealing to non-Afrikaners. 'If he were a woman,' said Helen Suzman, 'he would ride into parliament on a broomstick.'

But defence helped to broaden some of his attitudes: he promoted English-speaking generals and admirals, and even promoted some blacks to positions above whites. In his quieter moments he did have some worries about the clash of nationalisms and the humiliation of the blacks – and particularly the coloureds. 'The people I belong to,' he told Samora Machel the President of Mozambique in March 1984, 'know the feeling of powerlessness in the face of an external force greater than ours.' He was certainly more thoughtful than his predecessor. 'He remains a political enigma; a mixture of sentimentality and intolerance . . .' wrote his liberal parliamentary opponent Van Zyl Slabbert. 'His political instinct told him that to pursue the old road would deepen the crisis of government, even if he did not know where the new road was or where it led. He initiated the search we are involved in and he is going to receive very little gratitude from the hard right or left for it.'*

* Frederik Van Zyl Slabbert, *op. cit.*, p. 147

Other Afrikaner leaders, facing the black danger and the 'total onslaught', were also modifying their old hostility to the English-speakers; and the mythology of the Boer War was beginning to fade. 'Afrikaner interests now required the co-operation of English-speaking white South Africans,' wrote the historian Leonard Thompson, 'and the sympathy and governments of America and Europe, including the United Kingdom.'* Botha wanted to produce a new image, particularly to businessmen, whom he met in November 1979 at a much publicised conference at the Carlton Centre in Johannesburg. Most of the tycoons were relieved, after Vorster's resentment of any business advice, to find Botha listening apparently intently. The prime minister outlined his proposals for a 'constellation of states', a plan which Oppenheimer said had 'imagination and charm'; but the businessmen were too flattered to utter much criticism. It would be an exaggeration to compare Botha's meeting with Hitler's first meeting with German businessmen as Chancellor in February 1933, when he rallied them behind him with promises to fight the Red Terror and to build up the army. But the South African businessmen proved almost as easy to manipulate. 'If the Carlton meeting is an indication of how organised business will deal with government in future when hard bargains need to be struck,' warned the *Financial Mail*, 'it is clear the prime minister has managed to stack the odds in his favour.'† Many businessmen later looked back at the meeting with recriminations. 'What we rather naïve businessmen failed to realise was that we were, in fact, being "set up",' said John Wilson of Shell seven years later: 'that those conferences were nothing more than a forum for the propagation of government policies.' By the time of the next meeting in Cape Town two years later many tycoons were already disillusioned: 'Perhaps the best lesson the business leaders learnt was that government has

* Thompson, *op. cit.*, p. 212
† *Financial Mail*, Johannesburg, November 30, 1979

no plans to modernise apartheid,' said the *Financial Mail*. '. . . it would be naïve to believe that, in the South African context, economic power determines political power. The history of Afrikaner nationalism and the modern history of black nationalism refute this theory.'*

Botha and his government did give way to businessmen on one critical area: on recognising black labour unions. The outbreaks of illegal strikes from the early 'seventies had strengthened the case made by many industrialists that it was safer to deal with black grievances inside a union than outside. Tony Bloom of the Premier Group had called for recognising black unions in 1974, and Anglo-American followed. 'After 1979 I was sure the right thing for the mining houses was to help the blacks to build up a powerful trades union leadership,' recalled Gavin Relly, soon to become chairman of Anglo. 'It was an illusion for the mines to think that the old paternalistic process could continue to work. And the self-interest of the unions may not make them the natural bed-fellows of the black political leaders.'† 'I was not so foolish to suppose that this would make the life of industrialists like me easier,' Oppenheimer recollected later, 'but I still thought that it was much better to have this than to sit on the safety valve.'‡

In 1979 a commission on industrial relations, which had been appointed by Vorster two years before, chaired by Professor Nic Wiehahn, reported that to recognise black unions would provide 'a more structured and orderly situation' and would allow official surveillance and 'responsible behaviour'. Wiehahn recommended that job reservation in industry should be abolished and that (as in the army) industry might work under blacks. He also paid a significant tribute to foreign business pressure: 'The presence of subsidiaries of multinational enterprises within a country's borders creates a conduit through which strong

* *Ibid.*, November 20, 1981
† Interview with author, May 6, 1986
‡ Interview with ABC TV, March 20, 1985

influences and pressure can be exerted on that country's policies and practices.' The Botha government faced a storm of protests over the Wiehahn report, particularly from the white unions. 'It was the greatest treachery against the white employees of South Africa since 1922,' said the secretary of the (white) Mineworkers Union. But it was supported by most industrialists, including the Afrikaanse Handelsinstituut which now saw black unions as 'a new safety valve so that we do not land in the minefield without warning'. After much wrangling and many exemptions, Botha was persuaded that legal unions could be effectively controlled, and could defuse political agitation; and the government accepted most of the recommendations. It was a much more radical reform than most of its authors realised. 'Not only did the unions gain unprecedented power in the workplace,' wrote the Labour correspondent Steven Friedman looking back on it afterwards, 'but they soon began to use it to press for political rights . . . The reform achieved the opposite to the one its architects intended – and if they were surprised, so too were the commentators, including this one, who believed the reforms were the product of a sophisticated plan which would bolster white control within the factories and outside them.'*

The new leaders of black unions still faced many obstacles. The union movement was split, between the white-based group TUCSA which worked closely with management and now formed its parallel black unions, and the federation of independent black unions FOSATU which saw the TUCSA unions as stooges of the managers; while the old ANC unions of SACTU still had a shadowy existence. The black unions still had to be registered, and were strictly forbidden from engaging in politics. In November 1979 black Ford workers went on strike after one of their colleagues, Thozamile Botha, was dismissed for belonging to a militant community group in Port Elizabeth, PEBCO.

* *Weekly Mail*, May 30, 1986

The dispute was settled after three months, but the government detained Botha and three of his colleagues without trial. When black municipal workers in Johannesburg struck because their union was not recognised, the government deported some workers back to the Bantustans and detained others, to encourage the rest back to work. But many black unions, by providing organisation and communication, were soon helping to politicise the workers; and the political steam among workers was far too strong to be released by this kind of industrial safety valve. As Sam Nolutshungu wrote: 'Even "reform" under such conditions merely highlights to the deprived the enormity of their political disabilities.'*

The most spectacular manifestation was in the goldmines which had so long rejected black unions. The most right-wing mining groups – Gold Fields of South Africa, the only British-owned group, and Gencor controlled by Afrikaners – still refused to recognise black trades unionists. But the others, including Anglo-American and Anglo-Vaal, preferred to deal with organised workers who were now represented by the black National Union of Mineworkers. Its young secretary Cyril Ramaphosa was already thoroughly politicised: as a student at Turfloop university he had been chairman of the local black consciousness organisation SASO: he was detained for a year, rejected from the university, and detained again. He now found himself organising half-a-million black mineworkers and building up 100,000 fee-paying union members in the next four years. He soon realised the political potential: 'You only need to attend our meetings to tell how radical they are. It began as soon as they realised that the union organisation gave them a chance to show their real feelings.'† He knew he was creating a much more disciplined organisation than the political parties, and he never concealed his political interests. 'We have to make a link

* Nolutshungu, *op. cit.*, p. 128
† Telephone interview with author, August 1985

between economic and political issues,' he said later. 'We all agree that the struggle on the shop floor cannot be separated from the wider political issues.'*

Botha's government could also reassure businessmen by pointing to some progress in providing for a black middle class. By 1980 the blacks had 30 percent of the GNP, compared with 15 percent fifteen years earlier.† Already by the 1970 census there were 44,000 black teachers, 28,000 nurses, and 9,700 'working proprietors'; and in 1979 there were 6,800 Africans at university (and another 9,000 doing correspondence courses). It was certainly a long way from 1924, when Z K Matthews had become the first black graduate of a South African university. But the figures were still tiny compared to 118,000 whites at universities of both kinds, and in 1970 there were no black architects or senior engineers in the population of 15 million. And the apartheid system continued to ensure that black professional people could still not be absorbed into any kind of white world: those that did go abroad often returned in a more rebellious mood, while many teachers had been radicalised by the events following Soweto in 1976. Black graduates were still forming the spearhead of radical movements. The hope that the growing middle class would provide a bourgeois buffer was negated by the segregation which pushed graduates back among their own people.

But many white South African businessmen believed that Botha was bringing in the new era of industrial liberalism which Oppenheimer had so long asked for. Apartheid was no longer a complete obstacle to economic expansion. Blacks could now perform skilled jobs; a few earned wages comparable to whites. Soweto had a few two-storey houses and a handful of black millionaires (in rand), and Botha was much more willing than Vorster to seek out the views

* Interview with Barry Streek, *Africa Report*, March 1986

† Symposium on Current Issues Facing American Corporations in South Africa, New York, Interfaith Center on Corporate Responsibility, September 28, 1981, p. 53

of more moderate blacks. He was the first prime minister ever to visit Soweto, arriving by helicopter and talking to some residents. 'We are all South Africans,' he told the Sowetans, 'and we must act in that spirit towards each other.' And his sophisticated economic adviser Simon Brand warned that 'blacks must be allowed to take part fully in the free enterprise system if we want them to accept it, defend it, and make it their own'.

Not only businessmen, but also some persistent overseas critics of apartheid were persuaded. 'South Africa had changed almost beyond recognition,' wrote the influential South African exile Colin Legum having returned to his home country after twenty years. 'The army, I discovered, has become the outstanding institutional model for the kind of multiracial society South Africa could one day become . . . in South Africa's first line of defence, apartheid (as preached) no longer exists.' Legum found that, even though the political system had not altered, the Afrikaner establishment had fundamentally changed its attitudes to apartheid.*

Pretoria was making renewed efforts to reassure businessmen overseas after the embarrassing images of Soweto, Biko and the Muldergate scandals. In November 1979 a delegation of South African businessmen, led by Gerry Muller, the chief executive of the Afrikaner group Nedbank, came to Britain to encourage trade: at a conference at Ditchley Park they explained how rapidly government attitudes were changing, and Simon Brand quietly and convincingly described how the prime minister had a new blueprint, a total strategy for modernising the country, and how the government was becoming much more business-like, less military. The Afrikaners admitted that their reforms had been the result of international pressure, though they still seemed to lack interest in black opinion. 'We will know there's progress,' said the American scholar Sanford Ungar, 'when the blacks tell us.'

* Colin Legum, 'An Enemy Goes Home', *Observer*, April 26, 1981

British businessmen were glad to forget about Soweto and Biko, and to share the renewed South African optimism, helped on by the revived growth rate and the mounting gold-price. Their trade association UKSATA, with its 300 corporate members, boasted in a new pamphlet in 1979 that South Africa still made up 10 percent of all British direct investment overseas, which together with portfolio investment amounted to about £7 billion; while trade brought in about £2 billion a year. It warned that 'the managerial class must extend far into the black and brown sectors of the population', and that 'an enormous investment in the human infrastructure of the country is necessary if the South African economy is to grow, and if black advancement is to develop'.

British governments still encouraged investment and trade: even the Labour government before it lost office in 1979. Their ambassador to the UN, Ivor Richard, had insisted that while Britain should disapprove of South Africa's policies 'it should be treated in precisely the same way as any other country with which we have economic relations . . . Gesture politics don't work. It is transparent, intellectually dishonest, and morally specious . . .' But when Mrs Thatcher became prime minister in 1979 she showed a more positive sympathy for white South Africa – one of the few topics on which she was influenced by her husband Denis, with his business friendships. It was true that she was soon very pragmatic in agreeing to negotiations with terrorist leaders from Rhodesia–Zimbabwe, which led to independence under Robert Mugabe; but she never expected Mugabe to win the elections, and she still saw the African National Congress in terms of the terrorists of the IRA or the PLO. It was left to Thatcher's predecessor and rival Edward Heath to try to dissociate British business interests from apartheid, more extremely than Macmillan in his 'wind of change' twenty years earlier. 'Neither in peacetime nor in war', Heath said in Johannesburg in August 1981, 'would the West stand in strategic alliance with South Africa as long as she pursues a system which she considers to be profoundly insulting to the rights of the overwhelming majority of her population . . .'*

˙ The international bankers were also rediscovering South Africa's charms. For two years after Soweto even the Swiss bankers had been wary of lending. Robert Studer, senior vice-president of the Union Bank of Switzerland, had warned that apartheid could lead to revolution, civil war or even open war between West and East. 'The very existence of these incalculable risks,' he told a conference, 'would result in the decline of the flood of foreign capital in the future, or in it drying up completely.'† In 1978 the South African government was exasperated to discover that it was paying interest rates as high as Tanzania's, when it borrowed $12 million from the Bank of America. The next year the genial minister of finance Owen Horwood complained that 'there is not one foreign bank that talks to us that does not say that if they looked at this country from an economic point of view there is no reason why terms and conditions should not be better'.‡ Swiss and German banks continued to lend at high rates and in 1980 the Deutsche Bank caused a stir by appearing publicly at the top of a 'tombstone' advertisement announcing a loan to South Africa. But most British and American banks had stopped lending to the government or public corporations. In London Anthony Tuke, the chairman of Barclays, came under heavy fire for lending to a new SASOL oil-from-coal plant in 1980: 'I find it difficult to understand why it should be good for countries in the Western world to develop alternative energy sources,' he told an angry shareholder, 'but that it's bad for South Africa to do precisely the same thing.'

But South African businessmen were fostering a more humane image. Harry Oppenheimer made a forceful

---

* Speech to conference on international political prospects, Carlton Centre, Johannesburg, August 31, 1981

† *Africa Contemporary Record*, 1977–8, p. b876

‡ *Euromoney*, June 1979. *See also* Anthony Sampson, *The Money Lenders*, Chapter 11, London, Hodder & Stoughton, 1981

speech at a bankers' meeting in Mexico in 1978: 'Those who seek to bring about change in South Africa's racial attitudes by cutting us off from the capital markets of the world,' he said, 'should understand clearly that in practice, if not intent, they are aiming at change by violence.'* (It was the dead opposite of the argument of Oliver Tambo, the President of the ANC; that only through foreign pressure by disinvestment could much further violence be avoided.)

By 1980 gold was once again working its unpredictable magic, and had shot up to an all-time high of over $800 an ounce, while the growth rate was back to 8 percent. The South African government tried for the first time since Soweto to raise a major loan – which they presented as being 'socially productive' for the benefit of blacks. 'We did not really need the money,' the finance minister Horwood significantly explained, 'but it is important to fly our flag in the international capital markets.' The South Africans approached their friends in Citibank in New York, who were still feeling exposed. 'I feel that Citibank has borne the brunt really,' their voluble spokesman, Bill Koplowitz, explained, '. . . because we are so vulnerable to public pressure by selling our stock and taking accounts out of our bank.' Since Soweto, Citibank had lent nothing to the South African public sector, but they now (said Koplowitz) agreed to lead a syndicated loan of $250 million, for *moral* reasons:

> It caused us to re-examine the question of moral content of our earnings . . . We made that one loan because it was the right thing to do, as well as good business. The houses, the hospital, the 26 primary schools and 32 secondary schools, the facilities that are going up daily, are impressive.

The Citibank loan caused an uproar among the American churches and other big shareholders. Harvard University

---

* London *Times*, May 24, 1978

sold $51 million of Citibank's securities, and many churches stopped buying Citibank notes. 'Citibank assisted in building South Africa's moral and financial credibility as well as providing hard cash for apartheid,' said William Howard, the President of the National Council of Churches, with unconcealed menace. 'Those banks continuing loans to the South African government will be met with massive withdrawal of deposits, accounts and divestiture of securities. There will be a financial price to pay, in the United States, for supporting apartheid.'* His words were truer than most bankers could have imagined.

American industrial companies were also again being lured. In June 1978 *Fortune* magazine had carried an influential report on 'The Case for doing Business in South Africa' by one of its editors Herman Nickel – a veteran *Time* correspondent with an admiration for Afrikaners – who was struck by the progress in what *Fortune* had called 'the only real industrial complex south of Milan'. He described how average incomes in black households had gone up by 118 percent in the five years to 1975, whereas white households had gone up by only 58 percent; how the ratio of black to white incomes in industry had been narrowing steadily, from 1 to 5.85 in 1970 to 1 to 4.44 in 1976; while the white share in total incomes had been going down by 1 percent each year, to 63 percent in 1977. Nickel was confident that the 'Oppenheimer thesis' was being vindicated, that economic growth – until the recession – had led to many more good jobs for blacks, while 'the contradictions of the system were bound to become ever more glaring, even to many of its Afrikaner supporters'. As for public criticism: 'All the Carter Administration has managed to achieve with its rhetoric so far has been to stiffen the will of the forces of resistance, and complicate the task of black leaders struggling for reform.'

Many American companies could now justify their presence by obeying the 'Sullivan Principles', and General

* *Symposium*, p. 40

Motors was still in the forefront. It was barely profitable in South Africa before 1979, when it injected $24 million into its plant – not (it stressed) to expand production but to improve efficiency and conditions. Roger Smith, who succeeded Murphy as chairman in January 1981, felt a personal commitment to oppose apartheid and back up Leon Sullivan on the board. 'We have the opportunity to be a positive force for change in that government's apartheid policies,' said a spokesman, Bob McCabe, in 1981.* General Motors every year earned top marks under the Sullivan code – 'Making Good Progress' – and after its previous embarrassment over orange and blue lavatories it now provided integrated lavatories, dining rooms and lockers. By 1985 it even claimed to have twelve black car dealers.† But Sullivan kept his options open, insisting: 'My aim is not to keep the American companies there. They can leave. But the companies must become part of the fiber of the liberation movement. If you can use the American companies, like a crowbar, to move a great big rock, you have to.'‡

It was a romantic idea, that companies should become 'part of the fiber of the liberation movement'; but it was far from being reciprocated inside South Africa – where many blacks accused them of encouraging apartheid and helping to build up the military machine. 'Multinational corporations are not yet involved in the business of helping to destroy apartheid,' said Desmond Tutu, later bishop of Johannesburg, in an open letter in September 1981. 'They are making apartheid more comfortable rather than dismantling it.'§ Donald McHenry, the former US ambassador to the UN, concurred: though there may have been some improvement in employees' lives, 'there has been little or

* *Symposium*, p. 2

† Interview with President James McDonald, CTC Reporter, New York UN Centre on Transnational Corporations, Spring 1985

‡ Interview with Lindsey Gruson, *International Herald Tribune*, September 18, 1985

§ *Washington Post*, September 23, 1981

no structural change in South Africa'. Ramaphosa of the mineworkers union in Johannesburg later insisted that the Sullivan principles '. . . have had absolutely no effect. None whatsoever'; and he claimed that the American mining company Union Carbide was far worse than the South African company Anglo-American.* Ramaphosa was being unfair to the Sullivan rules, which had not only improved black working conditions and wages, but had shown that apartheid could be broken down without industry collapsing. But several American companies were still supplying equipment to the South African military or police – including computers for black pass-books – evading an embargo laid down in 1978. 'Most firms have been able to continue sales,' said a confidential cable from the American Embassy (quoted by the columnist Jack Anderson in May 1981), 'by shifting to non-US sources for components.' The American company Control Data had supplied disk-drives to the British ICL, which then supplied computer equipment used by the South African police. General Motors promised not to sell any 'vehicles with US content or technology' to the army or police; but they still sold them trucks and cars: stopping those, said their spokesman McCabe, would reduce GM's capability in the country, and thus prevent it from promoting change.†

This indeed was the nub of Pretoria's bargain: they wanted multinationals for their capital and technology, which they could also use for their military machine. This contradicted any notion of companies 'becoming part of the fiber of the liberation movement'. As the Botha government extended its military forces and its security net, foreign investors were inevitably locked more closely into the defence system. After the ANC had bombed SASOL oil plants the government passed the 'National Key Points Act' which put many industrial installations including oil refineries under special controls with great secrecy; and

* Africa Report, March 1986
† *Symposium*, pp. 33, 37

foreign industrialists found themselves working with government in planning and running their plants, in some cases keeping secrets from their own company head-quarters.*

The renewed friendship between Botha and American business gained a new warmth from the arrival of Ronald Reagan in Washington after the cold years of Jimmy Carter. Reagan knew little about South Africa, which he seemed to envisage as a kind of very Deep South on its way to reform through prosperity. He explained in one interview in 1985 how it 'had eliminated the segregation that we once had in our own country – the type of thing when hotels and restaurants and places were segregated – that had all been eliminated. They recognise now inter-racial marriages and all.'† Reagan's ambassador to the United Nations, Jeanne Kirkpatrick, was openly sympath-etic to the Botha regime and had talks with its military and intelligence leaders; while both the American and British secret services began co-operating with South African in-telligence, reversing Carter's policy and giving Pretoria information about the ANC in return for information about Soviet shipping and other movements.‡ Reagan's first choice as ambassador to Pretoria was Patrick Buchanan, the right-wing polemicist who had written speeches for President Nixon. The eventual choice was Herman Nickel, the *Fortune* editor who had written hopefully about South Africa's prospects, who stuck to his view that its expanding industrial economy was constantly undermining the apart-heid system.

A further signal of warmer relations was the appoint-ment of Chester Crocker to be the chief formulator of American policy on South Africa, as assistant secretary of state – an urbane academic, passionately interested in South Africa and married to a white Rhodesian. Crocker

* *The Dilemma of Code Three*, SA Council of Churches, 1981, pp. 5–6
† Telephone interview with WSB Radio in Atlanta, August 24, 1985
‡ Seymour Hersh in the *New York Times*, July 23, 1986

was seen by Senator Helms and other conservatives as too liberal on Africa; but he was contemptuous of the 'verbal flagellation' of apartheid by the Carter administration: 'Indignation by itself is not foreign policy,' he explained. When I once asked him if he could really trust the Pretoria government he replied: 'Trust is a matter for lovers or families, not for diplomats. My job is to deal with the real forces in the region.' He called his own policy 'constructive engagement', which chimed well with Reagan's own faith in the free market as an instrument of diplomacy, and which proved not very different from Kissinger's 'tar baby option' ten years earlier. As Crocker described it just before his appointment: 'Our market economies will apply normal political risk criteria in the reading of the South African investment climate, thereby signalling a message of both hope and concern . . . engagement in its economy can be constructive for the majority . . . if there is a "tilt" in such a policy, it is in favour of sustained and orderly change.' But to many blacks inside South Africa it looked like a tilt from black to white; the black paper *City Press* reckoned that in three years from January 1982 Crocker only had formal meetings with fifteen black South Africans – all of them in the US.*

Crocker acclaimed Botha's economic reforms, achieved by 'tight-fisted Friedmanites' who had freed the foreign exchange, labour and capital markets: 'The private sector will now be set free to become the engine of job creation and black socio-economic advancement.' He left it open as to whether economic expansion would strengthen the military machine, or create a more liberal climate, but he saw 'a window of opportunity to create such a climate in Southern Africa'; and he suggested that the defence chiefs were themselves 'a lobby of modernising patriots'.† And

* Johannesburg *City Press*, May 19, 1985. *See also* Sanford Ungar and Peter Vale, 'South Africa: Why Constructive Engagement Failed', *Foreign Affairs*, Winter 1985–6

† Chester A Crocker, 'Strategy for Change', *Foreign Affairs*, Winter 1980–1

when the Secretary of State Al Haig was due to meet
Botha's foreign minister Pik Botha in 1981, Crocker wrote
a secret briefing explaining the '. . . possibility for a more
positive and reciprocal relationship between the two countries based upon shared strategic concerns in South
Africa'.*

Crocker, Nickel and Kirkpatrick all encouraged American companies and bankers with the same hopeful message: that after the shocks of Soweto, South Africa would
be helped by American capital and trade along the road
to democracy; and over the next years Washington showed
few signs of criticising Pretoria. It was a tragic misreading:
for while capital in the long term might bring reconciliation
and peace, in the immediate future it could be easily
manipulated into building up a still more dangerous military system. And the Washington analysis showed little
understanding of the extent of black anger that was sim-
mering behind the white wall.

With all the apparent reforms since Soweto, most blacks
now saw businessmen as closely arrayed on the same side
as Afrikaner politicians and policemen, maintaining white
oppression against them – all the more since their new
public cosiness. 'More and more blacks – especially young
blacks – are beginning to identify apartheid with the capitalist system,' Allister Sparks, the editor of the *Rand Daily
Mail*, warned in September 1979, 'and to see the struggle
to overthrow apartheid in terms of a struggle to overthrow
the capitalist system as a whole.' A survey of migrant
labour conducted by Schlemmer and Moller in 1982
showed that 82 percent thought that business leaders work
with and support the government, 72 percent thought they
did not care about blacks, and 94 percent thought that
they ran to the police whenever there was a dispute. 'Many
big businesses in South Africa have, over the last ten
years, moved on to what one can call liberal capitalism,'
commented Hermann Giliomee, professor of political

---

* Washington, TransAfrica News Report, August 1981

science at Cape Town, 'which demands a well-paid and secure labour force rather than badly-paid and repressed workers. But this does not get these big businesses out of the dock. A vast underclass of migrant labourers – men turned into atomised strangers in their own land – will always be a living indictment of the exploitative nature of capitalism.'*

Businessmen increasingly looked towards new moderate black leaders; and particularly towards Chief Buthelezi in KwaZulu, who was now becoming a more independent and unpredictable power with a strong tribal base. By 1980 his Zulu party Inkatha was claiming 350,000 members. Its real democratic following was hard to analyse, since its leadership virtually corresponded with the government of KwaZulu which commanded much patronage, and had its own private army of Zulu 'impis' who could intimidate any opponents. Buthelezi had very variable relationships with other black leaders, above all with the ANC: he praised Mandela while criticising Tambo and his 'mission-in-exile', and publicly opposed the armed struggle and the policy of disinvestment. The ANC executive agreed to meet Buthelezi secretly in London in 1979 'to explain the position of our movement and ensure unity of approach to the main strategic requirements of the struggle'.† But Buthelezi made the meeting public, explaining that Inkatha and the ANC would form a united front; after which the ANC faced a storm of criticism for collaborating with him. By the following year, as the ANC stepped up sabotage and encouraged schools boycotts, the deadlock between Buthelezi and Tambo had hardened further.

Many business leaders inside and outside South Africa were beginning to see Buthelezi as an attractive 'third force' who was opposed to violence and encouraging to free enterprise. He supported the 'constructive engagement' of foreign companies, while concerned that there should be

* Leape *et al.*, *op. cit.*, p. 151
† *Sechaba*, December 1985. *See also* Time Running Out, p. 196

more jobs in rural areas and that 'economic progress of blacks in South Africa should not be measured by the performance of a few dozen large multinationals'.* He was a favourite guest of the South African Foundation; he was supported by the Institute of Race Relations; and he was befriended by British and American corporations, including Barclays Bank and Mobil. Above all, he was supported by Anglo-American and Harry Oppenheimer, who invited him to his seventieth birthday party. 'No one, the ANC included, has done more to halt the ideological thrust of apartheid than Buthelezi,' said Gavin Relly of Anglo-American later. 'Because he has rejected violence as an instrument to bring about national change, he naturally stands in a better light for many than those who do not. It is easy today to forget that he was the only black leader with an authentic power base to have faced the heat, a long time ago, of a government still determined to enforce apartheid . . . You can't expect us to run away from the single black leader who says exactly what we think.'†

While none of the ANC leaders could be quoted, Buthelezi was the most publicised black leader in South Africa. He had his public relations team of white ex-journalists, including an 'Information Centre on South Africa' in Amsterdam, which was far more professional than the ANC's organisation: his long speeches were handed out to the press before being delivered. He could switch quickly from demagogic speeches to Zulu crowds in tribal costume to friendly and intimate discussions in a dark suit with Western businessmen. The more the ANC escalated their violence, the more attractive Buthelezi looked to businessmen – and even to Afrikaner politicians.

When Buthelezi first met Botha just after he became prime minister he was impressed that 'unlike his predecessor, at least this man was a human being'. Botha told

---

* Memo to Leon Sullivan, September 1980. *See* Kane-Berman in Leape *et al.*, *op cit.*, p. 36

† Interviews with author, May 1986

Buthelezi that the whites must either adapt or die, and that as a Christian he would work for people of all races; and Buthelezi decided to give him a chance. Botha visited KwaZulu in August 1979 and invited Buthelezi to Cape Town six months later, together with the heads of the other homelands; but Botha, true to his ethnic theories, would only see them one by one; when Buthelezi's time came he wanted to make it public, lest his people would accuse him of negotiating secretly: Botha (according to Buthelezi) lost his temper, and for the next four-and-a-half years they did not meet.*

Buthelezi went his own way, developing his own links with businessmen and politicians in Natal. In 1980 he appointed a commission – whose members included Chris Saunders, chairman of the important Tongaat Group – to discuss how KwaZulu could work more closely with the whites in Natal. The 'Natal option' was beginning to take shape, which Saunders and other local industrialists began to see as a way of having harmonious relations with blacks without being dominated by a future black majority. Harry Oppenheimer persuaded Buthelezi to extend his commission to consider black rights in central government. The commission's report published in 1982 concluded that all the racial groups in Natal – including whites, Indians, coloureds and blacks – could accept multiracial governments in the province. 'Through the involvement of some of the leading corporations and business organisations in South Africa,' wrote John Kane-Berman of the Institute of Race Relations who was close to Buthelezi, 'it elevated "constructive engagement" to new heights. It took engagement beyond the conventional areas of industrial relations and wage levels into the realms of economic planning and development, social policy, urbanisation, and, of course, politics.'†

But the armed struggle was beginning to become more .

* Interview with Hugh Murray, *Leadership*, December 1985
† Leape *et al.*, *op. cit.*, p. 37

194

deadly on both sides, with reprisals and counter-reprisals. Umkhonto, the military wing of the ANC, was by 1981 launching more effective raids, attacking the oil-from-coal plant at Sasolburg, the Koeberg nuclear power station and the defence headquarters at Voortrekkerhoogte. After the ANC representative in Zimbabwe was murdered in 1981, the ANC retaliated by exploding a bomb a few days later in the centre of Port Elizabeth. By 1982 the ANC's raids constituted, according to the historian Tom Lodge, 'the most sustained violent rebellion in South African history and all the indications are that it will develop into a full-scale revolutionary war'.* (The ANC welcomed Lodge's assessment while complaining that 'he has not yet grasped and imbibed the spirit of the times'.)†

Pretoria's counter-attacks were fiercer. In August 1982, Ruth First, the veteran communist supporter of the ANC, was killed by a letter-bomb in Maputo where she worked in a study-centre. Her husband Joe Slovo, a key military organiser for the ANC, claimed that she was murdered because she was obstructing Pretoria's new plans to make bargains with surrounding states including Mozambique.‡ The South African defence forces wanted to eradicate the ANC bases in the border countries. In 1981 they raided the ANC offices in Maputo, Mozambique, killing thirteen people; the next year they raided Maseru in Lesotho, killing forty-two. In Lusaka, Oliver Tambo decided that 'something must be done about this succession of massacres' and in May 1983 a car-bomb exploded outside the air force headquarters in Pretoria, killing nineteen people and injuring two hundred, most of them civilians. In his jail in Cape Town, Nelson Mandela heard about it and regretted that people had been killed: 'We don't believe in assassinations,' he said. Tambo later explained: 'I can quite understand why he would regret it. It was a military

* Lodge, *op. cit.*, pp. 339–40
† Francis Meli in *Sechaba*, February 1984
‡ *Sechaba*, February 1985

target, but the press highlighted the civilian casualties . . . He was expressing the horror we ourselves used to have about hurting civilians.'*

Pretoria's forces remained far greater than anything the ANC could mount, including armies of informers. In 1982 the head of security, General Coetzee, told Joseph Lely- veld of the *New York Times* that the ANC was crippled by the risk of informers inside South Africa: 'I have them all the way to Moscow.' Tambo seemed to concur. 'He was right . . .' he told Lelyveld. 'They've been giving us a rough time, making us work very hard. At one time there was a group of ten, and only one of them was genuine . . .'† The chief of police Mike Geldenhuys seemed equally confi- dent. 'I will only begin to worry about the ANC', he told an American diplomat, 'when we can't identify from our files every one of their guerrillas when we catch them: from their fingerprints we can trace exactly where they've been.'

Oliver Tambo, in his base in Zambia, remained an improbable terrorist leader. 'He seems far too gentle to head the revolutionary African National Congress,' as Andrew Young described him. 'His tone is too calm and reasoned; an almost casual objectivity pervades his spirit. His eyes glow with warmth and affection . . .'‡ He still seemed more like a monk manqué than a militant leader, with none of the fiery style of Buthelezi. His wife Adelaide, a formidable hospital sister, lived in London with his family, and their daughter married an English banker in St Paul's Cathedral. The ANC had offices in London, in a shabby house in Pentonville: the British government gave it some protection, but no recognition. Most of the London support for the ANC came from the Anti-Apartheid Move- ment and the International Defence and Aid Fund (IDAF)

---

* Interview with author, July 1985. *See also* Benson, *op. cit.*, pp. 222–3; Interview with Lord Bethel, *The Mail on Sunday*, London, January 27, 1985

† Joseph Lelyveld, *op. cit.*, pp. 331–2

‡ African–American Institute, New York, Africa Report, March– April 1986

set up by Canon Collins, which both included a large intake of South African exiles.

Yet the ANC was never as ineffectual as it looked. Tambo always insisted that it must have its 'four pillars' – the underground structure, the united mass action, the armed offensive and the international pressure.* He still looked to world opinion as the means of avoiding a bloodbath, and the ANC developed an increasingly sophisticated diplomatic approach, with the help of its chief of publicity Thabo Mbeki (the son of the jailed leader Govan Mbeki) who had been educated at Sussex University, and Johnny Makatini, its representative in the US. Tambo and Mbeki travelled in tandem, seeking support from the West, particularly from America. Tambo put little faith in Washington's policy: 'Under the US policy of "constructive engagement",' he said in 1983, 'there has been an increase in US investments, loans and financing of apartheid; new movements of military and nuclear co-operation with the racist regime have been opened up.'† But by 1981 he was beginning to gain some support both from black American movements and from some business interests who were beginning to look to a black future (*see* Chapter 11).

And within South Africa the traditions of the ANC had survived the battering of twenty years of banning and suppression far more effectively than either the military or the business leaders had realised. Mandela had been in jail for fourteen years when Botha became prime minister in 1978, but his name was more famous than ever, proclaimed in chants and graffiti. Two years later the Soweto paper *The Post* launched a new 'Release Mandela' campaign. The ANC was still a baffling mixture of purpose and muddle, radicalism and conservatism, Christianity and communism; but it remained the chief forum for the aspirations of the blacks.

* *Sechaba*, March 1984
† *Sechaba*, October 1983

10

Slamming the Black Door

The most perilous moment for a bad government is when it seeks to mend its ways. Only consummate statecraft can enable a king to save his throne when after a long spell of oppressive rule he sets to improving the lot of his subjects.

De Tocqueville, *Democracy in America*, 1840, Part 3,
Chapter 4, p. 196

It has become something of a cliché to say that whenever a country experiences a period of reform there is bound to be uncertainty.

P W Botha, *Wall Street Journal*, May 15, 1986

It was when Botha put forward his new constitution in 1983 that he provided businessmen with their most difficult and decisive choice. Determined to co-opt some other racial groups into the parliamentary system, he had tested his strength with a general election, which gave broader white support to his National Party. The liberal PFP had increased its seats and the right-wing HNP – still led by Jaap Marais – had gained votes, while the following year eighteen more right-wing MPs seceded from the National Party to form another right-wing group, the Conservative Party led by the Transvaal leader Andreas Treurnicht. But Botha gained support at the election from many English-

speakers including businessmen, and retained a commanding majority.

Botha could thus put all his energies behind major
constitutional changes; and in 1983 he proposed separate
parliamentary assemblies for eighty-five coloured representatives and forty-five Asians on top of the existing 178
members of the white parliament. Each chamber would
be responsible for its people's 'own affairs' – education,
welfare, housing, local government – while all the three
chambers would separately vote on finance, foreign policy
and defence. An electoral college drawn from the three
chambers – with whites in an overall majority – would
choose an executive president. The Africans, the overwhelming majority of the population, were firmly shut out.
To many Afrikaners it seemed rational to include the
coloureds, predominantly Afrikaans-speaking and de-
scended from Afrikaners, while keeping out Africans
whom, they claimed, had different ethnic roots and their
own homelands to vote in. But most Indians and coloureds
opposed the new constitution, and for Africans it was the
greatest provocation, to introduce reforms which gave
concessions to others but took no notice of them.

Botha got his constitution through the white parliament
and then submitted it to a referendum of whites, preceded
by a passionate two months' debate. It was an awkward
choice for the more far-sighted business leaders: they were
worried about excluding the blacks, but more worried
about undermining Botha's reforming leadership and reducing overseas confidence. 'It is all too likely that "no"
would be an act of despair that would lead to the fall of
P W Botha, if not of his government,' wrote the *Financial
Mail*, 'the reduction of even our tentative reform process
to stasis and a freezing of our international links from
cool to frigid.' A few business leaders lobbied against
the constitution, including Harry Oppenheimer and his
ex-son-in-law Gordon Waddell, Clive Menell, the vice-
chairman of Anglo-Vaal, and Tony Bloom, the chairman
of the Premier Group. Oppenheimer himself gave a lunch

for Van Zyl Slabbert, the leader of the PFP liberal party
who was campaigning against the constitution because it
excluded blacks, to try to persuade businessmen to vote
No: 'Almost without exception they agreed with my
reasons for rejecting the new constitution,' said Slabbert,
'but at the same time it was clear to me that most of them
were going to support the Yes vote.'

For Oppenheimer, who had retired from the chairman-
ship of Anglo after twenty-five years in December 1983, it
seemed a sad conclusion. He believed that the central issue
was bound to be the black majority: Botha's constitution,
he thought, might have been workable thirty years earlier
– just when the government abolished the coloured vote –
but not in the 'eighties. He was not entirely critical of the
government and thought the homelands policy was now
irreversible. But he was convinced that the blacks should
have far greater mobility and freedom, and he was proud
of his political role as an industrialist. 'We have produced
the circumstances which have caused this great black
population to accumulate in the towns', he told the
London *Financial Times*, 'and where there simply aren't
enough white people to do the jobs.'* But he had never
fully faced up to the political consequences of that
movement.

In the referendum the Yes lobby was much more powerful, assisted by a convincing advertising campaign mounted
by Saatchi and Saatchi. A group of business leaders –
including the local chairman of Rio Tinto Alastair Macmillan, the former chairman of Goldfields Adriaan Louw and
the chairman of Nedbank, Frans Cronje – set up a Reform
Fund to persuade others, on the grounds that a No would
discourage foreign investment. Influential businessmen –
including Gavin Relly who succeeded Oppenheimer, Raymond Ackerman of Pick 'n Pay and Raymond Parsons,
the head of the Associated Chambers of Commerce (ASSO-
COM) – publicly said Yes. And several multinationals wel-

* Interview with J D F Jones, *Financial Times*, January 31, 1983

comed Botha's proposal as far as it went. 'It is a step in the right direction,' said Michael Peacock of ICI. 'It could be a tentative step in the direction the country must go,' said General Motors. 'It is a move to reform which will increase confidence abroad,' said the Swiss Ciba-Geigy, 'provided it is followed by real change.'*

In the context of purely white politics the Constitution could appear as the bold beginning of a new road. As Henry Kissinger explained, playing devil's advocate over breakfast to Slabbert, it showed 'how a dominant minority intent on maintaining control could manipulate patronage by co-opting clients to assist it'.† Many foreign diplomats were hopeful, and both the British ambassador, Ewen Fergusson and the American Ambassador, Herman Nickel – to Slabbert's chagrin – welcomed it as a positive step. Two major English-language newspapers, the *Sunday Times* and the *Financial Mail*, condemned the constitution but advised their readers to vote Yes. But to the blacks that Yes was the last straw, the final provocation to revolt; and a few white liberals gave clear warnings. It was 'a step backward in terms of evolutionary change and stability,' said John Kane-Berman of the Institute of Race Relations. 'It made absolutely no sense,' said Slabbert, 'if you accepted that the legitimacy of reform also depended on the acceptance of the constitution by a significant number of blacks, deliberately to exclude them from the constitution itself.'

The referendum was hailed as a triumph for Botha: of the 76 percent of the white electorate who voted, 66.3 percent said Yes, 33.2 percent said No. Botha was soon installed with his new title of State President, presiding over whites, Indians and coloureds – but not blacks. For them, he set up a seven-member committee to discuss their future in the cities. Most businessmen who had opposed the constitution now thought they must defend it abroad.

---

* *Financial Mail*, November 11, 1985
† Slabbert, *op. cit.*. pp. 113–14

'It is quite wrong to think of the new constitution as a sham, or as a device to entrench apartheid in a new form,' Oppenheimer said in New York in October, 'even though the division of parliament into separate racially constituted chambers is a clumsy device which reflects the prejudices of the past.'* But blacks saw it as much worse than a sham: it denied them any hope of a political role, just when they were being allowed an industrial role through trades unions. It proved the decisive watershed in alienating a new black generation, and in provoking a far more serious confrontation which threatened to damage business interests irreparably.

Western governments continued to see Botha's constitution as part of a new era of peaceful development and stability; and the referendum had been followed in March 1984 by a striking diplomatic achievement. The president of Mozambique, Samora Machel, who had taken over his country nine years earlier with such high hopes from young black radicals, had seen his country devastated by a combination of economic disasters and sabotage by guerrillas backed by Pretoria; and he had to plead to Washington for help. Chester Crocker and his deputy Frank Wisner secretly pressed Botha to reach a diplomatic detente: the South African generals wanted to crush Machel, while the security service wanted to make a deal with him, to eject the ANC guerrillas from Mozambique. The Americans could exploit the split, and in March 1984 Botha signed an agreement at Nkomati on the Mozambique border with Machel, in which both sides undertook to prevent guerrilla incursions. The small figure of Machel in military uniform looked up at Botha's big smiling head in front of the television cameras, the symbol of successful white paternalism. It seemed to many Western observers and businessmen that the 'Nkomati Accord' was the beginning of a new recognition of Pretoria's true power. 'For two decades,' said *The Economist* on March 24, 'the politics of the region

* Speech to Foreign Policy Association, New York, October 11, 1984 have been distorted by fanciful predictions of continued black revolution.'

For Botha, the accord with Machel opened the way to a new detente with the West, and two months later he made a tour of nine Western European countries, beginning with Britain – the first visit by a South African head of government since Verwoerd was forced out of the Commonwealth twenty-three years before – where he met Margaret Thatcher (while her husband Denis watched rugby on television with Botha's security men).* The British press were told that Thatcher gave Botha a dressing down and she explained later that she told him that the forced removal of blacks was 'totally and utterly and particularly repugnant to us';† while the South Africans were told the talks were 'fruitful, extremely frank but not acrimonious': either way it was the beginning of a candid relationship through correspondence. Botha complained to Thatcher about the ANC office in London, which he insisted was master-minding terrorist attacks, and he pressed his argument through Europe that the ANC was a communist tool with no broad following inside South Africa.

Certainly the ANC saw the Nkomati Accord as an unexpected blow which had, as they admitted, 'surprised the progressive world'. They had been deprived of an important base for guerrilla activity, which had been indispensable for Mugabe's Zanu army in attacking white Rhodesia. Yet the setback had its compensations, for the ANC was now compelled to think more seriously about its internal activity. 'Our principal task,' said the secretary-general Alfred Nzo just after the accord, 'is, and must be, to intensify our political and military offensive inside South Africa.'‡ Botha's own preoccupation with military power and the 'total onslaught' of communist forces distracted

* Graham Leach, *South Africa*, London, Routledge, 1986, p. 59
† Interview with Hugo Young, *Guardian*, July 1986
‡ *Sechaba*, May 1984

the attention of both government and businessmen from the more serious danger of a fundamental black revolt inside the country; while the provocation of the new constitution provided the ANC with many new supporters. 'Its diplomatic defeat at Nkomati,' as Adam and Moodley put it, 'turned into a psychological victory at home.'*

Botha returned to Pretoria with a new authority among whites as the architect of a new detente with Europe; and his political triumphs were beginning to reassure investors and bankers after some lean years. On top of the world recession South Africa had suffered two years of serious drought which had cut down the maize crop; exports had declined and the gold-price had sunk back again, to below $400 in early 1984. But the basic potential of the economy still impressed bankers, and it looked more attractive again in the light of Botha's promised political stability and apparently sound financial management which was in welcome contrast to the rest of Africa. The short-term opportunities for capital soon won over the longer-term dangers, as South Africa began to look like a golden boy of free enterprise in the continent.

The finance minister Owen Horwood, a chubby figure who enjoyed literary quotations, had been in office since 1975; and in 1981 the Reserve Bank in Pretoria acquired a new governor Gerhard de Kock, a donnish economist, the son of a previous governor, who had impressed Western bankers at the IMF – particularly Americans. He believed firmly in freeing markets and the benign consequences of economic expansion: 'Economic forces shape political history,' he said later. 'I think Indians, coloureds and blacks will come into the cabinet because the economy needs them. Like in the southern US, economic advance will lead to political advance.'† De Kock had already chaired a commission on monetary policy which had recommended liberalising the financial markets, and

* Adam & Moodley, *op. cit.*, p. 250
† *Euromoney*, December 1985, p. 67

his free-market theories fitted well with Botha's own promises to businessmen, and with the prevailing mood in New York and London. Bernard Simon welcomed de Kock's arrival in *The Banker* magazine in May 1982:

> A new era is bursting on South Africa's banks, transforming them from an over-protected, over-controlled and downright stodgy sector of the economy to one more competitive and innovative than most others in a country not renowned for its free markets . . . South Africa is fortunate that its present appetite for foreign loans has coincided with a period of relative political stability at home and turmoil in some other countries far more heavily in debt to the banks. Pretoria is on good terms with foreign bankers. It has never defaulted on a foreign loan, nor has it asked for a renegotiation of debt repayments . . . Nonetheless, South Africa's uncertain political future and unrelenting pressure on many banks not to help maintain minority rule hamper Pretoria's credit rating.[*]

Faced with the declining exports de Kock and his deputy Chris Stahls actively encouraged South African corporations to borrow abroad, where dollar interest-rates were far lower than the local rates: 'We replaced lost real income with short-term finance,' said Stahls.[†] Most American and British banks were prepared to lend to public corporations, if not to the government, and as South Africa looked politically less risky again the extra interest-rate or 'spread' on its loans began to come down. The biggest borrower was the state-owned electricity company Escom – the symbol of South Africa's industrial expectations – which now planned to triple its generating capacity by the end of the century; and Escom's contracts for power-stations

---

[*] *The Banker*, London, May 1982

[†] *Euromoney*, June 1984. Supplement on 'South Africa – Land of Change', p. 68

aroused frenzied competition from overseas bidders in spite of the political risks.* The power-stations also required big loans which reached a new peak in 1984 when Escom raised a loan of $50 million for three years at a spread of only ⅝ percent above the standard interest-rate Libor. 'The political premium has disappeared,' said Escom's financial manager, Len te Groen, 'but there is still an economic risk in a country that is heavily dependent on exports of one product – even if that does happen to be gold.' Owen Horwood still complained that the spreads were too high. 'The banks tell us, without exception, that if they were to look at it simply on an economic and financial basis, we would be right among the top. But then they say: "How do we assess the political factor?" We can't.'†

By the summer of 1984 South Africa was once again a favourite of international bankers, and their magazine *Euromoney* published a glowing special report with no political clouds on the horizon. The dual exchange rate designed to protect the currency had been abolished the previous year. Of the two dominant banks, Barclays' profits were up by 24 percent in 1983 over the previous year, while Standard's went up by 47 percent; and they were both bringing funds into the country. 'The fact that they are not seen on a so-called tombstone does not mean that they are not responsible for channelling a lot of money into the country, and I dare say out as well,' said Owen Horwood. The third runner, Nedbank, was growing fastest of all: it liked to compare itself to Morgan's and in 1983 opened a branch in New York. 'I want Nedbank to be an international bank,' said its chief executive Rob Abrahamsen, 'which happens to have its headquarters in Johannesburg.'‡ It was a heady atmosphere for dynamic South African financiers who felt they were opening up to

* Leape *et al.*, *Business in the Shadow of Apartheid*, Lexington Books, 1985, p. 5
† *Euromoney, ibid.*, p. 19
‡ *Euromoney*, June 1984

the world; and there were few warnings that money could flow out much faster than it flowed in.

Yet there were already signs that the new constitution had triggered off a wave of fury among the blacks, with a new leadership. The leaders could not come from the old political parties which were banned or exiled; they could only emerge from less obviously political organisations – from the new trades unions, from sports or social bodies, and perhaps most important from the churches which were now forced into politics as never before, and which threw up two spokesmen whose voices could carry round the world.

The most surprising of them, Allan Boesak, had emerged from the Cape coloured people: an intellectual theologian with a high-pitched voice who belonged to the Dutch Reformed Mission Church, the coloureds' offshoot of the Calvinist Afrikaner church. Boesak had been reluctantly involved in politics: after seeing his own suburb bulldozed to conform to the Group Areas Act he had decided in the early 'sixties that he could not reconcile apartheid with Christ's teaching; but on the advice of another dissident Afrikaner theologian, Beyers Naude, he stayed within his church, seeing it as a potential agent for liberation rather than oppression. He was so successful that by 1982, as President of the world's Reformed Churches meeting in Ottawa, he had apartheid denounced as a heresy. He became increasingly politically involved, grappling with the problem of violence and deciding that: 'it is irresponsible for me to tell people to protest non-violently if I know that the response will be violent'. The proposed new constitution outraged him, as an insult to the humanity of the blacks, and he joined cause with Indians who had revived the Transvaal Indian Congress, an old ally of the ANC which had never been banned. In January 1983 Boesak called for a united front of all kinds of bodies, to 'inform people of the fraud that is about to be perpetrated in our name'.

Eight months later in August a meeting of 10,000 people

near Cape Town launched the United Democratic Front (UDF), which was pledged to oppose the new constitution. It was a federation of 570 different bodies ranging from bicycle clubs to trades, unions with members of all races: its structure was deliberately planned to make its leadership less vulnerable to picking-off, and to spread across the whole country. 'We thought Cape Town would be our weakest region,' one of its anonymous founders told me, 'so we sent most of our organisers down there . . . We knew the leaders would be cut off, but others could always take over.' The UDF took care not to challenge the existing exiled organisations, and its own declaration was even vaguer than the ANC's Freedom Charter: it stood for 'a single non-racial, unfragmented South Africa, free of Bantustans and group areas' and it was against 'economic and all other forms of exploitation'. In the words of its young general-secretary Popo Molefe – who was later arrested and tried for treason – 'it was the voice to say that there was still a chance to bring about change without loss of life'. The ANC in Lusaka which was also calling for everyone to reject 'dummy institutions' soon warmly welcomed the UDF which included many former ANC figures among its patrons. 'The UDF mobilises all people into one mass movement and co-ordinates community resistance,' wrote *Sechaba* in October, 'but it does not purport to be a substitute movement to accredited people's movements.' The ANC did not claim credit for creating the UDF, and explained that its members did not necessarily support the Freedom Charter; but it saw the UDF as a 'historic development in our people's march to freedom'.* In fact the UDF was much less radical in its economic attitudes than its rival AZAPO which criticised both the UDF and the ANC for not being sufficiently revolutionary against the existing racist-capitalist system. AZAPO had also formed its own coalition called the National Forum just before the UDF and in the following months the rival groups had bitter

* Interview with Mac Maharaj, *Sechaba*, March 1984

and sometimes violent conflicts – with some apparent
connivance from the police who were noticeably more
permissive towards AZAPO.

By the end of 1984 another black priest was achieving
international political importance. Desmond Tutu had become the general-secretary of the South African Council
of Churches in 1978, and eight years later became the first
black bishop of Johannesburg – a position which gave him
high exposure and unusual mobility as he moved between
his small house in black Soweto and his big house in
a white suburb – where the front lawn could (he said)
accommodate ten Soweto houses. As a child Tutu had
been much influenced, like Tambo, by Father Trevor
Huddleston (after whom he named his son). Tutu's
mother, an uneducated woman, worked in a menial job at
the school for the blind run by Arthur Blaxall. 'I'll never
forget seeing this tall white priest walking by, and *raising
his hat* to my mother. I realised that here was a white man
who treated everyone as human beings.' Later when he
was seriously ill he had regular visits from Huddleston,
and from him and others he gained a picture of the church
as both compassionate and militant. Tutu liked to re-tell
the old joke about how the blacks first had the land, when
the whites came with the Bible: then the whites had the
land, and the blacks had the Bible. 'But perhaps it was not
such a bad exchange,' Tutu reflects. 'The Bible was very
revolutionary. It was a tremendous idea, to be the partner
of God in the dusty streets of the townships.'

Tutu was quite prepared to mix politics with religion,
speaking with both passion and wit – rather like Cardinal
Sin in the Philippines – grinning and rubbing his hands as
he went into the attack. He made increasingly political
statements, and when in 1980 he predicted that Mandela
would be prime minister in five to ten years the government
did not intervene. He did not overtly support the UDF or
the ANC; but he did not criticise them and he kept his
distance from Buthelezi. Many blacks talked of him as
'Mandela's caretaker': but he also took risks by mediating

with the police. He warned American and European businessmen that they could not duck out of political involvement: 'By coming out here you make a political statement.' When in December 1984 Tutu was awarded the Nobel Peace Prize – twenty-three years after Albert Luthuli's in 1961 – he reached a new level, on which even President Reagan felt obliged to receive him. He soon became a persistent public commentator on successive crises: the first black South African to gain regular and effective access to the American media.

By September 1984 the UDF and other opposition groups showed the first signs of their strength when coloureds and Indians were elected to parliament under the new constitution. The UDF had called for a total boycott and out of the potential voters who had registered only 30.9 per cent of the coloureds and 20.3 percent of the Indians voted. And at the same time there were already signs of a new wave of black discontent, focussing once again on the inferior education. The new radical students union COSAS, set up in 1979, was an important ingredient of the UDF and was agitating both for better schooling and also mobilising pupils behind the broader policies of the UDF. During the elections black and coloured schoolchildren were protesting violently against their schools and the constitution. The black anger was increased by sharp rent increases, particularly in the townships in the 'Vaal Triangle' south of Johannesburg, which the black local councillors had to enforce on behalf of the government. On the same day that new members of parliament arrived in Cape Town a demonstration in Sharpeville – where the massacre had occurred twenty-four years before – led to riots, burnings and reprisals against black councillors. The new parliament coincided with the beginning of an almost continuous upsurge of protests and violence in black townships all over the country.

The links between the new resistance and either the UDF or the ANC remained very uncertain. But at the beginning of the new year Oliver Tambo delivered a dramatic new

year message called RENDER SOUTH AFRICA UNGOVERNABLE.
He claimed that the ANC had already 'taken impressive
strides towards rendering the country ungovernable' – by
such measures as boycotting community councils and the
new constitution – and he warned that: 'In the coming
period we shall need to pursue, with even greater vigour,
the task of reducing the capacity of the colonial apartheid
regime to continue its illegal rule of our country. The
destruction of the organs of government weakens the
regime and is a necessary part of our continuing mass
offensive.'* The new slogan was still part of a broader
strategy. As Tambo explained it later: 'There are many
ways of making it unworkable of course, not just by
violence. We think that economic sanctions, disinvestment and so on have the effect of creating problems for
the apartheid system – therefore making it less efficient,
less desirable as a system to the people of South Africa
overall.'† But it was not clear how far the ANC had really
expected, or was ready to control, the escalation of
violence that was to follow.

Many black townships were certainly becoming virtually
ungovernable by the official authorities. The police now
dared not suppress many demonstrations which openly
advertised the ANC and the name of Mandela. Nor did they
try to silence Winnie Mandela, who was now a major
politician in her own right and who had herself almost
become a no-go area, talking of the government with
undisguised contempt. 'Just about every aspect of our lives
is deteriorating,' she said in January 1985. 'When the army
has to be called in to surround a township because people
are demonstrating against the increase in rents – because
people are protesting as they do in every democratic
country – then that political situation must have deterio-
rated to zero. Things are cracking up. They are losing
control.'‡ By March 1985 the twenty-fifth anniversary of

---

* Message of the NEC of the ANC, January 8, 1985
† Telephone interview with author, July 1985
‡ Telephone interview with author, January 1985

Sharpeville precipitated a new wave of protests beginning in Uitenhage, an industrial town near the Volkswagen factory in the Eastern Cape. A procession of blacks walking to a funeral was met by the police who, unaware of the anniversary, panicked and killed nineteen.

No one could be sure how far the riots and protests were inspired by the ANC and its 'underground structures', how far they came spontaneously from a grass-roots fury, or from groups of children. Tambo had no formal organisation inside South Africa to compare with that of his rival Buthelezi, whose organisation was always free to hold meetings and who insisted that 'the myth that the ANC is the dominating black political force in South Africa is being falsely propagated'.* But the ANC still invoked its past record of defiance and martyrdom, and it could look back on its own warnings. As Winnie Mandela recalled: 'The leadership prophesied when they went to prison in 1964 that if violence is not controlled – which is what they were trying to do, to contain it, to direct acts of sabotage – violent revolution would be inevitable. Well, from that day we have picked up children's bodies from the streets because they dared to protest.'†

In June while the riots and protests were escalating Tambo presided over the second 'consultative conference' of the ANC in exile, at Kabwe in Zambia, attended by about 250 delegates including some who had just escaped from South Africa. They elected an enlarged national executive, with thirty members instead of twenty-two, embracing for the first time some non-Africans including the veteran white communist Joe Slovo. 'Some white participants opposed this admission,' Tambo said later. 'They thought it was wrong, ill-timed. But the conference ultimately came round to accepting that the time had come to practise complete non-racialism.' The chief leaders were re-elected uncontested, including Tambo. Some Congress-watchers

---

* Letter to the author, January 1985
† Telephone interview with author, March 1985

suggested that Tambo was not the real boss of the movement, and that the real power lay with the 'Revolutionary Council' which included more guerrilla leaders. Certainly Tambo's measured statements in private often contrasted with the fierce rhetoric of the ANC's 'Freedom Radio'. But Tambo had a very visible command over his colleagues; and he was able to unify them with all the authority of his friend Mandela behind him. Tambo told the conference that the violence in South Africa would inevitably escalate, and that it would be much harder to make the distinction between hard and soft targets. The ANC had so far been careful to avoid acts of pure terrorism against civilians, like those of the PLO; and in the previous August Tambo had reprimanded the people who had exploded a car-bomb in Durban, killing five.* But he now saw the country coming much closer to civil war. As he explained later: 'I didn't call for a general uprising. I can't say that because I wouldn't get it. But we did say that the black policemen must begin to prepare to turn their guns against their masters. We called on them to join our ranks rather than fight to defend the apartheid system.'†

Botha and many business leaders were now stepping up their warnings that the ANC was the tool of foreign communists 'marching to the beat of a distant drum'. Certainly the enlarged executive included many members of the South African Communist Party, which worked closely with the ANC – which was hardly surprising since the ANC in its quarter-century of exile had depended on financial and military support from the East, while most doors to the West had been closed. The fact of exile had inevitably shifted the balance, and many ANC politicians looked to the release of their leaders and the unbanning of their party to redress it. What was threatening to the West was not so much foreign communist influence as the hatred of capitalism by the young blacks inside the

---

* Lodge, *op. cit.*, p. 85
† Telephone interview with author, July 1985

townships, who had never even heard of Marx but who naturally identified white business with apartheid. As Tom Lodge analysed the situation after the Kabwe conference:

> With the renaissance of popular political culture during the post-Soweto era there has developed a profound and widespread antipathy to capitalism . . . It is evident in the anti-capitalist polemic of virtually every black trade union spokesman regardless of his organisational affiliation . . . If in the future the ANC shifts to the left in its social and economic prescriptions this will not be the result of any kind of manipulation of the movement by communists; it will rather be a reflection of the wider political culture of which it is part.*

Tambo still insisted that the ANC remained ideologically uncommitted. 'Our broad movement for national liberation,' he said in the political report to the conference, 'contains both a nationalist and a socialist tendency.'† And to avoid a catastrophic civil war he still looked for intervention from the West – and particularly from the United States.

---

* Tom Lodge: The Second Consultative Conference of the African National Congress, South African International, 1985
  † *Sechaba*, October 1985

11

The American Crusade

For America, 1985 has become the year of South Africa. A great nation has been stirred by the presence of a monumental evil in a small country. The moral sensibilities of our citizenry have been roused to a pitch that has no parallel elsewhere in the world and few precedents in our own history.

Franklin Thomas, President of the Ford Foundation,
in his speech to Commonwealth Club of California,
May 31, 1985

I'm going to keep order in this country. And nobody in the world is going to stop me keeping order . . . South Africa is a tough country. We nearly brought the British Empire to its knees. And I would advise some superpowers not to try and destroy us.

President Botha, to ABC Television, March 22, 1985

It was the United States, much more than Europe, which quite suddenly provided new hope for black South Africans despite Reagan's policies. But the outcome remained very uncertain: how far would Americans really intervene?

Black Americans were now the prime movers, as they found a common cause and exploited their leverage in Washington. For years black South Africans had been advised to follow the example of the Israelis whose survival had depended on mobilising American Jews. Why not likewise use the political pressure of the 27 million black Americans – more than the 20 million black South Africans themselves? But they had faced a much harder task than the Israelis. Most black Americans had been bored with Africa, preoccupied with their own campaigns, impatient of the passivity of black South Africans: others were full of romantic cross-purposes about tribal life. Black South Africans had their own superiority, conscious that they were in a majority in their own continent, and worried that American blacks were in the end too American, too caught up in materialism and capitalism.

Andrew Young, now mayor of the prosperous city of Atlanta – 'the city too busy to hate' – personified the new reconciliation of middle-class blacks with capitalism. He had seen the snags of socialism in Africa, when aid programmes took two years to get through to socialist Sudan, three months to capitalist Nigeria. 'I've made peace with capitalism,' he said later. 'There's nothing better for coping with sin. It rewards people for working hard.'* Young was convinced that the experience of the civil rights movement, including its financial pressures and boycotts, was relevant to black South Africans, as they became more urbanised and industrialised. 'Atlanta's future twenty-five years ago was no more certain than South Africa's is today,' he explained. 'The saving grace was that Atlanta's white business leadership recognised that conflict was self-defeating; they sat down with the black leadership and began working out ways to accomplish their goals together.' Many civil rights veterans shared the same faith in peaceful pressures. As Franklin Thomas, the black president of the Ford Foundation, later put it: 'The civil rights cause was best served not by the violent gestures and anarchic agendas of the Black Power movement – though it helped draw attention to the issue – but by the persistent and purposeful efforts of established leaders

* *International Herald Tribune*, June 7, 1986

who were familiar with the levers of change.'* And the
coalition of interests, including blacks, churches and liberal
businessmen, who had come together for the civil rights
campaign but who had been frustrated in other fields,
found a more hopeful common interest in South Africa.

Civil rights could be a misleading precedent. 'There was
one fundamental difference,' as Bishop Tutu put it. 'The
law in the United States was on the side of those campaigning in the civil rights movement, claiming their rights under
the constitution. Here, the constitution and the law are
against us.'† Black Americans who were proud of the
discipline of their passive resistance and boycotts were
often worried by the ANC's commitment to violence in
South Africa. Yet it was the violence, demonstrating that
blacks were at last beginning to fight back, which was a
major cause in attracting American attention. 'Without
the blacks rising up,' said the black American columnist
William Raspberry, 'the story was not complete.'‡

The example of Israel had first been taken up by a small
lobbying group called TransAfrica which had first been set
up after a conference of the African-American Institute in
Lesotho in December 1976, just after the horrors of
Soweto. The black American participants, including
Andrew Young, inspired by their 'physical communion
with the land of our forefathers', resolved 'to take vigorous
action for positive policy changes'.§ TransAfrica planned
to lobby for black Africa as the American-Israel Public
Affairs Committee lobbied for Israel. It was run by Randall
Robinson, a conservative-looking young aide to Congressman Charles Diggs of Michigan, whose brother Max was an
anchorman for ABC. He had been brought up in segregated
Virginia, graduated at the Harvard Law School and worked
for a year in Tanzania. He was more radical in his approach

* Thomas, *ibid.*

† *Witness to Apartheid*, Channel 4, April 4, 1986

‡ Media Conference on South Africa in the News, Harvard, March
12, 1986

§ Statement by the Afro-American participants. The African American Conference, December 2, 1976

to South Africa than Leon Sullivan. The political scientist Robert Rotberg argued in 1980 that 'the tough task of the West is to help Afrikaners recognise that their self-interest lies in resolving questions of power by negotiation rather than by confrontation and repression. The ultimate interests of Americans and white South Africans are probably not very different', Robinson quoted the second sentence and insisted that was 'fundamentally misguided. The long-range interests of the United States lie in accommodation and identification with the black majority, that will inevitably inherit South African Society.'*

TransAfrica was a small outfit which for years hardly dented the American apathy about Africa: but by the early 'eighties it was becoming more effective. In June 1981 it sponsored a conference in Washington attended by Oliver Tambo which concluded with a 'national declaration' advocating a massive educational drive about Southern Africa and stating that: 'We, as a people, have an immediate, direct hands-on impact capability.' Randall Robinson continued to maintain close links with the ANC, and with other radical groups in Africa and the Caribbean. Right-wing groups liked to depict TransAfrica as a leftist menace: 'TransAfrica is a spokesman, not for black Americans,' said the right-wing Lincoln Institute in Washington, 'but for the Soviet and Cuban supported terrorist groups.'†　But many Republicans as well as Democrats came to be impressed by Robinson's campaign. 'It was not a Congressman, a Senator, or a President who brought the matter of South Africa to the attention of the American people,' said Senator Lowell Weicker in 1986: 'It was a citizen – Randall Robinson.'‡

But the ANC was also beginning to gain some friends in business circles in the United States, through the African-

* Robert Rotberg, 'How Deep a Change?' and Randall Robinson, 'Investments in Tokenism', *Foreign Policy*, Spring 1980

† *TransAfrica, A Lobby of the Left*, Washington, The Lincoln Institute, 1985

‡ US Senate debate, August 14, 1986

American Institute in New York under its senior vice-president Frank Ferrari. In June 1981, Oliver Tambo had his first meeting in New York with representatives of American companies including General Motors and Ford, and had a very friendly talk with the President of Gulf Oil International, Melvin Hill. In spring 1985 he visited New York and Washington, where he addressed Congressional staffers, spoke to the Council of Foreign Relations, and met more businessmen and bankers including David Rockefeller. 'I found it interesting to talk to business people in the United States,' Tambo said in July 1985. 'I suppose they look at things slightly differently, but they are businessmen all the same . . . I was really impressed by what was going on (in America): the situation has been changed by people at all levels: Congressmen, Senators and the population generally.'*

The campaign of Jesse Jackson in the 1984 presidential elections gave some encouragement to black South Africans, but without much obvious response, and Reagan's re-election gave little indication of an impending crusade. 'I'm not naïve politically,' commented Buthelezi. 'Both Mondale and Jackson made apartheid an election issue, but people still elected Reagan.' Then in November 1984 – just after Reagan's re-election, and after Tutu had won the Nobel Peace Prize – Robinson planned a new kind of protest: he and two other black leaders, Congressmen Walter Fauntroy and Mary Frances Berry, a member of the Civil Rights Commission, protested outside the South African embassy until they were arrested and taken to jail. It was on the eve of Thanksgiving Day (chosen, said Fauntroy, because 'there's nothing to report but turkeys'). At first it only made a news story for black Washington, but the national media quickly took it up. Robinson hastily called his campaign the 'Free South Africa Movement', and persuaded others to follow. Many people saw it as a distraction from the humiliation of the Democrats and the

<hr>

* Interview with author, July 1985

black lobbies in the election, and Robinson did not conceal his resentment that the Reagan administration had 'almost entirely shut out blacks'. But the campaign very soon became bi-partisan and went far beyond black politicians: by March, 2,000 people, many of them newsworthy, in-cluding Republican Senators, had been arrested outside the embassy in Washington. Robinson was now stepping up his campaign. 'We have a commitment to be relentless,' he said. 'The South African regime won't negotiate in good faith until they're certain that the US is prepared to impose the stiffest of sanctions.'*

Many black politicians now saw American business as sharing the blame for apartheid, and insisted on sanctions as the only effective response. Already by 1982 the black Congressman for Pennsylvania William Gray – who be-came chairman of the budget committee – had introduced the first proposal in Congress for sanctions against South Africa. 'Apartheid may have been nurtured by a degener-ate theocracy born in the seventeenth century,' he said later, 'but profits sustain it in the twentieth century . . . I decided that America cannot be loyal to its own democratic creed and at the same time provide the economic fuel for apartheid.'†

By early 1985 there was much more pressure for sanc-tions – ranging from banning the gold Krugerrand coins to banning all trade and investment or withdrawing landing rights for airlines from South Africa (which Andrew Young had long advocated). The pressure was now much more intense in America than in Europe. The motives were mixed and often muddled: some were crudely punitive; some self-righteous; many were ignorant of conditions inside South Africa, or the problems of opposing sanctions. But the consistent theme in the American campaign was the determination to pressurise companies and banks operating in South Africa, as part of the growing concern

---

* *Wall Street Journal*, October 10, 1985
† *Africa Report*, March 1986

for the social responsibility of capitalism. The activists were determined that capitalism should not be allowed to give support to apartheid and oppression, and to pull the levers of investment away from the all-white world.

Television, as it began to show nightly scenes of riots, whippings and police raids, was bringing South Africa much closer to American homes. In January 1985 Senator Edward Kennedy visited South Africa, invited by Tutu and Boesak, emulating his brother Bobby's visit nineteen years before – to show support for the blacks and to take up the cause of disinvestment. He was received in a blaze of TV publicity, with little overt support from the ANC or the UDF, and with angry demonstrations from the black consciousness party AZAPO, which the police were glad to allow. When he addressed a lunch of businessmen, Ambassador Nickel introduced him with a very critical speech. The white press reported Kennedy's travels with mockery and vitriol, and depicted the visit as a fiasco. In fact it did much to pressurise local businessmen into committing themselves further against the apartheid system: and Kennedy stopped in Zambia on the way back for a friendly meeting with Tambo and the ANC. 'It took a Kennedy to emphasise the conditions we have had to live with to the rest of the world,' said Winnie Mandela later. 'It was one of the most significant political visits. But the Reagan administration is a lost cause. That clown is committed to constructive engagement to protect his investments.'*

Bishop Tutu also impinged on American TV with the suddenness of a jack-in-the-box: he had been granted a passport after pressure from Washington, and he proved to be one of the few black beneficiaries of constructive engagement, projecting a quite new perception of South Africa. Before him the main spokespeople for the blacks had been distinguished white liberals, like Helen Suzman

* Interview with author, August 1985

or Alan Paton, who had emphasised the horrors and inhu-
manity of apartheid without necessarily supporting any
black agenda. But Tutu invited a much clearer identification with the black side by-passing the white Liberals –
to the chagrin of many. He always insisted that Western
politicians and businessmen had a responsibility to intervene, to avoid further bloodshed; and in May 1985 he
spoke to huge student crowds – including 30,000 on three
California campuses – stressing repeatedly the blacks' desperate need for Western help. 'Every time we have called
for a change,' Tutu explained back in South Africa, 'the
effect has been not even a minimal change but a tightening
of the rules . . . If international pressure doesn't work, we
are for the birds . . . We need the world. Most business
people know we can't make it on our own. I would not
like to see this country destroyed.'* Tutu never at this
stage specifically called for economic sanctions or disinvestment – which were illegal to advocate inside South Africa.
But he gave an impetus to the sanctions movement in the
United States.

Washington now saw a far wider coalition against apartheid than the familiar band of campaigners, as Senators
and Congressmen began proposing laws to enforce differ-
ing degrees of sanctions; and the assumption that investment was in itself benign was fast fading. Senator
Proxmire, the senior Democrat on the banking committee,
said that 'at long last, people like myself feel we ought to
begin doing something about it,'† and proposed legislation
to ban any new investment. Stephen Solarz, the liberal
Democrat who had been four times to South Africa, argued
that 'the apartheid system is more entrenched today than
ever before'. He doubted that American corporations
could be a major vehicle for change, and insisted on
external pressure: 'I know of no examples in history where

* *Leadership* magazine, Johannesburg, special issue on Disinvestment, July 1985, pp. 15–16
† *Leadership*, *ibid.*, p. 37

ruling establishments have voluntarily divested themselves of their power, and their position.'*

Inside South Africa nearly all whites, from right or left, were appalled by the idea of sanctions; and the liberals were among the most vociferous. 'The best hope for reform in South Africa lies in economic advancement of the blacks,' said Helen Suzman. 'Anything that retards the economic advancement of blacks is counter-productive.' Alan Paton insisted that 'punishment is no proper treatment for erring countries . . . The Afrikaner nationalist is ready to behave better . . . He is in fact attempting to return to the West.' Harry Oppenheimer continued to insist that new investment and business initiatives had helped to liberalise South Africa.† The black political leaders were divided. Chief Buthelezi warned that 'only those working for a future communist state see disinvestment as being in the best interests of South Africa.' But the UDF leaders and most activist groups insisted that sanctions offered the only alternative to mounting violence and chaos. 'Disinvestment is a practicable, possible and necessary tool for pressing against apartheid,' said Allan Boesak, one of the UDF founders. 'I do believe that without economic pressure on the South African government, there will be no movement towards change.'‡ The opposing views about sanctions helped to widen the gap between blacks and white liberals, and to emphasise their different economic perspectives.

American viewers came still closer to South Africa when in March 1986 Ted Koppel of ABC television went out there to film every night for a week which coincided with the anniversary of Sharpeville and the police killings at Uitenhage. Koppel brought together South Africans on the same screen, many of whom had never exchanged views before – revealing all the tragic fragmentation. 'We have stirred

---

* *Ibid.*, p. 50
† *Leadership*, ibid.
‡ *Corporate Examiner*, Vol. 14, No. 6, 1985

up in South Africa what we tend to take so much for granted in the US,' Koppel said at the end of the series, 'debate and the public exchange of views.' The head of the black mineworkers' union Cyril Ramaphosa appeared on the same programme – though in a different studio – as the head of the white mineworkers union Arrie Paulus: it was the closest they had ever got to actually meeting.*

Harry Oppenheimer told Koppel that disinvestment 'could only cause change by bringing about a state of despair amongst black people, which would lead, not to peaceful change, but to violent change'. Louis Wilking of General Motors said that his company was 'in the vanguard of enticing South Africa to make many of the political changes that you see today'. But Ramaphosa asked: 'Why would the white South Africans make noises in the US and all over the world about their disinvestment campaign if they were not worried about it? . . . In recent months it has finally resulted in making the government make a number of changes, which people would never thought could be made in this country.' 'We want US business to voluntarily get out,' said the more extreme Imrann Moosa of AZAPO, 'before we have to force them to move out.' Finally President Botha himself appeared: 'I have the impression – and I think my impression is right – that you Americans are fighting your elections in America on South African grounds . . . You have too many elections, that is my complaint against your country. You can't lead the Western world with all the elections you have – you're weakening yourself.'†

It was only part of the bombardment of South African news. TV teams and special correspondents poured into the Republic to follow the daily trail of violence. Foundations and commissions sent out researchers and fact-finding groups to interview the small stage army of famous blacks. Black and white South Africans were flown over to Amer-

* Interview with Ramaphosa: *Africa Report*, March 1986
† ABC News, March 18–22, 1985

ica for seminars, conferences, fellowships, scholarships. Television and direct dialling could by-pass Pretoria and bring restricted black leaders like Winnie Mandela into the global community. The centre of real communications was no longer in Pretoria or Johannesburg where TV screens and newspapers were muzzled, but in the airwaves where the voices of Botha, Tambo, Buthelezi or Oppenheimer could all come together as they could not at home. The American interest and hospitality undoubtedly helped to boost the morale of black leaders, particularly if they were granted passports: unlike the Afrikaners they could now see themselves as citizens of the world, and could be more widely informed than most whites. But the embrace of the black elite could easily cut them off from the youth in the townships who were setting the pace, and becoming increasingly anti-American and anti-capitalist; and the world of the American media and liberal universities was very different from the world of the American government.

How far was the United States becoming an actor, as well as a spectator, in the South African melodrama? Were the media only raising false expectations? 'Blacks are getting the idea that external pressure and non-governability of the townships will give them victory just round the corner,' said the progressive MP Helen Suzman later in the year. 'The risk is that Western powers are inadvertently encouraging blacks to launch violence against whites, and then the government is really going to unleash its terrible power on these kids.' The *Wall Street Journal* quoted a black student saying, 'America is with us,' and commented: 'But America isn't with them. The US Marines aren't going to land in Soweto or New Brighton or any other black township if the South African defence forces, mightiest in all Africa, are unleashed on blacks. All they can expect is a rush to the television cameras by US congressmen, Reagan administration officials and American businessmen to deplore the killings.'*

* Karen Elliott House in the *Wall Street Journal*, November 1, 1985

Certainly President Reagan still showed little desire to identify himself with black South Africans, or with sanctions. By September 1985, Reagan felt impelled to preempt a Senate bill for sanctions with his own half-hearted executive order which agreed on a modified package, including a ban on all computer exports to South African apartheid agencies, restricting nuclear technology and banning imports of Krugerrands. Reagan, like Thatcher in Britain, never concealed his reluctance to impose serious sanctions. And despite the growing friendship from Congress black South Africans became increasingly hostile to Washington – paradoxically more hostile than towards London, though the British investment was much bigger they were more hostile as Reagan began overtly supporting Savimbi, the anti-communist rebel leader in Angola, whom they saw as in league with Pretoria, threatening a legitimate black state. Yet many black leaders looked to individual Americans and organisations as allies in their struggle; and American companies were now under much more pressure than the British to confront apartheid visibly and boldly. The campaign for sanctions, though it fell short of its object, achieved an important by-product in improving black conditions in the meantime. The more vociferous the demands for disinvestment the more companies felt the need to justify their presence in South Africa. Leon Sullivan was aware that his original principles had been outdated by the rising militancy, while his supporters in the companies were developing their own missionary zeal to convert blacks to capitalism – and to award marks to companies like schoolboys. In 1985 Sullivan could point to 178 signatories, compared to 128 the year before. Of the 146 companies which reported, thirty-six were Making Good Progress, including most of the biggest such as General Motors, Citicorp and IBM; while only four Did Not Pass Basic Requirements – including Ashland Oil and McCann-Erickson.* The most zealous

* *America Magazine*, New York. August 2–10, 1985, p. 53

of Sullivan's apostles was Sal Marzullo, the exuberant government relations manager of Mobil who was a close ally of Chief Buthelezi, who was determined to restore Mobil's reputation among blacks after its elaborate sanctions-busting in Rhodesia in the 'sixties, and who shared Mobil's faith in publicity and advertising: 'The process of urbanisation and industrialisation has done more to doom traditional apartheid,' he promised in mid-1985, 'than any other single influence.'*

While Randall Robinson was launching his 'Free South Africa' campaign in November 1984 Sullivan was announcing his 'Fourth Amplification' which would press companies to recognise black unions and to campaign publicly against specific apartheid laws; and he now called for dismantling apartheid within two years. It was a call for external political interference in bold contrast to all the earlier philosophy of multinationals, and it soon provoked angry responses from inside the Republic. 'The only effective role for United States interests,' Arthur Hammond-Tooke, the director of economic affairs for the Federated Chamber of Industries told executives in New York in May, 'is to latch onto the internal pressures and developments which are moving under their own power in the right direction.'

The most far-reaching American pressures were from the church and other groups who were now pressing shareholders and investors to take stronger stands; and in New York the Interfaith Center on Corporate Responsibility was stepping up its long crusade under its persistent director Tim Smith. Christian shareholders were steadily chipping away at the big corporations, submitting resolutions on all kinds of social issues, but increasingly featuring South Africa. The Grey Nuns of the Sacred Heart, with six shares in Eastman Kodak, called on the company to withdraw from South Africa. There were also universities,

* Ninth Report on the Signatory Companies to the Sullivan Principles, Arthur D Little, Cambridge, October 1985

foundations and institutions with far bigger shareholdings which were demanding disinvestment, while American cities and states were threatening to refuse to order goods from companies investing in South Africa. In May 1985, while Tutu was touring America, fifty-four Protestant and Catholic groups announced a new campaign against twelve 'key investors in apartheid' which all had, said the churches, 'long histories of providing products and services which have built South Africa's racist economy and way of life'. They included three computer companies (IBM, Control Data, Burroughs) – 'user-friendly to apartheid' – three oil companies (Mobil, Texaco, Chevron), two car companies (Ford, General Motors), together with Fluor, General Electric and Newmont Mining. The church groups called on the companies to tell Pretoria that they would not stay in South Africa unless eight drastic conditions were met by the end of 1986 – including releasing all political prisoners, unbanning all organisations, repealing the Group Areas Act and abandoning the homelands policy. To press them, the churches would organise further shareholders' resolutions and meetings with businessmen, and if necessary start divesting securities and launch campaigns for selective buying.*

The persistent protests at company meetings – together with nightly television coverage from South Africa, and, often, nagging from children and wives – were gradually wearing down the resistance of chairmen and directors, and changing their perspectives. Whatever the commercial benefits from their South African investment – which were now anyway dwindling – the 'hassle factor' was already looming much larger as boards were compelled to think more carefully about their involvements with apartheid. The typical American corporation, it was said, had 1 percent of its investments in South Africa, producing 2 percent of its profits – but occupying 10 percent or

* New York: Interfaith Center on Corporate Responsibility: *The Corporate Examiner*, Vol. 14, No. 4, 1985

even 20 percent of its chairman's time. While black South
African radicals continued to blame American capitalism
for their oppression, American companies, many operating
at a loss, were identifying themselves more closely with
blacks than the administration.

They were much more active than the British, who still
had four times the investment but were far less vulnerable
to calls for disinvestment or sanctions. Leon Sullivan was
very keen to involve British companies in his stepped-up
campaign: 'No one can have more impact than the British,'
he told me, 'but they need a crisis to move them.' In March
1985, with the help of Edward Heath, he summoned a
secret conference of chief executives at Leeds Castle, the
moated mansion in Kent much favoured for discreet pal-
avers. It was a high-powered British team – including Sir
Peter Baxendell the head of Shell, Sir Peter Walters of BP,
Sir Tim Bevan of Barclays and Sir Alistair Frame, the
very conservative chairman of Rio Tinto-Zinc – while
the American tycoons included Roger Smith of General
Motors, Rawleigh Warner of Mobil and John Reed of
Citibank (who had asked to attend after Sullivan had
pulled out a New York pension fund from Citibank, forcing
it to stop new lending to South Africa). In the castle they
discussed the role of the business community in a just
society, education and job creation, and Sullivan talked
vaguely about windows and goal-setting. 'I don't want the
crisis, when it comes,' he said, 'to be so great that it's
uncontrollable.' But the South Africans, who included
Tony Bloom of the Premier Group and Judge Steyn of the
Urban Foundation, turned out to be the most radical,
while the British chairmen explained that they were not
under much pressure from shareholders, and saw no need
for bold commitments. To Sullivan's disappointment they
would only agree on a weak communique about their
'common concern' which he wisely tore up.

The British were much less pressed by their shareholders. The great bulk of British church investments were
held in a single portfolio by the Church Commissioners

which in 1986 included nearly £300 million of investments in South Africa, including £21 million in four British companies – British Petroleum, Thorn EMI, BET and BPB – which paid some workers below the minimum rate stipulated by the EEC 'code of conduct'.* But the Commission insisted that profits were their main criteria and that they could not use investment as protest. The all-party British demonstrations and protests against apartheid in the 'fifties and 'sixties had dwindled to a narrow base, and the Anti-Apartheid Movement was almost exclusively the province of the Left. High unemployment, the long fiasco of sanctions against Rhodesia and the economic disasters of black Africa, had all contributed to the British protest fatigue; and there was no black political lobby in Britain to compare with the American campaigners.

While Americans liked to see South Africa in the image of their own Deep South and the civil rights campaign, the British were still inclined to see it in terms of African colonial wars, and particularly the Boer War eighty years earlier; and Mrs Thatcher among many others invested the Afrikaners with a legendary resistance and stubbornness. While Americans instinctively looked to economic pressures which had prevailed in the South, the British constantly warned that overt pressure on Pretoria would make the Afrikaners 'retreat back into the laager'. British businessmen had longer traditional links than Americans with their white South African counterparts, often reinforced by relatives and friends, which made them more reluctant to defy local customs and attitudes, even if they disagreed with them. The headquarters of British multinationals traditionally gave much more freedom of action to their subsidiaries than their American equivalents, so that if the London boards suggested that their South African companies might be bolder in opposing apartheid or promoting black managers they were easily shut up by warnings of the dangers of a white backlash – warnings which

* *Financial Times*, July 7, 1986

usually turned out (*see* page 266) to be without real basis.

The British trade lobby UKSATA, run by the former diplomat John McQuiggan, still stayed close to Pretoria and South African officials – 'it's really the commercial arm of the South African Embassy,' said one of its members – while the new South African ambassador Denis Worrall, a sophisticated political scientist, was agile in deploying the network of potential friendships. McQuiggan and his chairman Neil Forster also kept closely in touch with the Foreign Office, and in July 1985 they were reassured by the official in charge of Africa, Ewen Fergusson (the former ambassador to Pretoria), that UKSATA would be consulted before any changes affecting companies were made. The Foreign Office was equally cut off from black opinion and politics, having virtually no contact with the African National Congress, while its embassy in Pretoria was more nervous than ever of offending the Afrikaners, and the Secret Service still co-operated with Pretoria's intelligence services in return for information on Cubans and communists in the North. The job of keeping in touch with blacks was delegated to the deputy-consul in Johannesburg, whose reports were filtered through the embassy. British diplomats in London had their own traumas about implementing sanctions after their experiences with Rhodesia; and most of them accepted Pretoria's argument that sanctions would either be ineffective, or would hurt the blacks without persuading the whites. In fact the argument that sanctions would not work was not proven. Robin Renwick, the senior British diplomat who had run the Rhodesia department and was a key negotiator of Zimbabwe's independence, had written his own study of past sanctions which pointed out many snags but concluded: 'The idea that sanctions have no effect, impose no penalty, or that their avoidance (or termination) offers no incentive, is contrary to the evidence, as it is to common sense . . .'*

* Robin Renwick, 'Economic Sanctions', Cambridge, *Harvard Studies in International Affairs*, No. 45, 1981

While British and American politicians debated sanctions in theoretical terms, the mounting violence and counter-violence inside South Africa was moving the ground beneath them. Pretoria's iron control was looking much less certain; the old religious faith in apartheid was fading; the might of the military machine looked less relevant. Businessmen and bankers were becoming less confident of the *status quo* that they were defending, and more reluctant to invest anything more. They thought that the blacks might well be winning; and while the transition would be bloody and unprofitable they might do business with them in the end. Without much likelihood of orderly white reforms the case for sanctions was already looking stronger. 'What is marginal in conditions of relatively internal calm,' wrote Ian Davidson in the *Financial Times* in July 1985, 'may become critical in conditions of unrest and uncertainty . . . Western governments need to consider whether, for the sake of the white South Africans as well as for the blacks, their intervention may improve the odds of a better outcome, however unlikely it may appear to be.'*

But the emotional clamour in America for disinvestment, and the eagerness of many chairmen to escape from the hassle, tended to distract attention from the more critical question of what would happen afterwards. For any thoughtful view of South Africa's long-term survival, disinvestment and sanctions could only be part of the strategy: they would have to be accompanied by much more constructive measures by both companies and governments, including a more decisive alignment with the black opposition, more support for the neighbouring black states and the building up of an alternative infrastructure of rail and air routes, to limit the dangerous dependence on South Africa. It was an error of many campaigners for disinvestment that they too easily allowed both businessmen and politicians to opt out and evade their real long-

* *Financial Times*, July 29, 1985

term problem: how to safeguard the continuity of Western interests and influence in Southern Africa by gaining much broader black support.

12

Emergency

We've got a new breed of children. They believe that they're going to die – and the frightening thing is they don't care. Because it is their view the only language the government understands is violence.

Bishop Tutu, *Witness to Apartheid*, Channel 4 TV,
April 4, 1986

By the middle of 1985 the Botha government was convinced that its authority was being seriously undermined by the growing black revolt. The ANC's policy to 'render South Africa ungovernable' was looking more credible inside the townships. The young blacks were beginning to build up their own 'alternative structures' with their own crude form of discipline and government. For months, many black families had refused to pay higher rents. The government-sponsored community councils were boycotted. Police terrorism and torture were opposed by counter-terrorism against black police and suspected informers. The 'necklace' – the tyre filled with petrol and set alight round the victim's neck – had already become black South Africa's grim contribution to the language of revenge.

The government blamed as the chief culprits a group of radicals within the students' body COSAS, which they accused of conspiring secretly with the ANC, and which they soon banned. The well-briefed BBC correspondent Graham Leach reported:

> The government was disturbed by evidence that the radicals were trying to carry through a classic two-stage revolutionary programme in some of the townships. The first phase was to make the townships ungovernable as the ANC had urged. Local government in many areas had collapsed following attacks on black councillors and the resignation, out of fear, of others. Black policemen, also the victims of violence, had been evacuated from their homes and, along with their families, were living like refugees in tented camps behind barbed wire on the outskirts of townships. Law and order had broken down with even the simplest burglary unable to be investigated unless an officer entered the township accompanied by armoured personnel-carriers carrying police and troops. Indeed it appeared to the authorities that the second phase of the activists' programme was becoming evident.*

On July 20 President Botha announced a state of emergency in thirty-six magisterial districts. It was just over twenty-five years since the previous emergency after Sharpeville, whose anniversary had helped to precipitate the new crisis. Two days afterwards I asked two rival black leaders how they thought it would compare with Sharpeville. From KwaZulu, Chief Buthelezi of Inkatha said:

> You'll remember how Sharpeville broke down people's morale to the extent that you could hardly hear a whisper. So now one does fear that everything might reach its lowest ebb. I doubt very much whether the emergency will increase the opposition, knowing how cruel the police can be. You know how tough the Afrikaners are:

* Graham Leach, *op. cit.*, p. 174

they cling together once they feel an onslaught on them. Apartheid has been here for thirty-seven years. It would be a mistake to think the Afrikaners have lost the will to rule. It's true that they are very confused about where they want to go. Dr Verwoerd was cock-a-hoop about apartheid, whereas this regime is ashamed now about apartheid, to the extent that Botha, I'm sure, wants to dismantle it. They do worry about what they are doing, and this does give some encouragement to the blacks. But that is very different from losing the will to rule.

From Zambia, Oliver Tambo of the ANC said:

Martial law will sanction the killing of hundreds of people without police or others being asked to account for it. There will be a lot of 'disappearances'. But a greater degree of repression produces a greater upsurge. My expectation is that the emergency is preparing conditions for a much more violent conflict – moving towards a real explosion . . . The townships are struggling against the apartheid structure. But the struggle will soon go far beyond the townships, questioning the whole right to rule.*

When I visited Johannesburg a month after the declaration of the emergency both sides seemed to think that anything might happen, with the same discrepancy between ideas and realities that was so striking after Sharpeville: the premature optimism of the young blacks, insisting 'This is it!', while the white businessmen pursued their business as usual, and their suburban life was untouched. But this black revolt was now far more widespread; and the balance of confidence, if not the balance of power, had clearly changed. 'Sharpeville was a revolt of the parents,' as the veteran photographer Peter Mugabane put it. 'Soweto was the children. Now it's both.' 'In 1976 the kids began it,

* Telephone interviews with author, July 1985

almost spontaneously,' said the editor of *Drum*, Stanley
Motjuwadi. 'But now the parents can't control the children
as they could in '76, and the kids don't care about the
consequences. The more kids they arrest, the worse it
becomes.' The revolt had spread from town to country –
even to the downtrodden farm labourers in the Eastern
Transvaal – and from middle-class to workers: the activists
of the UDF were a much more proletarian group than earlier
middle-class leaders such as Mandela or Tambo. The police
were helping to unite black businessmen and workers
against them, and militant blacks sounded confident that
when the real terrorists emerged they would find it easier
to hide. 'There are safe houses for freedom fighters,' one
boasted, 'even in small Afrikaner towns in the Orange
Free State.'

Could it really be the prelude to a revolution? Could the
state really be losing control? President Botha repeatedly
warned that it had still only used a small part of its fire-
power; and while the 50,000 police were clearly over-
stretched and prone to panic, the government still had a
potential army of 300,000. The violence was largely limited
to the townships, and no casual visitor to the white suburbs
would notice any cause for worry. Yet the army com-
manders knew that they could not impose a purely military
solution in the heart of an advanced industrial state; and
General Magnus Malan, the Minister of Defence, had said
long ago that they must win 'hearts and minds'. Each
confrontation was now losing more hearts and minds, and
the young Afrikaner police were visibly provoking more
resistance with their brutality and arbitrary arrests. The
co-opting of the army into many townships had created
its own problems by providing the appearance of a civil
war.

Most whites had clearly expected the emergency to
restore order quickly, but the first weeks revealed unsus-
pected resistance; and the UDF's grass roots surprised
everyone including the police. In Cape Town where the
UDF had thought they would be weakest the organisation

was the most effective; and it was there that its co-founder Allan Boesak planned a march on Mandela's prison to 'turn South Africa upside down', until he was himself arrested and jailed. Black militants were emerging everywhere, and it was hard to find 'Uncle Toms', for most blacks were convinced that they were winning. They gave different time-frames, but rarely less than ten years, before they would share political power – or control it. They disagreed widely about the cost of it, whether it would be achieved after far more bloodshed or after the intervention of the West. But the heightened expectations reverberated through the townships: any middle-class black now thought carefully before he identified himself too closely with whites, on the losing side.

The blacks had very few guns and faced massed forces and weaponry. Their optimism seemed absurd: yet many whites including Afrikaners now seemed convinced that part of their system was crumbling. A poll taken in August 1985 showed 63 percent of whites as well as 59 percent of blacks saying that apartheid would not exist in ten years' time. Businessmen and politicians were talking in commonplace terms about the post-apartheid era and power-sharing with blacks; and even conservative Afrikaners including Anton Rupert were insisting that apartheid must be buried. The conditions seemed to be ripe for at least two ingredients for revolution: the rulers had lost confidence in their theories, and the ruled were convinced that they could win. But between words and action there remained a huge gap. The white language of power-sharing and post-apartheid remained coded, with far vaguer connotations than among Westerners or blacks, while the means of transition to any kind of black government were still quite undefined. And in the meantime the political pressures were still pushing the two sides further apart. When the same poll asked blacks what would happen, 69 percent thought there would be a civil war, and only 29 percent that it would be resolved peacefully: compared to 30 percent of whites who expected civil war, and 59 percent who ex-

pected a peaceful resolution.* The lack of common perceptions, and the suppression of news suggested that the civil
war had already begun. Riots and shootings were officially
described as 'unrest'. The television films of baton-charges
and whippings which were screened round the world were
never glimpsed inside South Africa. Blinkered from the
real news, the two sides were diverging still further.

Nine years after Soweto, the black children were still
more in the centre of the revolt; and again the most
explosive issue was black education which was deteriorating still further. The schoolboys were now further alienated
from existing structures, with a conviction in their own
cause which had changed the frontiers of politics. As the
sociologists Adam and Moodley described it:

> The hysteria that sweeps the school and townships re-
> sembles the Children's Crusades of medieval Europe.
> Immune to the strategic reasoning of parents, teachers
> or even Bishop Tutu, it cuts its deadly path outside
> conventional politics and traditional ideologies. Politi-
> cal socialisation now starts with tear-gas fumes.†

Pretoria was quick to compare the militant children with
the teenage Shi-ite warriors in the Middle East, or the
Khmer Rouge in Cambodia. But the teenagers who called
themselves 'comrades' in the townships owed little to religious or ideological teaching, and much more to their
street-schooling in the townships which had taught them
to expect nothing from the white world, whether government or business. They continued to be enraged by their
formal schooling, which they equated with enslavement.
The traditional belief in education as the means to compete
with the whites, which had permeated the earlier ANC
political leaders, was being undermined by the schoolboys'

---

* Robert M Worcester of Mori, in *Public Opinion* magazine, AEI
Washington, September 18, 1985
  † Adam and Moodley, *op. cit.*, p. 114

slogans: 'liberation before education' or 'freedom now, education later'. But the schools and syllabi were still part of the battleground.

Behind many of the protests and boycotts there proved to be more organisation than at first appeared. The students' union COSAS had since 1983 produced a network of local 'youth congresses' such as the Soweto congress SOYCO or the Port Elizabeth congress PEYCO, influenced by the ANC and the Freedom Charter as their acronyms suggested. One of the key organisers was Daniel Montsisi who had been a prominent student leader in the Soweto uprising in 1976 before spending four years on Robben Island; and he saw the development of local congresses in the tradition of the ANC and the Youth League to which Mandela and Tambo belonged in the 'forties: 'we regarded ourselves broadly as a logical progression of that type of tradition,' he told Shaun Johnson. The organisers saw the youth as essential to the struggle, but not necessarily decisive. As Montsisi put it:

In the formation of street and defence committees, the youths are central. They are the first to be detained, the first to be shot. But this should not be confused with us thinking we are in the vanguard of the struggle. That role belongs to our working parents.*

As the schoolchildren became more militant, boycotting the schools and setting up their own committees and discipline, the older black leadership of the UDF and the ANC were more anxious to harness and control this new power; and the parents, first in Soweto then across the nation, set up their own bodies. By the end of 1985 they had called the First National Education Conference to persuade the children to return to school, in return for an ultimatum to the government to meet their demands – including the

* Shaun Johnson, The Youth in South Africa. Report for the David Davies Memorial Foundation, London, 1986

unbanning of COSAS, reinstating sacked teachers and releasing detainees – within three months. For the time being the two black generations seemed to have reached some understanding; but as the death toll increased, and the feuds between rival political groups became more violent, the control was clearly tenuous. And the build-up to March 1986 became increasingly tense.

By the end of 1985 official figures stated that the police had killed 763 people over the year, of whom only three were white and 201 were children, while 2,571 had been shot and wounded.*

The most obvious contrast between this emergency and Sharpeville was the blacks' involvement with industry. Johannesburg was no longer primarily a city of mine-dumps and compounds: it was ringed with shining new factories, assembly plants, supermarkets and shopping centres – with black operators and checkers in place of whites. Many more blacks were now involved in the economic system, including trades unions which had been legalised six years before. And Botha now faced a basic contradiction between industry's need for formal unions with which to negotiate, and the determination of his security services to cut off the black leaders, including unions. 'The black trades unions were illegal in 1960, and they're now legal,' said Tambo. 'But the curious thing is that trades unionists are now being charged with high treason – because they've organised trades unions.'†

The black union leaders had already been flexing their muscles. 'The members of those unions are beginning to see what the government is doing,' said Cyril Ramaphosa of the mineworkers', the most powerful of them, in March 1985. 'The government has been promising for a number of years to make a number of changes, and the government hasn't lived up to its promises. So they are beginning now to feel that they should take things into their own hands.'‡

* *Weekly Mail*, March 7, 1986
† Interview with author, July 1985
‡ Interview with ABC TV, March 20, 1985

Ramaphosa knew that unions were the critical means of political organisation while the major parties were banned, and that they could produce more radical leaders. 'We have a very strong base,' he said a year later, 'maybe even much stronger, for instance, than the ANC . . . We believe that the workers should take leadership positions because we would like to see a country that is going to be ruled in the interests of the workers who produce the wealth of the country.*

Ramaphosa had a trial of strength with the mine-owners in August 1985, when his workers went on strike for higher wages. He could claim some progress: the six great gold-mining houses had been split as never before, with Anglo-American as usual on the liberal wing and the Afrikaner-controlled Gencor and the British-controlled Gold Fields on the extreme right. 'Gencor and Gold Fields wish they had never opened the doors to unions,' Ramaphosa said. 'They show that in their negotiations: though they can't afford to press to abolish them.'† But the mine-owners were still able to dismiss striking workers and the strike was broken. 'You can commence a strike,' Ramaphosa said afterwards, 'but if the bosses still have the right to dismiss your members, then you don't have a strike anymore.'‡

As the emergency continued the unions became more associated with the broader struggle for freedom. By November 1985 Ramaphosa was taking the lead in bringing black trades unionists together to form a new confederation called COSATU, with the mine-workers' vice-president Elijah Barayi as president. Barayi had been in the ANC Youth League with Mandela and Tambo, which shaped his political awareness; he took part in the defiance campaign in 1952; and he saw COSATU as being 'part and parcel of the liberation struggle'. He believed in socialism 'as

* Interview with Barry Streek, Africa Report, March 1986
† Telephone interview with author, August 1985
‡ Africa Report, March 1986

practised by the Labour Party in England' and wanted to nationalise the mines: 'Black people are the people who are digging up gold and in return are paid peanuts. Once we nationalise the whole industry, our belief is that everyone will reap the fruits of his sweat and toil . . . This country is in crisis because of capitalism. If we at least took the big firms, nationalised them, then the government would look after its people and the people would look after the government.' But he believed firmly in the democratic system: 'I don't want a one-party state. I believe that is a dictatorship of the worst kind.'*

The new confederation was launched at a meeting of 10,000 blacks in December in Durban, where the wave of strikes had begun twelve years earlier. 'The wealth must be shared by all the people in this country,' said Ramaphosa in his opening speech. 'It is important for us to make our politics the politics of the oppressed people of this country.' COSATU soon claimed half-a-million members of its affiliated unions, but there remained deep rivalries with other groupings split between political leaderships including AZACTU (the Azanian conferation of trade unions), the arm of the black consciousness group AZAPO and UWUSA, the Zulu unions linked to Buthelezi's Inkatha movement, while the ANC lamented that 'there are 560,000 workers organised in "white-dominated", racist trade unions, and only 14 percent of the total workforce is organised in any trade union'.† But the ANC rejoiced that 'a powerful new voice has been added to the politics of South Africa'. There were potential tensions between COSATU leaders and the ANC in exile; but Tambo knew that when the ANC was legalised the unions would be critical to its re-organisation.

Both government and businesses were confused by the politicisation of the unions. The government had expected to be able to infiltrate and monitor them, to clamp down before they became dangerous; the companies were caught

---

* Interview with Philip Van Niekerk, *Africa Report*, March 1986
† *Sechaba*, January 1986

between their need for leaders to negotiate with, and their dread of radical leadership. The mine-owners compared Ramaphosa with Arthur Scargill, the militant miners' leader in Britain. 'The more radical elements are naturally drawn towards the power base of the unions,' said Robin Plumbridge of Gold Fields. 'It's awkward if they abuse their power.'

But the most immediate demonstration of black economic influence was the success of local consumer boycotts, which could exploit their purchasing power, pulling the strings of capitalism at the consumer end, while shareholders tugged at the investing end. Consumer boycotts were not new to South Africa: rural black families had boycotted potatoes in the late 'fifties in protest against farm jails; and there had recently been 'black Christmases' boycotting the shops. By early 1985 blacks were organising political boycotts in the Eastern Cape to persuade white shopkeepers to bring pressure on government, or to dissuade black and other shopkeepers from collaborating with the government.

One of the most influential was in the small coastal town of Kenton-on-Sea between Port Elizabeth and East London, where 2,000 blacks lived with one water-tap, no electricity or sewerage and a rubbish dump for the whites in the middle of their township. Just before the emergency they petitioned the local development board, and were faced by the police who tear-gassed them and arrested a hundred. They responded by boycotting white shops which had treated them badly, carefully excepting friendly shopkeepers. The boycott soon showed practical results: the white community formed a liaison committee to discuss the blacks' grievances, arranged for more water-taps, removed the rubbish dump. Then the emergency was declared, the police arrested four black members of the committee, beat them up and interrogated them as agitators.*

But the emergency further inspired the boycotters, par-

* *See Financial Times, October 29, 1985*

ticularly in the politicised Eastern Cape, near the big
car-plants and other factories. In Port Elizabeth a debonair
young black building worker Mkhuseli Jack emerged as
the chief spokesman: he had been a student leader in the
Soweto revolt and had been jailed many times since. He
became prominent in the UDF, and became the 'loud-
speaker' for consumer boycotts just before the emergency.
He insisted that the boycotters must keep negotiating,
using both carrots and sticks: 'If we just say we won't talk
they'll be united against us.'* His committee had striking
successes with white shops which agreed to their terms;
and when the police detained him under the emergency
the whites complained that they had no one with whom to
negotiate.

The Port Elizabeth boycott was so damaging to white
shops – forcing many to shut down – that the Chamber of
Commerce complained to Pretoria that the emergency had
wrecked their negotiations, and the mayor appealed in
vain to President Botha to relax it. The movement spread
to the Western Cape, including the prosperous town of
Worcester: 'Why should we make Worcester rich,' asked
Allan Boesak, 'when these people vote for the National
Party and keep P W Botha in power?' As boycotts spread to
the Transvaal, the Association of Chambers of Commerce,
ASSOCOM, met to discuss the need for better communication. Raymond Ackerman, the retailing tycoon and
champion of consumer sovereignty who ran the Pick 'n
Pay supermarkets – who only a few years earlier had keenly
supported the government – now formed a committee to
'press for reform and to promote dialogue' and emerged
as a lifelong 'foe of apartheid'.

The boycotts had limitations; they never really worked
in Soweto, which was too big and divided to be effectively
monitored and enforced; and when the young 'comrades'
tried coercion – for instance by forcing housewives to drink
the oil they had bought from white shops – the older

* *Wall Street Journal*, April 28, 1985

people turned against them. The movement was only really effective for remedying local grievances, and could not penetrate the more powerful financial interests. 'It has taken the struggle on to white doorsteps,' said the ANC magazine *Sechaba*. 'It has not yet taken it into the inner corridors of power.'* But the blacks had learnt to work the economic pulleys, like the blacks in America, to achieve immediate results; and they had also rapidly persuaded many big retailing companies that they must campaign openly against the government if they wanted to keep their black customers. Shopkeepers, supermarkets, cinemas and retail chains became bolder in pressing for radical and rapid reforms, all the more as recession bit into their business. The old Marxist picture of a monolithic capitalism could not fit the whole spectrum of different interests – from mining and engineering through manufacturing to retailing – each with their conflicting pressures from black custom and unions on one side, and government patronage on the other. Nor could immediate commercial interests altogether explain the very different responses of companies to the crisis. For most South African business was still controlled by a handful of individual entrepreneurs, each with his own background, conscience and perspective. It was personality and judgment, as much as economic interests, which explained differences of behaviour. The emergency was causing agonised rethinking by the more far-sighted business leaders in all sectors, who were aware of their hateful image among blacks, and most of all among the schoolboys who should be their future workforce. They knew that they could not achieve political stability without a settlement with the blacks; while opinion polls were recording the growing hostility.

Chief Buthelezi looked more attractive to many businessmen, particularly in Natal, as the violence increased. He insisted that investment was a strategy *for*

* Jean Middleton, 'The Consumer Boycott: A People's Weapon', *Sechaba*, April 1986

liberation and always gave a friendly welcome to visiting businessmen. He explained the horrors of violence and the evils of the ANC, and after the ANC's ·special congress in June he told American business visitors that its delegates had been 'faceless nobodies' who were to blame for inciting blacks against blacks. He remained ambivalent towards the ANC, praising Mandela – with whom he had a friendly exchange of letters – while denigrating Tambo. In September he ferociously attacked the ANC to a crowd of 15,000 in KwaZulu, explaining how their so-called armed struggle had been a dismal failure. 'The fundamental difference in approach between Inkatha and the ANC mission-in-exile revolves around the use of violence.' He condemned both Botha and Tambo for being out of touch: 'It is the people in the end who will triumph and Inkatha is rooted in the people's power.'* But in the angry black townships round Johannesburg or Port Elizabeth, Buthelezi's Zulu traditions could not attract Xhosa or Basuto; and his Zulu *impi*s were practised in violence. 'He has left the nation,' said Dr Motlana of the VDF, 'and joined the tribe.'

The predicament of businessmen was much more fundamental. 'There can be no real change until business takes the side of freedom,' Winnie Mandela said to me in Johannesburg in August. 'In the past white businesses haven't used their clout because their profit margins were soaring with the help of influx control, decentralising and slave-wages,' said Percy Qoboza, the veteran editor of the black *City Press*. 'Now the tables are turned and apartheid is hurting them. I sense they feel helpless: they don't seem psychologically able to use their collective muscle.' Many businessmen privately agreed; but the gap between thinking and acting was as wide as ever, and they each looked to leadership from the other. There was special agonising among the Jewish community whose families had first come to South Africa to escape racial persecution in Tsarist

---

* Speech at Umlazi, September 28, 1985. *See also Clarion Call* (the official magazine of the KwaZulu government, Ulundi), Vol, 13, 1985

Russia or Nazi Germany. As Mendel Kaplan put it, in his history of Jewish entrepreneurs:

> Businessmen as a group, until the second half of 1985, have been often mere spectators in the battle to remove, not only general discriminatory practices, but those specifically affecting the economy of which their companies are a part. If Jewish businessmen, in particular, fail to give leadership in the movement to abolish all discriminatory practices, they will be betraying their heritage in the country which gave the Jewish people their freedom and opportunities.*

What really hit businessmen was the state of the economy, and the collapsing currency. The rand had already been sloping downwards over the previous year, as foreign investors became more concerned about the political stability. The declaration of the emergency had been quickly followed by the Chase Manhattan's refusal to continue lending (*see* Chapter 2) which, with the French ban on investment, caused a massive loss of confidence. As the rand fell further, threatening any business with short-term loans in dollars, the businessmen looked forward hopefully to President Botha's speech to the National Party Congress on August 16 which was heralded as promising crucial reforms to reassure the bankers. But Botha at the last minute modified his speech, leaving out references to sharing political power with blacks and slamming the door on Mandela, whom he untruthfully portrayed as a self-confessed communist. Nothing was left to placate the blacks – except a reference to pass-laws being 'outdated'. And Botha's main emphasis was on defying foreign pressure: 'Don't push us too far . . .'

The blacks were outraged: '*He* has pushed *us* too far,' said Winnie Mandela. '*He* has pushed the rest of the world too far. It's incredible – not even Hitler would have done

* Kaplan, *op. cit.*, p. 389

that. That peculiar Afrikaner tribe, they get themselves into their corner and then ask people to negotiate to get them out of that corner.'*

But Botha's 'Rubicon' speech had also slammed the door on businessmen and bankers as it precipitated a new collapse of the currency, which went on falling for the next days; and a week after Botha's speech the stock-exchange was closed while the government re-imposed its emergency controls to prevent further capital flight (*see* page 44). The connection between politics and business now seemed total. 'I used to say that we should only be involved in politics when it directly affected our own financial interests,' the chairman of Barlow Rand, Mike Rosholt, said to me the day after the rand had collapsed, 'but now where can you draw the line?' Rosholt hoped that the economic crisis would concentrate minds in Pretoria, and was sure that businessmen must play a bolder role. 'When you think about it, compromises are part of our daily activity, every time we make a deal. We're more used to them than politicians.' And behind the scenes a group of business leaders, including Rosholt, had been seriously considering: might they possibly be able to do business with the ANC?

* Interview with author, August 1985

13

Tycoons and Revolutionaries

The longer the white minority regime persists in its racist policies, the greater the likelihood that black South African mythology will become overwhelmingly anti-capitalist and anti-Western.

Leonard Thompson, *The Political Mythology of Apartheid*,
New Haven, Yale University Press, 1985, p. 243

Since Harry Oppenheimer had retired as chairman of the Anglo-American Corporation in January 1983 there had been constant speculation about the character of the new leadership. Few people were very surprised at the choice of his successor, Gavin Relly, who came from the heart of the Anglo tradition: a former Rhodes Scholar, he had been private secretary to both Harry and his father Sir Ernest before climbing the Anglo ladder: he had run its Zambian mines at the time when President Kaunda had half-nationalised them – which shocked him much less than Oppenheimer – and he later ran its North American business from Toronto. He personified the 'Anglo style' which combined the manner of an English public school with being (as Relly put it) 'much tougher than one looks'.* He was more naturally conservative and much less politi-

---

* Interview with Alan Cowell, *New York Times*, November 18, 1985 cally experienced than Oppenheimer, but he was thrust into politics as a director of Anglo and as president of the SA Foundation. He thought that South African business-men were more exposed to the international disapproval of apartheid than governments which were 'involved in the delicate egg dances of the diplomatic world', and he insisted that business was 'entitled to say when it thinks those politics are jeopardising its ability to create wealth'. He had his own doubts about capitalism: 'I am not keen on calling ours a capitalist society,' he said in 1985, 'because I think capitalism in certain circumstances is not very free. For instance, while Nazi Germany was a capitalist society it was never free in any proper sense.'*

Harry Oppenheimer still had an office in the Anglo building; his only son Nicholas, who became deputy chairman, was talked of as Relly's successor, and the family firm, E Oppenheimer & Son, was still the largest single shareholder in Anglo. Harry still made some speeches round the world, and made no secret of his political worries: with the emergency he was totally disillusioned with Botha's promises to businessmen. Gavin Relly commissioned an immense volume weighing sixteen pounds full of flattering tributes to Oppenheimer and the Corporation,† but he made clear that he would not necessarily follow in his predecessor's footsteps: 'I don't intend to have to fill his boots. I intend to fill my own.'‡ He was less subtle and reflective than Oppenheimer: he had the bluff outdoors style of many Anglo executives; he held forth articulately, looking over his spectacles; he enjoyed robust argument and giving interviews, using phrases like 'I would judge that'. But he never had Oppenheimer's intellectual curiosity or love of listening, and did not pretend to. He was not deeply informed about black politics, and had never taken the ANC very seriously. It was all the more

* Interview with Hugh Murray, *Leadership* magazine, Johannesburg, 1985

† HFO: Some Personal Perspectives, 1985

‡ *New York Times*, ibid.

astonishing when, soon after the declaration of the emergency, he agreed to join a small group to fly up to Zambia to talk to Oliver Tambo.

Relly had a more awesome responsibility than the bankers: a huge industrial company could not simply cut its losses and pull out, as the bankers had done; it had a massive stake in the country's future, whatever its government. And Anglo now dominated the South African economy more than ever. One survey compiled in 1985 (fiercely disputed by Anglo) showed that it controlled, directly and indirectly, 54.2 percent of the Johannesburg stock exchange (which is said to represent 26 percent of South Africa's wealth), four times as much as its nearest contenders, Sanlam and SA Mutual. 'We're living in a country controlled by cartels and lobbyists,' wrote Robin McGregor, the author and publisher of *The Investor's Handbook* '– and a government only too keen to satisfy the lobbyists at the expense of 25 million people.'*

Percentage of control over Johannesburg stock exchange

Anglo-American	54.1%	Rembrandt Group	4.4%
Sanlam	11.3%	Liberty Group	2.3%
SA Mutual	10.9%	Anglo-Vaal	2.1%

To many black radicals Anglo seemed to come close to Lenin's picture of 'monopoly capitalism', as Relly was fully aware. Would it not be better, I asked him, if it were broken up? 'But where would you start?' he replied. 'We've got a quarter of a million shareholders. We don't deal in price-fixing businesses. Gold doesn't rape the public. All our companies are very separate. The government knows that they would fiddle with Anglo at their peril – because there'd be no logic for preventing other fiddling.' But Relly was aware that Anglo and the other major corporations would have to be fundamentally changed to

* *The Investor's Handbook*, Purdey Publishing (Box 47, McGregor, 6708, South Africa)

make them acceptable to any future black, or partly black, government. 'I don't stand by rigid paternalist capitalism; we need a change in the process of shareholding. But free enterprise should mean above all a freedom of choice.'*

The economic strength of Anglo was not easily translated into political power; and its semi-monopoly was a source of weakness as much as strength. It was always acutely vulnerable to Pretoria, whether through government contracts or broader political leverage; and it was reluctant to interfere with the autonomy of its hundreds of subsidiaries for fear of being accused of monopoly. A tragic example was its attitude to the country's most liberal newspaper, the *Rand Daily Mail*, which it controlled indirectly through the newspaper group SAAN. The *Mail* had a large black readership in Soweto, so that it formed (as Gavin Relly himself put it) 'a bridge between black and white thinking'. And Relly was personally concerned that white South Africans would 'get into a position where for lack of nitty-gritty investigation or comment by the press, we may come to be deluded as to the real nature of our society, and how it is developing'.† But the *Mail* was not popular with most businessmen or advertisers, who preferred the conventional Johannesburg *Star*, the traditional spokesman of the Chamber of Mines. By the 'eighties the *Mail* was losing several million dollars a year, and SAAN wanted to close it down: the journalists appealed to Oppenheimer and Relly, but in vain, and on April 30, 1985 it stopped publication, to be replaced the next day by *Business Day*, which was proclaimed as the 'national newspaper for decision-makers' and which had few black readers. To knock down the *Mail*'s bridge, just when the country was becoming rapidly polarised and businessmen were looking anxiously for contacts with blacks, raised more serious doubts as to whether South African businessmen were really acting in their own interests.

* Interview with author, May 1986
† *Leadership*, ibid.

But as the wave of violence moved into the emergency, Relly was becoming more aware of the long-term dangers of Anglo's identification with Pretoria; and though he dreaded the 'African quagmire' he had seen in Zambia a peaceful transition to black rule. Already before the emergency there had been tentative moves to make contact with the ANC in exile from several businessmen, who included Ian Sims, the New Zealander who ran BP in Cape Town and Chris Ball, the chief executive of Barclays in Johannesburg. The most determined and open was Tony Bloom, the debonair young Harvard-trained lawyer who had taken over from his father – as the fourth generation of his family – to become chairman of the Premier Group in 1979. Premier's bakeries, stores and factories were increasingly dependent on black custom and thus concerned with their political image; but Bloom was also personally an intellectual, and one of the most courageous of the business leaders. Others outside business were also pressing for contacts with the ANC, including Hugh Murray, the entrepreneurial editor of *Leadership* magazine who had struck up a warm relationship with President Kaunda in Zambia, and believed that 'the ANC *is* a reality that South Africans will have to come to grips with – sooner or later'; and Harald Pakendorf, the adventurous young editor of the Afrikaner daily *Vaderland*, who had decided: 'it is only really the ANC which at the end of the day can be said to have a truly national following – if not for its methods at least for its ideals.' Pakendorf insisted that South Africa must 'grasp the nettle of the ANC, full well knowing that it may be dangerous, but not as dangerous as not doing it'.*

The South African Foundation, which was now much more independent from Pretoria, was also favouring contact with the ANC, and in January 1985 its man in London, David Willers, had already met two officials from the ANC in London, Solly Smith and Seretse Choabe. Willers assured them that South African businessmen were now

* *Leadership*, 1985

committed to fundamental reforms, for reasons of self-interest, and preferred the ANC to be legalised: the Foundation would like to exchange views with the ANC and to find common ground; they were also 'anxious to try to avoid becoming a sabotage target of the ANC'. Solly Smith said that the ANC would be glad to have talks with anyone, provided they were not formal negotiations; and warned that if the ANC were to be undermined by more radical elements, the task of reconstruction would become much more difficult.

The revival in the reputation of the African National Congress had taken nearly all whites by surprise. It was still officially banned, unquoted in the press, and most of its leaders had been in jail for twenty-two years; but Mandela had never been so famous. The power of the ANC, with their fragile organisation confronted by all Pretoria's military machine, seemed as mysterious as that of the Ayatollah Khomeini before the Iranian revolution, and in some ways more baffling; for it had no strong religious backing, and no network of mullahs and mosques. But it still represented the long tradition of black protest, martyrdom and freedom to which the young rebels now rallied. Many younger white businessmen were now seriously wondering whether they might not be dealing with an ANC government in their lifetime. 'Within the Republic,' wrote the historian of black politics, Tom Lodge, 'the conviction that the ANC constitutes the only viable alternative and successor to the incumbent administration is one that is beginning to affect not just the political responses of black people but those of whites as well.'*

In Lusaka, Oliver Tambo was still looking for international economic pressure to avert the need for greater violence; and he believed that businessmen could do far more to influence the Pretoria government. He was supported by his more left-wing colleagues, including the

---

* Tom Lodge, The Second Consultative Conference of the African National Congress, South African International, 1985

white communist Joe Slovo, and he took care to keep in touch with his contacts inside South Africa, to explain to them why he was talking to capitalists.

By early August a group of South African business leaders had agreed to take the bold step and to fly up to Lusaka. Originally they were to include not only Gavin Relly and Tony Bloom, but also Chris Ball of Barclays, Mike Rosholt, the chairman of the conglomerate Barlow Rand, and two influential Afrikaners: Anton Rupert of the Rembrandt tobacco group and Fred Du Plessis of Sanlam. But the first meeting on August 28 had to be postponed; then Ball had to attend a strategy meeting, and Rosholt explained he must go to his son's wedding. And when the plans were leaked Du Plessis and Rupert dropped out, fearing the anger of the president. But Botha did not try to stop the visit: 'He was cross, but not very cross,' said Relly. The foreign ministry in Pretoria even gave the businessmen's party a very superficial three-page briefing about the ANC.

On September 13, the little party flew up in an Anglo plane to Zambia: the businessmen Relly and Bloom, augmented at the last moment by Zach de Beer, the former Progressive MP who was now a director of Anglo, Peter Sorour of the South African Foundation and two newspaper editors, Pakendorf and Tertius Myburg of the Johannesburg *Sunday Times*. But Relly was far the most significant, as head of the dominant corporation; and he had agreed against the opinion of Oppenheimer, who did not conceal that he felt 'twitchy' about the excursion.

They met at the presidential hunting lodge of Mfuwe, the game park in Zambia, where Kaunda received them, and brought them together with the team from the ANC: Oliver Tambo, as President; the young director of information Thabo Mbeki, whose father Govan was still in prison with Mandela; the Indian Mac Maharaj, who had been on Robben Island; and Chris Hani. The blacks wore ties and neat suits, while the whites looked unkempt with open necks: 'If you'd been asked to say which were the businessmen, which were the revolutionaries,' said one of the whites, 'you'd have got it the wrong way round.' Kaunda spoke briefly, pointing out that they were all South Africans: he offered to leave them together, and was pressed to stay. Tambo insisted that they should not sit in two phalanxes facing each other, like opposing camps, but should be distributed round the room. He called Relly 'Gavin' and asked to be called Oliver. The atmosphere, everyone agreed, was soon extraordinarily friendly. 'It was one of the nicest days I've ever spent,' Relly said afterwards. 'A picnic among South Africans talking about their future together.' 'A more attractive and genial group would be hard to imagine,' said Bloom. 'It was a marvellous meeting,' said Tambo. They talked for six hours – continuing through lunch where Tambo said grace to the whites' astonishment – about the problems of violence, reconstruction, nationalisation and the country's economic future. Bloom was struck by the blacks' sense of patriotism after years of exile: they loved to talk about places and people in the Republic. He also thought they were highly intelligent leaders – 'streets ahead' of most black leaders inside South Africa – with whom there could be serious negotiations and compromise. He remained worried by the communist component and the ANC's links with the SACP, but he was struck by the lack of Marxist dogma: Sweden seemed to be their model, rather than Eastern Europe or Russia. The businessmen predictably asked about the threat of nationalisation, which was implicit in the ANC's Freedom Charter of thirty years earlier. Tambo insisted that some major corporations would have to be taken under state control: 'They represent tremendous wealth in the midst of unspeakable poverty.' He also asked the businessmen to stop supporting the state arms corporation, Armscor, and warned that the ANC would attack economic installations. But he adopted a very conciliatory approach, and talked about a future mixed economy in South Africa. When asked about the violence, Tambo said he personally abhorred it – 'I even take insects out of the bath' – but he and Thabo Mbeki explained that the intensification of the military struggle would inevitably mean that more civilians would die, though the ANC would not deliberately attack them. But Tambo insisted later that he had left them with no doubt that he would be 'compelled to allow violence' in the future.*

The whites left in a mood of some euphoria. Bloom believed it was a breakthrough and hoped for a follow-up. Hugh Murray insisted that there was 'considerable justification for further talks'. Gavin Relly was clearly moved by the goodwill. 'There are important areas in which one should be able to find fundamental agreement, starting with the recognition that we are all South Africans . . .', he said in London soon afterwards. 'All of us in that meeting wanted to see a new coherent society in South Africa based on demonstrable justice and a court-monitored bill of rights.'† And he later explained:

Predictably there remained great gaps between us. Businessmen do not embrace the prospects of nationalisation, either in practical or philosophical terms; they know as a matter of fact that economic thinking which derives from the shadowy, incompetent world of worn-out Marxism does not create wealth. On the other hand, who can deny that there are inequities in the generation and distribution of South Africa's wealth? A new society, reformed or revolutionary, would have to apply itself more diligently to the alleviation of deprivation in education, health and feeding.‡

The ANC still broadcast bloodthirsty threats against whites. On October 7 Radio Freedom from Addis Ababa said: 'We must attack them at their homes and holiday resorts

* *Financial Times*, September 14, 1985; *Weekly Mail*, January 17, 1986. *Also* author's interviews with Tambo, Relly, Bloom

† Interview with Jonathan Power, *International Herald Tribune*, September 23, 1985

‡ Article in the *Guardian*, London, October 7, 1985

just as we have been attacking black boot-lickers at their homes. This must happen to their white colleagues.' But Tambo soon afterwards explained in a broadcast on October 15 that business leaders could be an 'additional lever' in the ANC's struggle, even if they were motivated by their own self-interest: 'If they reach the conclusion that, indeed, the whole apartheid system is going to destroy their businesses, even the whole economy, at that point they will want to remove the apartheid system and will even join with forces which are set to destroy the system, provided they are sure that the system will not be replaced with something worse for their economy, for their pockets, for their profits.'

Tambo was also ready to talk with international businessmen, all the more after his encounters in New York the previous March; and in October 1985 he was invited by a group of friends to visit London, not just to talk to the Anti-Apartheid Movement and the Labour Party – the traditional allies of the ANC – but to meet businessmen, bankers and other politicians. In the first part of his London visit Tambo briefly overlapped with Bishop Tutu; and the Commonwealth Secretary-General Sonny Ramphal gave a dinner for both at the resplendent Commonwealth headquarters at Marlborough House underneath the frescoes of the Duke of Marlborough's eighteenth-century victories. It was attended by Commonwealth diplomats, businessmen and churchmen, including Bishop Trevor Huddleston who had been the mentor of both guests of honour; but it was boycotted by the British government. Tambo talked warmly about his meeting with businessmen in Lusaka, where they were all South Africans together: but he warned of much harsher confrontations with apartheid government ahead. And he told the British guests: 'When you say that you don't want sanctions because it would hurt us most, you're not honest. You don't want to hurt your trade – which you think depends on apartheid.'

Later in October, at a small private gathering, Tambo

met for the first time chairmen or directors of the biggest British companies investing in South Africa. Tambo began by saying that the meeting should have happened ten or twenty years earlier, since they both should have the same concern with a peaceful South Africa. He had welcomed the concern of American and South African businessmen; but the British were especially important with their huge investments, and he asked for their help in bringing pressure on Botha. They couldn't leave it to economic progress to break down apartheid. He was confident that the ANC were winning the fight for their rights – he would not be talking to them if he were not – but there would be much more violence, even a total catastrophe, unless international interests intervened. Every reform that Pretoria had made had been the result of international pressure. Already whites, including Afrikaners, were turning against apartheid as they began to feel the pinch: they would insist on a change of government as the pressure stepped up. Sanctions would never cause an 'economic wasteland' because the government would be changed long before that. A real wasteland would be produced if South Africa were left to itself.

The businessmen were reluctant to commit themselves, and they complained about the ANC's policy of nationalising the banks, mines and land in the Freedom Charter thirty-five years earlier. 'How can you expect us to help you, on behalf of our shareholders,' one chairman asked, 'if our only reward will be to be nationalised?' 'We do business in twenty African countries,' said another, 'often with the greatest difficulty. We have to be able to earn dividends. We're fed up with being told before independence "It'll be alright on the night." What guarantees can you give us?' 'But we are not committed to any dogma,' replied Tambo: 'we are committed to democracy, and we must wait for the people to decide what they want. Our chief concern is redistribution, in our country which has such great inequalities and concentrations of wealth.' Nationalisation had seemed the most obvious means; but there could be others, including perhaps a version of the American Sherman anti-trust act. He was impressed by the economic policies of Robert Mugabe in Zimbabwe (who though committed to extensive nationalisation had in fact stalled it and encouraged free enterprise).

Tambo asked them to make clear their total opposition to apartheid, and to press the British government to a much stronger stand. 'I'm talking to you not as businessmen but as human beings.' He was puzzled that a nation which had fought at such cost to defeat the Nazis should have such reservations in defeating apartheid. 'You British were determined to destroy Hitler – which meant that much of Europe became a wasteland – but you destroyed him. We see the Pretoria regime as like the Nazis.' The businessmen had varying views. 'Isn't there a constructive way,' one of them asked the others, 'of showing that business is on the side of the blacks?' But most were wary. 'It's much harder for foreign companies to criticise the government than for the South Africans,' one of them told Tambo. 'We exert a lot of pressure behind the scenes, but we can't press too hard or they'll chuck us out.' It was a worrying argument, that multinationals had to be more subservient to tyranny than local companies, and it contradicted the Americans' insistence that multinationals had a special political responsibility. But the British were under much less domestic pressure from shareholders and dared not risk offending Pretoria by appearing to consort with the enemy. They were beginning to hedge their bets, but not to change sides. Tambo was disappointed, he said later, that they had shown no 'change of heart'.

But in the following days Tambo, who had so often visited London, was for the first time received into the conservative areas of the city: he gave a speech at Chatham House, dined privately with bankers and entrepreneurs, and was welcomed by the two biggest banks, Barclays and Standard. He had tea with Tory MPs and gave evidence to the House of Commons' Foreign Affairs Committee – to

whom he explained once again the ANC's policy on violence
and reasserted that only sanctions could reduce the bloodshed and that condemnations and denunciations of apartheid meant nothing to Pretoria. 'However, they are very
very concerned now, since the position taken by the banks.
In fact the withdrawal of loans, the refusal to grant loans
or to roll them over, has demonstrated that sanctions can
be effective. One of the consequences of this has been that
the business community in South Africa has now been
moved not by appeals but by the reality of the threat of
sanctions, of disinvestment, to take very firm positions
against the Botha regime.'

The British government – even junior officials – still had
no contact with Tambo or the ANC; but a few dissident
Tory MPs, headed by Hugh Dykes and Tim Rathbone,
formed their own 'Talk to Tambo' group and later invited
a delegation from the ANC to a forthright lunch. 'Why do
you make it difficult for your friends by blowing up cars
with landmines?' asked the Tories. 'Why is this the first
time that Tories have talked to us in twenty years?' asked
the ANC.

In South Africa in the meantime the first euphoria after
the Lusaka meeting was soon evaporating, as President
Botha began to reassert his authority with a propaganda
campaign against the ANC, while bombings and explosions
shocked white opinion. In December a landmine exploded
near Messina, close to the Zimbabwe frontier, killing six
whites, followed by another near Stockport – the most
serious acts of terrorism for eighteen months. At Anglo-
American, Gavin Relly was facing recriminations. Harry
Oppenheimer, still outspoken in retirement, remained
twitchy about the meeting, puzzled that the atmosphere
was so friendly even though Tambo had conceded nothing,
particularly over nationalisation; and in November he had
told the American Chamber of Commerce that businessmen should offer 'neither moral support nor material support' for the ANC, since they want 'an economic system
that would destroy everything that we in this room stand

for'.* And Relly himself was beginning to backtrack. 'The Lusaka meeting was really much more of a watershed than any of the participants intended,' he said later. 'I've been blamed ever since for opening the floodgates of international business to deal with the ANC . . . It was important to establish a relationship between the wealth-producing sector and a new African economic policy. But I don't think that we have a role to get the government and the ANC together.'† When more bombs and land-mines were exploding, Relly explained that Tambo had misled him, and not warned him about future atrocities. Even Hugh Murray, the journalist who helped to organise the meeting, had second thoughts, worried about the communists in the ANC and the bloodthirsty broadcasts: he still favoured more talks, but he thought that Tambo would have no real success until he stopped selling violence-related policies. 'The ANC is *not* about to seize power, no matter how it is hyped up . . .'‡

By the end of the year the honeymoon was emphatically over, after a more gruesome act of terrorism which gave a warning of the black anger and chaos to come. Andrew Zondo was a schoolboy of fifteen when in 1983 (he later told the court) he was recruited into the ANC, and in exile at seventeen he joined the military wing Umkhonto. He had been appalled by the tear-gassing of black students by the police: 'From that day onwards whenever I look at a policeman I see him as an enemy.' Then in May 1983 he heard news of a South African air attack on Mozambique, which persuaded him that 'there was no chance to improve the life of blacks in South Africa except through violence'; and before Christmas 1985 he decided to take his own reprisals. With the help of an accomplice, Mr X, he planted a limpet-mine with a thirty-minute fuse in a refuse bin in the shopping centre of Amanzimtoti, the seaside town near

* *New York Times*, November 18, 1985
† Interview with author, May 1986
‡ *Leadership* magazine, 1985

Durban: intending (he explained) to give warning before it went off. But he could not find a free telephone, and the bomb went off, killing five Christmas shoppers. Zondo was caught and Mr X turned state witness at his trial, claiming that he and Zondo had been instructed by Umkhonto and the ANC; while Tambo later disclaimed knowledge, insisting that ANC strategy did not call for attacks in supermarkets, schools, or cinemas. But the Amanzimtoti deaths just before Christmas caused a wave of white indignation. The father of a child killed at Amanzimtoti, Kennie Smit, actually urged the government to begin talking to the ANC about peaceful co-existence; but the killings effectively sabotaged further businessmen's talks with the ANC over the following months. At a press conference in the New Year (which South Africans were given special permission to quote) Tambo warned that civilian casualties were unavoidable in escalating warfare and promised that the ANC would organise 'mass units' drawn from local populations; while he again asked business leaders to stop supporting the state arms corporation, Armscor. But most businessmen were now in no mood to listen. Ken Owen in *Business Day* in Johannesburg now said that 'the gap between the ANC and the SA government is simply too wide to be bridgeable', and the *Star* said that Tambo 'has done incalculable harm to the cause of real reform in South Africa'.*

It was back to the classic deadlock: Relly and most business colleagues insisted that the continuing violence prevented future talks; while the ANC insisted that without violence no one would talk. 'It was *because* of the violence,' Tambo said, 'that Relly came to Lusaka.' The political pressures were now pulling both sides further apart, as extremists thrived on the confrontation: the ANC dreaded the emergence of a military state, while the businessmen foresaw a black anarchy ruled by a Khmer Rouge of

* *Business Day*, January 10, 1986. *Johannesburg Star*, January 10, 1986. *Weekly Mail*, January 17, 1986, *Sechaba*, August 1986

ruthless schoolboys. But they both faced a common night-mare of a chaotic country in which no one could do business.

14

Multinational Twilight

A major challenge to business is quite simply to save the system of capitalism from being fatally undermined by cynicism among blacks that capitalism and white supremacy are in cahoots with one another.

Professor Hermann Giliomee, in a paper to
management seminar of Mobil Southern Africa,
Cape Town, 1982

The businessmen's paradise of the 'seventies was now looking far less alluring: the green bay tree was visibly wilting. Already in the early 'eighties South African manufacturers were worried by the declining competitiveness of their products and the poor economic growth. In the decade up to 1982 South Africa's performance had compared miserably with its major trading partners in the West: its productivity, in terms of output per hour, had actually decreased by 18 percent in the previous twelve years. Between 1980 and 1985 the gross domestic product had grown by an average of only 0.7 percent per year, compared to 3.6 percent in the 'seventies, 5.9 percent in the 'sixties and 4.4 percent in the 'fifties. South Africa had a lower GDP per head than any of its major trading partners in the West; and it had risen more slowly than any of them

except Switzerland.* It was becoming more like another
African country.

The political causes were clear. The School of Business
Leadership in Cape Town had set up a 'Project Free Enterprise' which produced two reports in 1984 and 1985: they
found that black workers had little confidence in their management, that some of them were even actively sabotaging
production, and that 'both quality and productivity are irrelevant to workers who feel that they do not participate in, or
benefit from, the business system'. While many more blacks
had come into industry, few companies had seriously attended to black advancement, which was seen 'as a move
of economic necessity rather than strategic vision'. Many
executives had continued to delay promoting blacks for fear
of a backlash among their white employees. Yet eventually,
when they had to promote blacks from economic necessity,
'in no instance was any major white backlash experienced'.
It was a devastating response to all those multinationals who
deferred to the 'man on the spot'. As the report said: 'the
business sector has made itself guilty of paying "lip service"
for too long.'†

By the end of 1985 the political recession and falling demand were compounding the problems for exporting
companies. The car industry, into which so much investment
was flowing in the 'sixties, was now far too big: 'There is
plant capacity in South Africa for about 600,000 cars,' said
Walter Hasselkus the local managing director of BMW, which
had so rashly chosen the Republic for its only plant outside
West Germany: 'The market this year is about 200,000.' By
December 1985 even BMW was pressing for political change:
'Multinational corporations know,' said Hasselkus, 'perhaps better than our friends in government do, how intense
the Western world's impatience with South Africa has become. Let us create a political environment that takes the

* Survey for SA Foundation by the Bureau for Market Research, *see
SA Foundation News*, July 1986

† School of Business Leadership: Project Free Enterprise Final
Report, Cape Town, 1986

heat off foreign companies.' Pretoria was now proposing to
subsidise exporting car companies and with this incentive
BMW were having talks with General Motors about rational-
ising their production: but subsidies would inevitably increase the government's influence.*

The 'bubbling entrepreneurs' whom *The Economist* had
admired in the 'sixties now looked less daring as more
companies began to be cartelised round the two giants of
government on one side and Anglo on the other. The
economic crisis, with or without deliberate disinvestment
or sanctions, was making the big South African groups
relatively stronger, the foreigners weaker. The flow from
local pension funds still provided money to invest in local
industry and property, in a circle of self-sufficiency; but
without foreign investment and lending, the prospects for
growth were severely limited.

The one still-booming industry was defence, which provided through Armscor lucrative contracts in high-
technology for many apparently peaceful industrial
companies, making them increasingly dependent on Pretoria's patronage. The engineering conglomerate Barlow
Rand (linked through share ownership with Anglo-
American) appeared as a benign and liberalising company,
under its civilised chairman Mike Rosholt; but through
its subsidiaries, including C J Fuchs, Reunert and its
half-share in British General Electric, Barlow's had
secretly become a major producer of defence electronics
and computers. Since 1980 Rosholt, together with two
other members of Barlow's board, Goss of SA Breweries
and Cronje of Nedbank, had become a member of President Botha's new Defence Advisory Board – which placed
him at the heart of the military-industrial complex, both
profiting from it, and indebted to it.† It was hardly surpris-

* South African Report, December 6, 1985
† Report on 'The Barlow Rand Connection' in the International
Seminar on the UN Arms Embargo against South Africa, London, May
28, 1986

ing if Rosholt had decided not, after all, to make contact with the banned ANC.

But no industrialist could now ignore the political hazards and the visible unworkability of apartheid. In January 1986, the Federated Chamber of Industries, the most far-sighted of the business lobbies, chaired by John Wilson of Shell, produced a Business Charter of Rights – after consultations with black groups including the ANC and the UDF – which came out with bold-sounding prescriptions including removing all discrimination, negotiating 'genuine political power-sharing by all South Africans up to the highest level' and 'full equal citizenship for all South Africans'. It was soon endorsed by the American Chamber of Commerce and later by Project Free Enterprise, which insisted that 'political and economic policy are totally interdependent'.* But the Charter was not specific about actual black votes, and there was some wry comedy behind the rush of condemnations of apartheid by business leaders who had so long lain low. As they commuted back to their all-white suburbs, voted for their all-white MPs and subsidised the white army and police, most businessmen were now revealing themselves as lifelong enemies of apartheid in their annual reports, advertisements or charters: it was not difficult when even the State President had declared apartheid outdated. The word that had been so enthusiastically coined could be equally keenly discarded, leaving most of the structure and damage intact. And the charters were prepared to consider every reform except the one that political blacks were demanding: one man, one vote.

All the businessmen's worries about the future were multiplied by the projections of black population. A report by the Department of Health in 1984 had shown that black women were producing an average of 5.2 children, while white women produced an average of 2.08; and that at the present population growth rate the total South African population would be 47 million by 2000 and 79 million by

* Project Free Enterprise, p. 109

2020 – of whom 66 million would be black. The report warned that at this rate the balance between population and resources would be disturbed, 'seriously jeopardising stability and progress'. It was a forecast which seriously disturbed President Botha; * but it worried investors and businessmen as much. For it implied that South Africa would belong still less to the first world, more to the third world – and especially to the rest of the continent, which now faced more serious population problems than Asia or Latin America. The nightmare of sinking into the 'African quagmire' was becoming real. The big banks, looking at the projections of social costs and revenues, were beginning to reckon that South Africa, even without apartheid, had a very uncertain economic future.

But now the mounting black anger, the costs of repression, bad economic management and the withdrawal of loans all made the future still less hopeful. It was hard to solve the population problem without major black participation and consent; some blacks in Soweto, kept at home during the emergency curfew, were talking about having more children to 'make soldiers'. By the year 2000, according to one survey, an extra 3.6 million jobs would be needed, merely to absorb new work-seekers; or 6.8 million if unemployment were to be eliminated.† No long-term investor could take a positive view of the country unless it made major political changes; yet changes would add still further to the economic burden. The economic problem was only partly of the government's making; but its politics prevented any solution.

The foreign multinationals found the prospect still less appetising; for it offered not only diminishing profits but increasing political protests at home. They could find themselves on a hiding to nothing; while the apartheid crisis, which caricatured so much of the West, could shine a harsh floodlight on their corporate characters.

* Leach, *op. cit.*, p. 241
† Survey commissioned by the SA Foundation. *See SA Foundation News*, July 1986

   The British companies still had far the biggest stake with
between 40 and 45 percent of all the foreign investment*
– though its value had halved in the two years of the falling
rand. Watching the worsening profits and politics, the
British chairmen were increasingly bewildered. Many of
them now regretted their companies past enthusiasm for
investing, and those with big interests in black Africa
worried that they might miss some kind of black boat. But
they seemed transfixed like rabbits in the headlights by the
sheer size of their investments. They could not, like the
American bankers, simply decide to withdraw: they had
fixed plants on or under the ground which gave them an
unavoidable stake in the country's future and pressed them
to some kind of choice. They were hedging their bets, but
they still dreaded having to antagonise the existing Pretoria
government: however awful it looked, the alternative
could look far worse.
   They all preferred not to choose, in their different ways.
Unilever, the Anglo-Dutch multinational which had been
worried about apartheid since the 'sixties (*see* page 117),
still had a whole range of plants and products based on
Durban; while together with its trading subsidiary the
United Africa Company it had still bigger interests in black
African states. Their chairman Sir Kenneth Durham not
surprisingly opted for a very low profile in South Africa,
and his successor in 1986 Michael Angus stayed still lower,
hoping that blacks and protesting shareholders would not
notice the extent of their involvement. Courtaulds had
proportionately one of the biggest South African investments of all, and the big joint-venture in wood-pulp which
they had begun with the government in the 'sixties was
part of their international network. Their accounts showed
16 percent of their profits in 1985 coming from Africa
(mostly South Africa), with a return on capital of 25
percent: they remained very wary of antagonising Pretoria
and inclined to support Buthelezi rather than Tambo,

* British Industry in South Africa: BICSA, London, July 1986

partly because most of their plants were in Zulu territory.

Sir Alistair Frame, the Scots chairman of Rio Tinto-Zinc with its big copper mine at Palabora, was much more conservative than his predecessor Sir Mark Turner, and as mine-owners RTZ were less vulnerable to black opinion than manufacturers or retailers; while their political adviser David Watt, the former director of Chatham House, eloquently opposed any sanctions, both privately and as a columnist in the London *Times*. Lord Weinstock of General Electric, the British engineering giant, was deeply involved with Pretoria through contracts to build power-stations, while the collaboration of its subsidiary Marconi with Barlow Rand (*see* page 267) involved it more deeply in the military-industrial complex. Weinstock's chairman, James Prior, who had been Minister for Northern Ireland, was worried about where to draw the line between terrorists and a legitimate opposition.

The two oil companies, Shell and BP, both felt especially exposed with their global visibility and their past record in the 'sixties as sanctions-breakers passing oil via South Africa to Rhodesia. BP's London director Patrick Gillam and its New Zealander chief executive Ian Sims in Cape Town had done something to improve black conditions, and had encouraged approaches to the ANC. But the company was inevitably compromised by its dealings with government; and its limitations were embarrassingly revealed when the paperback edition of the Commonwealth Report on South Africa (*see* next chapter) published a photograph showing a BP sign in a service station above a notice saying 'Whites'. BP had to explain that they had no control over the service station which used their name under a ten-year franchise. Shell had its own vulnerability after it was boycotted by anti-apartheid campaigners in America and Europe, calling for it to disinvest; but its London chairman Peter Holmes, who had previously run Shell in Nigeria, insisted that it was improving black conditions in South Africa, while the local chairman John Wilson became more publicly critical of President Botha (*see* page 318) and closed Shell's offices on June 16, 'Soweto day'. But Shell remained suspect among many blacks, and in September 1986 one of its personnel officers, Thomas Nkadimeng complained that he had been sacked for refusing to report to Shell on subversive political activities in Soweto.* Shell denied the charge, and insisted in an internal memo that personnel officers had merely been asked to complete questionnaires to help explain the stresses under which they lived.† But whatever the facts it was clear that both the British oil companies would find themselves inevitably more closely involved with security reports as the military build-up continued.

The British chairmen remained frequently inhibited by their tradition of leaving their subsidiaries to run themselves. While IBM or GM wanted all their companies to follow a centralised corporate policy, the British still liked to give maximum scope to their local chief executive – usually a white South African subject to his country's laws and customs, who could find himself in conflict with headquarters, and even keeping secrets from them. Local managers – as Project Free Enterprise had exposed – often exaggerated the white backlash that would follow from bold instructions to defy apartheid or promoting blacks; while high-minded statements about equal opportunities could have little connection with the hierarchies below. As one investigator into German companies in South Africa found, the foreign firms 'put the foreigners into the highest positions, and then put the white Afrikaners between them and the workers and use these Boers as their front. It will always be a Boer who sacks a black worker.'‡

The influential British trade association UKSATA, run by John McQuiggan, was still close to the South African Embassy, and enjoyed easy access to the Tory government. When in February 1986 Van Zyl Slabbert called on Lynda

* *New Nation*, Johannesburg, September 1986
† Shell management brief, September 19, 1986
‡ 'The Dilemma of Code Three', South African Council of Churches, 198, p. 10

Chalker, the new Tory Minister for Africa, he was surprised to find her accompanied by McQuiggan who sounded more conservative than the Pretoria government. But by January 1986 some of its members wanted to defend their investments more robustly. Sir James Cleminson, the hunting-and-shooting chairman of the Confederation of British Industry, had recently visited South Africa; and the chairman of UKSATA, Neil Forster, who ran the British and Commonwealth shipping line, had close friends there. They called a meeting of eighteen companies and decided to form a new lobby called the British Industry Committee on South Africa or BICSA; and as its chairman they chose Sir Leslie Smith, a combative war-horse who had just retired after fifteen years as chairman of British Oxygen – whose South African subsidiary, though reduced, was still important. Sir Leslie loved a political battle, and was soon thoroughly gung-ho; in March he wrote to all the main company chairmen asking them to support BICSA and suggesting that they should raise their profile and no longer keep their heads 'down below the parapet'. 'We must either believe our South African investments are worthwhile and constructive (for both sides) . . .' he said, 'or we should not be there': and he promised that BICSA would 'ensure that UK business interests remain paramount, and do not get confused with political issues'. Sir Leslie's letter worried some of the chairmen: were not 'detailed political issues' exactly what they *should* be getting involved with? And was it wise to commit themselves so totally against sanctions, when the blacks were clamouring for them? Eventually fifty companies including most of the biggest joined BICSA, contributing £2,500 each, while Sir Leslie appeared to pipe down about sanctions.

Sir Leslie and BICSA insisted that British companies were working vigorously against apartheid; but between the high-minded statements of directors in London and the practices on South African shop-floors there was often a wide gap – which emerged dramatically in the Rowntree Mackintosh chocolate company, whose Quaker roots were still evident in the two trusts which were its biggest share-holders, one of which, the Joseph Rowntree Charitable Trust, was specifically committed to 'promoting peaceful change and development' for blacks in Southern Africa. The company's South African subsidiary in East London, Wilson Rowntree, had a record of low wages and poor labour conditions in the early 'eighties, and left-wing groups in Britain began boycotting their bestselling chocolates, Kit-Kat. Then a security policeman gave evidence in a trial that Wilson Rowntree with other companies had arranged to call in the police if workers threatened to strike; and the Charitable Trust was still more concerned when the parent company, Rowntree Mackintosh, decided to join Sir Leslie Smith's BICSA and its anti-sanctions campaign. In July 1986 the trust's secretary, Steven Burkeman went out to South Africa, and on his return the trust publicly attacked the company's association with BICSA, warning that by apparently aligning itself with Pretoria it would 'make it very much more difficult to operate under majority rule'.

The American companies were beginning to see apartheid as a more fundamental challenge to their corporate reputations after the waves of shareholders' revolts and black protests: if they did not pull out, they felt obliged not just to oppose apartheid, but to be seen to do so. They were much more self-conscious than most Europeans about their corporate image and standing, and about the role of capitalism in the developing world. The South African crisis was now calling many bluffs, and it required them to show what they could really achieve behind the rhetoric of social responsibility.

Mobil still had a big stake in South Africa where it supplied 20 percent of the gasoline, and it was the most determined to present a high and noble profile, spurred on by its ebullient government relations officer Sal Marzullo. The profits from its oil refinery in Durban were falling with the recession and with competition from the state oil company SASOL, while its dependence on government was increasingly embarrassing, but it was committed to stay to the bitter end. 'If we left South Africa tomorrow,' said Allen Murray, its chairman in South Africa in February 1986, 'the South African government would take over our operation in fourteen seconds and then you know where our people would be.' He was pained that Mobil should be attacked by anti-apartheid activists: 'We don't disagree over what should happen in South Africa. We disagree over the methods; and suddenly we're the enemy.'

The chief executive of IBM in New York, John Akers, was also under heavy fire, with a highly visible business in South Africa including a brown skyscraper in the centre of Johannesburg and a large range of government computer contracts which were often suspected of helping the police state. Akers promised that IBM would stay as long as it had a chance to be profitable, but that looked less likely as Pretoria began to look to alternative computer systems and IBM laid off workers. And by May 1986 Akers was publicly more pessimistic about the slow pace of change.

The chairman of Citibank in New York, John Reed, was still more besieged, with demonstrators in Manhattan and sit-ins in Johannesburg. His local managing director David Hexter insisted that he was contributing to black advancement, and in May 1986 he announced a new programme to lend to black businesses. He claimed, to the annoyance of Barclays and Standard, that there was 'a sizeable market which is not being served'. But Citibank's headquarters in Park Avenue could not persuade their dissident depositors and shareholders that their presence was justified.

The biggest and most exposed American company was still General Motors – still more since Ford had merged with Anglo-American – and its chairman Roger Smith was continually vulnerable, all the more with a large black workforce in Michigan and the unavoidable presence of the Reverend Sullivan on his board. Smith was an unlikely political campaigner: within the corporation he was seen as a cold numbers man, preoccupied with increasing pro-

ductivity and computerisation and with few social concerns. He was uncommanding in style, with a high-pitched
voice: Ralph Nader, General Motor's arch-critic, called
him 'the squeak that roars'.* General Motors in South
Africa employed less than 1 percent of GM's global total of
750,000; and had made a loss for the last few years: it
seemed odd that Smith should devote so much time to
this awkward fraction. Like other chairmen he now felt
challenged by the disinvestment campaigners to show that
capitalism could work for blacks as well as whites, all the
more through his commitment to Sullivan; and he refused
to be pushed around by demonstrators. 'Remember that
General Motors, like Pretoria, regards itself as a sovereign
state,' as one Ford man explained. But Smith was already
considering a dignified retreat.

   Would the corporate protests move beyond public relations? The most showy way to oppose apartheid was the
old Mobil way: to advertise. In the wake of the emergency
and the visit to Lusaka, ninety-one business leaders inside
South Africa published advertisements in the local papers
on September 29, headed: 'THERE IS A BETTER WAY'. They
explained they were 'deeply concerned about the current
situation', and while rejecting violence they advocated
accelerating reform by abolishing statutory race discrimination wherever it exists; negotiating with acknowledged
black leaders about power sharing; granting full South
African citizenship to all peoples; and restoring and en-
trenching the rule of law.

   Behind the scenes Roger Smith was lobbying his colleagues, and three weeks later a clutch of chief executives
advertised in American papers, including the *Wall Street
Journal*, proclaiming a new business group, 'the US Corporate Council on South Africa': they reproduced part of the
South African advertisement, adding 'Today, we add our

---

   * For a recent study of Smith's influence on General Motors *see* Ralph
Nader & William Taylor, *The Big Boys*, New York, Pantheon Books,
1986, pp. 62–142

voice to theirs', and pledging 'to play an active role in peace-fully achieving their goals'. It was signed by two co-chairmen, Roger Smith of GM and Michael Blumenthal, the chairman of the Burroughs Corporation, also in Michigan; and they were supported by a steering committee of eight more chairmen and chief executives heavily involved in South Africa: John Akers of IBM, James Burke of Johnson & Johnson, Robert Hanson of Deere, Reuben Mark of Colgate-Palmolive, John Reed of Citibank, David Tappan of Fluor, Rawleigh Warner of Mobil and Howard Yergin of Caltex.

The Corporate Council began with a fanfare, promising to support South African businessmen against apartheid, and to protest directly to Pretoria. They supported the existing Sullivan group, and the Reverend welcomed them as 'the beginning of a very important initiative'; though some of the old Sullivan hands soon suspected that the chief executives, arriving in their private jets for high-level talks as if no one had thought about apartheid before, were on their own ego-trips, more concerned with shareholders

---

Ten biggest American employers in South Africa, 1985 (source: *New York Times*, December 2, 1985);

Ford Motor*	6,700
General Motors	4,900
Coca-Cola	4,800
Mobil	3,300
US Gypsum	2,600
Goodyear	2,500
Caltex	2,200
Allegheny	2,000
R J Reynolds	1,800
IBM	1,800

* Merged with Anglo-American's Amcar, of which it owns 42 per cent

than blacks: half the ten companies on the steering committee had been targeted as 'key investors in apartheid' by American church groups (*see* page 227).

After their first splash the tycoons became very secretive. On November 11 four of them – Smith, Blumenthal, Reed and Warner – flew to London to meet South African tycoons including Relly of Anglo and Rosholt of Barlow Rand; two weeks later five South Africans – Wim de Villiers from Gencor, Oppenheimer and Relly from Anglo-American, Fred du Plessis from Sanlam and Anton Rupert from Rembrandt – met President Botha in Pretoria to discuss reforms. They looked a formidable joint lobby of Afrikaners and English, but de Villiers insisted that there was no confrontation and soon afterwards the local chief executive of Burroughs, Mias van Vuuren, insisted that the Corporate Council was 'not seen by anyone as a pressure group on government'.* If not that, what was it?

The Council did have a secret strategy: to offer large sums in return for specific reforms. James Burke of Johnson & Johnson said that if there were the right reforms he was prepared to raise a hundred million dollars with other American businessmen for education 'on a dollar-to-dollar basis with the American government' which would then have to be matched by South Africans.† That offer was never tested; but several individual American corporations were soon offering their own funds for black education and welfare. Coca-Cola based in Atlanta, with Donald McHenry on its board, was especially anxious and set up its multi-million dollar fund. Mobil announced a $10 million foundation for black housing, small business and education: 'We believe there is only one way to answer the justifiable anger among blacks at the shortcomings in the

---

* South African Report, December 6, 1985

† *See* transcript of Slabbert's interview with Botha on November 25, 1985, published in February 1986

education of their children,' said Mobil's local chairman George Racine. 'That is to improve teaching and the quality of education in one system.' Black education soon became the favourite cause for companies opposing sanctions; but unless it was firmly connected to black political groups it could easily become drawn into the traditional South African patterns.

Both British and American companies, like the diplomats, still preferred secretive discussions and seminars about apartheid on their home ground to any open activity and intervention out in the field. Apartheid became the hot topic in the conference industry, but most meetings were entirely with whites – in the old South African style. The most criticised gathering was in November 1985, at the Oxfordshire country house Ditchley Park, funded by both British and American trusts. The director Sir Reginald Hibbert set up a meeting about apartheid, to be chaired by Sir John Killick, an ex-ambassador who had been head of Dunlop South Africa; they invited South Africans, British and Americans, but no blacks at all. After some American guests fiercely protested, Cyrus Vance, the chairman of the American Ditchley committee, provided extra funds for last-minute black guests; but it remained a predominantly white occasion, to which the South African ambassador turned up unannounced. The black Americans, who included Donald McHenry and Judge Higginbottom from Philadelphia, treated it as a fiasco; while the black South Africans (as Sir Reginald later described them) 'intervened like a sombre chorus reminding the conference in each session that, as far as they were concerned, there was as yet nothing about which to negotiate; the South African government's policies and actions at home and abroad were comprehensively repugnant to the black population of South Africa . . . There could be no doubt about the authenticity of their moving words.'*

The Corporate Council held more secret meetings, and

* The *Ditchley Newsletter*, No. 15, January 1986

in March 1986 chief executives met discreetly again at Leeds Castle, chaired by Edward Heath and convened by Leon Sullivan and Roger Smith. The South African tycoons were now much more cut off from the others. 'They had begun to see Sullivan as a kind of shield against Western criticism,' said one informant, 'but now for the first time they found themselves as adversaries, while the West were clearly distancing themselves. They became defensive.' There were now some South African blacks including the businessman Sam Motsuenyane (*see* page 305); but the whites fought shy of black politicians, let alone the ANC. 'But we don't even know,' complained Roger Smith, 'whether they're the goodies or the baddies.' They made no public statement afterwards, and when I met Sullivan on the plane back to Philadelphia he would only reveal: 'It was very penetrating. Very penetrating. That's all I can say. But remember the bottom line: *end apartheid*.' The Anti-Apartheid Movement in London called it 'an attempt by foreign business to determine the future of South Africa without reference to those who will be most affected'. Certainly the conferences in castles and country houses seemed very aloof from the critical question: how does it play in Soweto? They seemed much more preoccupied with their corporate images than with the real problem of political realignment.

There was one bold public showdown. The outspoken chief executive of General Motors in South Africa, Bob White, insisted that 'our involvement in politics has to move to another level' and announced that his company would pay the legal fees of any black employee who chose to use the 'whites only' bathing beaches outside Port Elizabeth. There was a brief tension: soldiers patrolled the beaches and the government told GM to 'keep its nose out of South Africa's business'. But when White publicly attacked the beach segregation as 'abhorrent' he was supported by local businesses; and by April 1986 the Port Elizabeth council had voted to desegregate its beaches. As so often, the white backlash proved only a flick.

Sullivan himself was pressed to more open confrontation. In May 1986 he issued a sensational edict: he told the 192 American companies that had signed the Sullivan code that they must now adopt a 'stringent course of corporate civil disobedience to challenge actively all apartheid laws'. He asked them to 'assist blacks in the equal use of all private and public amenities, such as parks, beaches, hospitals, theatres, public transport, schools and housing'; and he warned them again that unless apartheid was completely dismantled by June 1987 he would endorse total economic sanctions. It was far more drastic than the 'Code of Conduct' which the European Community had revised in November 1985, which had been widely disregarded and inadequately monitored: and which the British government emphasised was 'not asking companies to act contrary to South African law'.*

Corporate disobedience! It was a unique instruction to multinationals who had always insisted that they must obey the laws of each country; still more in South Africa where they had so often used the local law and customs as an excuse for their own segregation. Many of the Sullivan companies were appalled; yet a few local companies were already becoming more openly disobedient, not just with mixed lavatories and cafeterias, but by defying more basic segregation including the Group Areas Act. At Barclays Bank Chris Ball in Johannesburg had publicly boasted on a video how his bank had frequently broken apartheid laws; and by June 1986 the bank was breaking new ground by installing a black executive in the midst of the white suburb of Wendywood, and even throwing a barbecue for his neighbours. Social reforms which managers had always said were impossible were now seen as essential, as business became more desperate to divorce itself from apartheid. But time was rapidly running out; and while the

* Code of Conduct for Companies with interests in South Africa. Command 9860, p. 3, HMSO, July 1986. *See also Weekly Mail*, September 12, 1986 for inadequate European definitions

white executives were contemplating more defiant acts against apartheid they were to be plunged into a new state of emergency which produced a still harsher confrontation, and made all those promises of discreet pressure and gradual improvements ring hollow.

15

The Road to Sanctions

*It is time we in the West realize that we are contributing
by default to an inexorable movement toward genocide.*

Robert McFarlane, *International Herald Tribune,*
August 5, 1986

The Western governments in the meantime had taken up
their positions towards South Africa with a remarkable
lack of concern for their own companies' long-term
interests. The British Foreign Office officially explained in
January 1986 that 'in essence the government's policy
towards South Africa is to further the considerable British
interests in that country, and as part of this effort to
promote early and peaceful transition to a genuinely non-
racial democracy'.* But many of those considerable
interests were becoming less sure that their government
was really furthering them. While American and British
industrialists and bankers were beginning to have talks
with the ANC as well as with Buthelezi, both Reagan and
Thatcher refused to have any relations with Congress, and
their diplomats' contacts with other black political groups
were fitful. Yet the Western capitals were already being

* For a discussion of British policy and its impact *see* Shaun Johnson,
British Policy Towards South Africa. David Davies Memorial Foundation. International Relations, May 1986, p. 445

pressed towards sanctions which would put an end to all hopes for expanding Western investment and 'constructive engagement'.

Both the American and British embassies in Pretoria remained constantly anxious not to offend Afrikaners. The American ambassador Herman Nickel, who continued vocally to oppose sanctions and disinvestment, was aloof from the black world, although the embassy had established an effective informal black network. The British Embassy in Pretoria, under a conventional new ambassador, Sir Patrick Moberly, was more preoccupied than ever with avoiding rows with the government – it had not even invited Bishop Tutu to the residence. It kept contact with black leaders only at one remove through the consulate in Johannesburg and its advice had played down the growing unrest as part of a cyclical trend. It was a worrying failure of information. After the Iranian revolution of 1979, which British diplomats and intelligence had so notably failed to predict, the Foreign Office had tried to ensure that it had better information about underground oppositions and revolutionary movements and had asked embassies in the Middle East to provide special reports in the light of Iran. But in South Africa the British still had very inadequate information about the black opposition – much less than the American Embassy whose financial interests were much smaller – while diplomats gave the same explanation as in Iran: they could not offend the existing regime.

But it was the perceptions at the top which influenced and limited the perceptions of diplomats and officials below, and which made governments often less informed even than businessmen. In Washington President Reagan still showed a startling lack of knowledge or interest and the White House often ignored the information and analysis of the State Department, while George Shultz suffered from the prevailing policy paralysis: appalled by the Afrikaner regime, but more appalled by the thought of any likely black alternative. Reagan was inclined to see white South Africans as embattled allies threatened by guerrillas and terrorists, comparing them either with Israelis, with the Shah of Iran or with conservative regimes in Central America. He always saw them in the East–West context, as anti-communists against communists. 'Too often in the past we Americans, acting out of anger and frustration and impatience, have turned our backs on flawed regimes, only to see disaster follow . . .', he said in a major speech on July 22. 'What foreign power would fill the vacuum if the ties with the West are broken?'

Reagan was happy to let Mrs Thatcher make much of the running, and she too was concerned with the Soviet menace: 'To me it is absolutely absurd,' she said in July 1986, 'that people should be prepared to put increasing power into the hands of the Soviet Union on the grounds that they disapprove of apartheid in South Africa.' But she was also much more personally fired by the issue. She had been to South Africa only once when she went out as Minister of Education in 1972 to open an observatory and was struck by the lack of apartheid in some areas: 'The first thing you see when you get off at Johannesburg airport,' she told Hugo Young, 'is that you go into a hotel which is totally non-colour conscious. You go into a dining room and there's all colours and backgrounds.' She thought that Britain should have had more contact with South Africa, not less: 'We would have influenced her more: she would have been able to see that multiracial societies do work in other countries.'* And her husband Denis had many South African business friends: in February 1986 at the height of the emergency he paid a visit to South Africa where he attended among other social events a dinner given for him by Mr Prime, the chief executive of a Durban car parts company with his colleagues.

She was totally sceptical about sanctions after the fiascos and hypocrisies over Rhodesia; and her scepticism was reinforced by successive South African visitors to Number 10 during 1985, including Chief Buthelezi, Helen Suzman

* Interview with Hugo Young, the *Guardian*, July 1986

and Harry Oppenheimer (who assured her that the blacks'
support for the ANC was much exaggerated). Some diplomats expected that she might suddenly switch as she had
switched over Rhodesia in 1979, accepting the need to
negotiate with armed rebels. But her personal detestation
of terrorism had, not surprisingly, increased since the IRA
had tried to murder her and her cabinet in October 1984.
She was determined that nobody in government, including
the Foreign Office, should talk to the African National
Congress. The resourceful South African ambassador in
London, Denis Worrall, was determined to paint the ANC
as a pariah like the PLO (though privately he thought it was
important to be in touch with them); and his embassy was
glad to disseminate the more bloodthirsty ANC propaganda
and Marxist rhetoric from Radio Freedom in Ethiopia.

Mrs Thatcher was convinced that she had a special
influence on President Botha, based on forthright exchanges without humbug. She believed that she could
influence the Afrikaner government towards peaceful and
necessary reforms more effectively if she did not threaten
or confront them; and she avoided any of the kind of moral
rhetoric that she directed against the Soviet Union. But
she was much less sensitive about her image with the
blacks; and both sides in South Africa saw her as a fundamental ally of the government who would stand by them
when the chips were down. The belief was already deep
in the Afrikaner's thinking: in the words of Mrs Thatcher's
predecessor as prime minister, Edward Heath – who had
been through his own ordeals with Botha's predecessor,
John Vorster:

> The South African government believe, that when it
> comes to the crunch, whatever and whenever it is, they
> will always have the support of the American adminis-
> tration and the British government . . . because they
> believe that they can always use the Communist threat
> as the argument with which to handle Washington and
> Whitehall . . . The irony of the situation is that the

longer South Africa continues its present policy, the more it drives its black population into Communist hands and the more it is encouraging the other black states in Africa to move towards a Communist outlook.*

Both Western leaders shared a loyalty to white South Africa and a dread of a black revolt; but they were up against very different political pressures. In Washington Capitol Hill, now effectively mobilised by the black caucus and liberal members of Congress, was pressing for bolder condemnation and intervention, particularly for sanctions; while members of parliament in London were much more muted, whether because of the effects of sanctions on unemployment, the gloomy record of black Africa, the fiascos of sanctions against Rhodesia, or the associations with black immigrants in Britain. After the declaration of the emergency, the Reagan administration had felt impelled to show its public disapproval; and Ambassador Nickel was recalled for several weeks. In September the European Community nations voted to withdraw their military attachés in protest; but the British government first refused to join in, until Mrs Thatcher climbed down reluctantly two weeks later complaining: 'It means we don't get as much information as we should otherwise.'†

Thatcher was now coming under heavy pressure for sanctions, not from parliament, but from the Commonwealth countries, particularly the black African states who felt impelled to show support for their black brothers who were now calling more vociferously for action. And the issue of sanctions came to a head at the two-yearly Commonwealth conference at Nassau in the Bahamas in October 1985. All the members except Britain were now pressing publicly for sanctions, led by Australia, Canada and India. It was true that the countries who were most ardent were often those which had least trade and invest-

---

* House of Commons, July 16, 1986
† Interview with Hugo Young, the *Guardian*, July 1986

ment, as Mrs Thatcher liked to remind them. And many
of the black states close to South Africa which publicly
clamoured for sanctions were privately fearful about the
effects on their own economies. But this problem of dependence already existed: South Africa had already been
exercising her own economic sanctions against any neighbours which caused trouble and harboured ANC refugees;
and in January 1986 she tightened her stranglehold on
Lesotho – the mountain kingdom surrounded by South
Africa – and toppled Chief Jonathan's government after
only two weeks' sanctions. As the Commonwealth stepped
up its demands for sanctions, so Pretoria increased its
threats to apply counter-sanctions against its neighbours –
whether by cutting rail and road links, by returning foreign
workers or by military raids and general destabilisation.
But the threats were a tricky weapon; for South Africa
earned a large surplus from her trade with her neighbours,
and her own sanctions spotlighted her own political domination through economic weaponry – which could
strengthen the argument for sanctions against herself.

The Western tycoons now watched apprehensively as the
pressures mounted towards sanctions and disinvestment
which would negate all their arguments that greater investment would bring greater freedom to blacks. While the
Corporate Council and the Sullivan Group in America
were promising to improve black conditions and to push
Pretoria towards dismantling apartheid, the clamour for
sanctions was undermining their claims.

At the Nassau conference the Commonwealth
secretary-general Sonny Ramphal tried to mobilise agreement and to bring pressure on Britain, as he had successfully done in Lusaka six years earlier, preparing the way
for the Zimbabwe negotiations. But Mrs Thatcher reacted
to the traditional emotional rhetoric of the Commonwealth with rising contempt. The other prime ministers
chose Rajiv Gandhi and Brian Mulroney from India and
Canada to lobby her personally, as two good-looking men
representing important countries; but with no success.

Eventually the prime ministers agreed on a 'Common-wealth Accord' which called on Pretoria to dismantle apartheid, end the emergency, release Nelson Mandela and unban the ANC. They settled only for minimal sanctions including a ban on Krugerrands, new government loans and funding of trade missions, which Mrs Thatcher could rightly claim were only 'a tiny little bit'. They agreed to appoint a Commonwealth group of seven 'eminent persons' to 'encourage political dialogue in South Africa with a view to establishing a non-racial and representative government'. If Pretoria had not made enough progress within six months the Commonwealth would 'agree to the adoption of further measures'.

The seven members included Dame Nita Barrow, a president of the World Council of Churches; John Malecela, a former Tanzanian minister; Sardar Swaran Singh, a former Indian minister; and Archbishop Edward Scott, the Anglican primate from Canada. But the most active were the two joint chairmen: Malcolm Fraser, the former Australian prime minister who had taken up a noisy stand against apartheid; and General Olusegun Obasanjo, the former Nigerian head of state who enjoyed unusual respect in Europe and America. For the British, the most important member was Mrs Thatcher's own nominee Lord Barber, who was chairman of the Standard Bank, one of South Africa's biggest creditors. He was expected to be cautious; in the Conservative government in the early seventies he had shown little interest in black Africa, and over the last ten years he had regularly visited white South Africa, where he had business and other friends, without showing much concern with apartheid.

The eminent persons, or 'The Commonwealth Group' as they preferred to call themselves, were at first received with scepticism by almost everyone. Botha thought they were interfering, while Tambo feared they would indefinitely be played along by Pretoria, like the Western 'contact group' over Namibia, with too high a profile for any useful negotiation. But Mrs Thatcher persuaded President Botha to allow the group to travel freely in South Africa; Fraser and Obasanjo insisted that they must see Mandela in prison, to which Botha agreed; and Tambo decided to co-operate fully. For the next six months the eminent persons were to be seen as the chief hope of achieving a peaceful settlement in South Africa, not just by the Commonwealth but by the Americans, who saw Obasanjo as their special link.

On their first visit to South Africa in February and March none of the eminent persons, as they later said publicly, 'were prepared for the full reality of apartheid'; while they were surprised how deeply the black resistance had penetrated, even into remote country areas. Lord Barber, as he told ANC officials, changed his whole view of South Africa after seeing the other side. But the group also found, to their surprise, that there might be a genuine prospect of agreement between the government and the ANC; and that a peaceful settlement could conceivably be achieved after releasing Mandela. The group prepared a 'possible negotiating concept': Pretoria on one side would release Mandela, unban the ANC, allow them normal political activity, and pull out troops (though not police) from the townships; while the ANC would agree to suspend violence and begin negotiations.

They saw the personality of Mandela as the key to any settlement; and Botha on his side was well aware of the exasperating paradox that after twenty-four years in jail – far longer than Gandhi or Kenyatta – Mandela was more influential than ever, and could be more dangerous inside prison than outside. Pretoria was looking for a way to release him in the most casual way: after he had a prostate operation in December 1985 he had been kept in a separate hospital wing and allowed special privileges even though he was in good health, while the government encouraged speculation about his future. 'It was quite obvious that they must have planned to release him after the operation,' his wife Winnie said later. 'They wanted to destroy the myth surrounding this man, to let him out in a position where he could not produce miracles . . . They were testing people's reaction, preparing for his release. Now they've overdone it. They're scared. They scare easy . . . The government are now the prisoners, and the prisoners are now the jailors.' By late February Botha had once again imposed conditions on Mandela's release – that he would renounce violence. Mandela could not agree to give up the only pressure which had had any effect; nor could he agree to being released while the ANC was banned. 'How could they have the *audacity* to impose conditions on Mandela's release after he's spent a lifetime in jail?' his wife said. 'They're not ready for it. I can't imagine them doing it in the present political climate, without moving an inch from twenty-four years ago.'*

Mandela in jail personified the South African deadlock between two forces which never met: against the military power of the state, he held the power of an idea: liberation. Botha knew that if he died in jail the fury in the townships could be unstoppable, and he recognised that if Mandela were released he could restrain the violence; but he dared not take the political risk, and continued to build up his own myth of Mandela the arch-communist. On his side Mandela still saw himself as a man of destiny: he was reading new Afrikaans literature, to prepare himself to be the leader of all South Africans, and he made clear to the Commonwealth group that he would seek to reassure the white minority, and to restrain black expectations. All the eminent persons were surprised by Mandela's mellowness, good judgment and humour; perhaps most of all Lord Barber, who exchanged jokes about his own escape from a Russian prisoner-of-war camp about which he had written. 'Lord Barber, send me a copy,' said Mandela. 'That could be very useful. And to make sure that I get it, send it through the British ambassador.'†

The Commonwealth Group were finding themselves

---

* Telephone interview with author, March 1986
† House of Lords, July 4, 1986

ineluctably pressed towards some form of sanctions. For Barber particularly it was a depressing and difficult conclusion, denying all those hopes that Western investment and business expansion would in themselves undermine apartheid. For the black states on the borders, too, it was desperate recourse, for only massive aid could compensate for the loss of trade and jobs with the South. But as South Africa appeared to be heading for civil war there was little alternative, short of military intervention, as a way to dissociate the West from Pretoria; while black South Africans saw sanctions as a key signal of support. By April Bishop Tutu had decided that he could no longer hold off, and made a long emotional speech concluding: 'Our children are dying. Our land is burning and bleeding. And so I call on the international community to apply punitive sanctions against this government to help us establish a new South Africa, non-racial, democratic and just.' Tutu did not explain what kind of sanctions but he hoped for 'something as painless as the run on the rand which suddenly inspired the private sector to discover that they did have tongues . . .' The State Department quickly replied that 'the United States does not believe that punitive sanctions will help promote change'; the Foreign Office said that 'Bishop Tutu has advanced no evidence to show that international financial and trade boycotts would help promote peaceful change'; the South African businessmen explained once again that sanctions would damage the blacks. But most black leaders now supported Tutu's call.

The eminent persons had left their 'negotiating concept' with the South African government, who neither accepted nor rejected it for two months. They thought that Pretoria was taking their ideas seriously, after seeing them on twenty separate ocasions. Obasanjo appeared to be specially trusted by the Botha government – including the defence minister Magnus Malan and the minister for the constitution Chris Heunis – as a general who understood the problems of a divided country. President Botha had made clear that he dreaded both sanctions and the escalating violence – which was approaching a new danger on the tenth anniversary of Soweto on June 16; while Pik Botha, who was in charge of the talks with the group, sounded sympathetic. On their next visit in May the group showed their negotiating concept to Mandela, who agreed that he could accept it as a starting point, though he could not speak for the ANC; they then showed it to the ANC and the UDF who asked for ten days to consider it. They then flew to Cape Town for a key meeting with the President's constitutional committee under Chris Heunis. An hour beforehand they heard reports that South Africa had raided three neighbouring countries, Zimbabwe, Zambia and Botswana: it seemed a deliberate insult, particularly to Obasanjo who had been nominated by Zambia and Zimbabwe. But they went into the meeting, where the government told them that they must insist on the ANC not just suspending violence but renouncing it for all time, regardless of negotiations. The group all thought this was 'unrealistic and wholly unreasonable'; and South African business leaders agreed with them. Obasanjo then urged that in the light of the raids they should abandon their mission; and they flew back to London hastily to compile their report. They had some disagreements: Barber at first wanted to produce his own minority report; but after consulting with the Foreign Office and modifying some of the 'nasty words' he agreed to sign a unanimous report.

The report, when it was published in June, caused a new furore; for the eminent persons were much more critical and forthright than most politicians including Mrs Thatcher had expected. They concluded that the Pretoria government was 'not yet prepared to negotiate fundamental change, nor to countenance the creation of genuine democratic structures, nor to face the prospect of the end of white domination and white power in the foreseeable future'. They put some hope in financial pressures (though Gavin Relly and others had told them that their views had little impact on Pretoria). They insisted that local businessmen had 'potential for exerting pressures upon the

Government to the benefit of the country as a whole'; they thought that businessmen were out of touch with black opinion, and could and should exert greater pressure on the Government. They were convinced that 'there can be no negotiated settlement in South Africa without the ANC; the breadth of its support is incontestable; and this support is growing'. In their final recommendations they carefully advocated 'measures' rather than sanctions; and the choice of measures was not for them, but for individual governments to recommend. But they left no doubt that some strong measures were essential: 'We are convinced that the South African government is concerned about the adoption of effective economic measures against it. If it comes to the conclusion that it would always remain protected from such measures, the process of change in South Africa is unlikely to increase in momentum and the descent into violence would be accelerated. In these circumstances, the cost in lives may have to be counted in millions.'*

Why had Pretoria decided so abruptly to reject the group's negotiating concept? There were varied explanations. Lord Barber said 'they simply could not bring themselves to take what seemed to them a leap into the unknown'.† Malcolm Fraser believed (as he told Mrs Thatcher) it was because the Commonwealth group had found important common ground between Mandela, Tambo and Buthelezi which therefore threatened Pretoria's policies of tribal separation and 'group rights':‡ and Obasanjo had the same impression. Sonny Ramphal thought that 'the Commonwealth group were doing too well for Pretoria's liking'. But the eminent persons were also conscious that: 'In recent weeks, the Government would appear to have moved consciously away from any realistic negotiating process'; and also that 'after more than

---

* *Mission to South Africa* (Eminent Persons Group), Penguin Books, 1986, p. 140
  † House of Lords, *ibid.*
  ‡ *See* Speech to Royal Commonwealth Society, July 31, 1986

eighteen months of persistent unrest, upheaval and killings unprecedented in the country's history, the government believes that it can contain the situation indefinitely by use of force'.* Behind the scenes the military in Pretoria were insisting that the government must show its true strength, both to the black rebels and to the right-wing Afrikaners. And the full extent of Pretoria's shift of policy was soon to become ominously clear as the government moved towards a showdown which faced business leaders with a more painful choice.

* *Mission to South Africa*, pp. 135, 138

16

The Boer Backlash

I wonder what it will be like
When we sit with Tambo
and tell him about the fall of the Boers

Song at youth rallies in the townships, 1986 (quoted
by Shaun Johnson, *The Youth in South Africa*)

How far could businessmen and bankers really influence
President Botha's policies in this crisis atmosphere? How
far was he really in control of the country? There were no
simple answers, for his behaviour was looking less and less
consistent.

Certainly the emergency had revealed him with a visible
loss of authority: the businessmen's visit to Lusaka in
September was due as much to disillusion with Botha's
policies as to any new-found confidence in a black alternative. Only a year before he had been acclaimed as the
masterly architect of the new constitution and the Nkomati
Accord, the friend of European prime ministers. But since
the emergency he appeared to have been brought low by
black schoolboys; while South Africa, in the words of two
Afrikaner political scientists in January 1986, appeared to
be 'stumbling from one political upheaval to the next,
inexorably sliding toward a civil war'.*

Botha still saw himself as a courageous reformer who had

* Deon Geldenhuys and Koos Van Wyk, 'South Africa in Crisis: A
Comparison of the Vorster and Botha Eras', *South Africa International*,
January 1986

shrewdly kept his following through difficult manoeuvres; like a de Gaulle or a Macmillan maintaining right-wing support while moving stealthily to the left. 'Under my leadership the whites have accepted much in South Africa . . .' he told the opposition leader Van Zyl Slabbert in November 1985. 'But I say that I represent more than the whites. I am now conceited enough to say that I represent the voice of more than 50 percent of the black people of South Africa who do not want to throw the rights they have attained into a pot and leave them there.'* He was determined to reassert his authority after it had been by-passed by the meetings with the ANC. He soon became much firmer in preventing liberal groups – including Afrikaner students and churchmen – from making the same journey to Lusaka, while his arguments were strengthened by the new outbreaks of sabotage.

But in the meantime the flight of capital and the collapse of the currency had been carrying their own message. Botha was being blamed from the right as well as the left for having undermined confidence, not just in the political system, but in the economy. After the emergency Jaap Marais, the leader of the right-wing Herstigte Nasionale Party, insisted that the economy had been weakened by his dangerous concessions. Under Dr Verwoerd, he argued:

We had a very strong economy, we had a strong international position and had internal order. What more do you want in a country? Look at the chaotic situation the country is now in. We can't pay our debts, we are sitting with an inflation rate of 16%, people are going bankrupt at an unheard-of rate, unemployment is increasing. The basic cause of all this is that government started with equality. If equality succeeds, it must succeed at the level of the economy and if it fails there it will succeed nowhere.†

* *See* transcript, published February 1986
† Interview with Willem de Klerk of Rapport, on SATV. *See South Africa International*, ibid.

Botha was fully aware that South Africa desperately needed external finance, and that only rapid concessions would appease the international financial community: and he went to great lengths to reassure bankers – particularly Fritz Leutwiler – that bolder reforms were on the way. By the end of 1985 he had been promising businessmen that he would unveil new reforms at his opening of parliament at the end of January; and with this expectation most of them, including Anglo-American, had decided to avoid any contacts with the ANC revolutionaries.

Botha's speech on January 31 – later known as 'Rubicon 2' – was certainly far more conciliatory in tone than the first Rubicon speech five months before: part of it might have been written specially for the world's bankers. 'We accept unequivocally that the Republic of South Africa is part of the international community. We have no wish to isolate ourselves from the world, particularly not from Africa of which we form an integral part. We accept that not all the pressure is necessarily malicious . . . But I wish to make clear that we do not need pressure to walk the road of reform and justice. We do it out of conviction.'

Botha spelt out reforms more specifically than before, outlining a 'programme of action' which included restoring South African citizenship to all black South Africans including those in the homelands; allowing freehold property rights to blacks; preparing to abolish influx control, to be replaced by a strategy of 'orderly urbanisation'; and replacing the hated pass-books with identity documents to be carried by all South Africans. He committed himself, however vaguely, to 'equal opportunity' and even 'equal education'; and 'all South Africans must be placed in a position where they can participate in government through their elected representatives . . .' He explained that: 'We have outgrown the outdated colonial system of paternalism as well as the outdated concept of apartheid.' And he proposed to establish a national statutory council, with himself as chairman, including leaders of black communities, to advise on constitutional structures for 'our multi-cultured society'.

The speech gave some immediate encouragement to the business community. Gavin Relly said it had 'brought South Africa back into the mainstream of western thinking'; and the rand soon climbed back to $0.45. But it represented a modernisation of apartheid, as the London *Financial Times* complained, not a dismantling of it; and it gave no indication of opening up to serious negotiations with blacks: even Buthelezi withdrew his support for a statutory council. Most blacks saw it as promising too little, too late. 'He has made promises that would have been considered treacherous if made by any of his predecessors,' said the black newspaper *The Sowetan*: 'If things were normal in South Africa he would have perhaps steered this country into better days. Things are far from normal. In fact we are poised on the type of precipice that only needs a push to land us in disaster. Taking a look at most of the prospective leaders who might succeed Botha, there is no hope for decisive change. This means South Africa needs a totally new government.' And Botha's liberal noises were soon drowned by contradictions. The minister of education, F W de Klerk, reasserted that education would remain segregated, which contradicted any claim that apartheid was outdated; and when the foreign minister Pik Botha referred to the possibility of a future black president he was humiliated by his boss. President Botha, said Hennie Kotze, professor of political science at Stellenbosch, 'took the political initiative but lost it in the space of one week'.*

The businessmen were more than ever confused. Botha had let them down again; but they could not come to terms with the ANC, while the middle road appeared suddenly to be reaching a new dead end. On February 7, Frederik Van Zyl Slabbert, the leader of the white opposition party the PFP, abruptly resigned both his leadership and his seat in

* *The South Africa Foundation News*, March 1986

parliament. It was a devastating blow, for Slabbert appeared as a special kind of bridge. He was an intellectual
Afrikaner who had rebelled against the National Party,
yet still commanded some respect among his own people.
He had been a rugby hero; he was warm and open, with
a boyish style and a turned-up nose, and he seemed to
personify the Afrikaner virtues without the isolation or
bitterness; even President Botha seemed to see him as a
kind of wayward son. Many saw him as the key to a liberal
future; while Slabbert on his side asked businessmen to
concern themselves more closely with politics:

> After all, businessmen have been politically involved or
> are politically involved in any other society. American
> politics couldn't survive if you didn't have your Demo-
> cratic and Republican businessmen. In South Africa you
> have this pretence that businessmen are not involved in
> politics, but then secretly they funnel a lot of funds into
> the dominant party because the dominant party has the
> patronage and determines contracts and so on.*

Slabbert did not ask businessmen to take a very radical
role. After he had toured Europe and America in
November 1985 President Botha invited him for a long
private talk (which Botha secretly tape-recorded and later
published); and Slabbert explained to him that business
people in the United States and Britain were not really
concerned about sanctions: 'They were concerned about
stability. What concerns them is the restoration of confidence
and especially how they saw their assets in this respect.'
Botha on his side complained about the contradictions of
overseas businessmen: 'On the one hand they want stability
and on the other they want concessions. But they don't
want an Africa situation, because if they wanted that, why
don't they invest in Zambia? Why don't they invest in

* Interview with Professor David Welsh of Cape Town University,
Leadership, 1985

Mozambique, which we plead with them to do?' Slabbert agreed about the hypocrisy of the critics ('If the average Australian had to come here he would vote slightly to the right of the National Party') and told Botha how people overseas 'have suddenly become aware of the dilemma of finding an alternative. It is something which had not been there before and which I think one can exploit.' The dialogue often sounded like two Afrikaners who were confident that they could get world business back on their side.

But Slabbert was becoming desperately disillusioned with his role as parliamentary leader of the opposition, and in his book *The Last White Parliament* he convincingly argued that it was becoming impossible to oppose a white system of government within the confines of an all-white assembly. He tried in February 1986 to persuade his white liberal colleagues to resign with him. But only one of them, Alex Boraine, agreed, and they left the other progressive MPs and their supporters in some acrimony. 'There is surely no precedent for the sudden resignation of an admired and trusted political leader,' said Harry Oppenheimer, his chief backer. He had 'gravely, and perhaps irreparably, damaged his own credibility in public life'. The Johannesburg *Business Day* angrily rebutted Slabbert's claim that the business community had let him down. 'He was above all the political creature of Big Business,' said the influential columnist Ken Owen. 'He was helped into politics by Big Business, sustained in it, supported and sponsored by Big Business.'

The Progressive MPs quickly elected a new leader, Colin Eglin, a more professional politician who lacked Slabbert's charisma but held his colleagues together, while Slabbert himself looked to a more radical role. When he was leader he had not shown much interest in the black opposition. He had visited Lusaka to talk to the ANC after the businessmen's visit, but did not seem very impressed. As he told Botha: 'The trouble with the ANC is that it is a myth – no, not a myth – it is a romantic image to those abroad . . . I told them in Lusaka that if they were really in control of the situation, why didn't they call a moratorium on violence for six weeks and say "We will show you?" . . . the ANC should not be held up as an organisation which is so powerful that they can handle the unrest.' He sounded equally unimpressed by Buthelezi: 'His big problem is that should Mandela die in jail he will become the Muzorewa of South Africa and he is well aware of it . . . He must be locked into an initiative.' (When Botha later released the transcript, Buthelezi was furious at being described like 'an uppity Kaffir' and Slabbert apologised; but Tambo was less touchy and explained that he understood that Slabbert needed to pacify Botha.)

Immediately Slabbert had resigned, the ANC in Lusaka welcomed the news fulsomely: 'An act of vision has made this February day a moment of pride for all the people in South Africa,' said the secretary-general Alfred Nzo. And other black leaders including the black consciousness party AZAPO and the United Democratic Front agreed. Slabbert reciprocated by having long talks with the ANC's publicity director Thabo Mbeki in London. But the ANC made it clear that they saw his role as working on white opinion, not black; and Slabbert's influence among Afrikaners had diminished after his resignation, while some of the more left-wing nationalists, 'the New Nats', had a more effective power-base. When Slabbert visited America again in April he was made aware, as he put it, that 'My trouble is, I'm not black.' He and Boraine remained active as intelligent brokers establishing links with black politicians. But the traditional role of the white liberal as the spokesman or lobbyist for blacks was now rapidly dwindling. The ANC and other black leaders appreciated white allies; but they knew that in the end they would strike the real bargains with the heart of Afrikanerdom, with the Broederbond or even the right-wing parties.

The English-speaking businessmen were now faced with a starker choice, between the government or the ANC; and they still looked anxiously to Pretoria for signs of economic pressures to liberate the government. Much now depended on the handful of prominent Afrikaner businessmen who had a major influence in Pretoria. Would they be prepared to retreat into a siege economy, or would they seek some reconciliation with the West?

Many liberals still put hopes on Anton Rupert, still at seventy the head of the Rembrandt tobacco group which now had most of its investments in other industries ranging from banks through life assurance to clinics. Rupert often represented Afrikaner paternalism in its most attractive and visionary form: he had actively encouraged black small businesses, helped to develop industries in Lesotho and believed genuinely in industrial partnership between whites and blacks. Through his cigarettes and his art-collecting he was also an international figure, a friend and admirer of David Rockefeller and a frequent visitor to New York, London and Germany. He saw his own country's problems as part of the world's. 'South Africa finds itself in the van of a crisis which Europe will eventually also have to face,' he said in 1985. 'The world should have more sympathy with South Africa because we are in the forefront of the unemployment problem.' He warned that black unemployment had doubled in the previous year, with job opportunities constantly disappearing; and he went on tactfully to suggest to his government that part of the blame lay in over-regulation. But while Rupert talked much about the common patriotism of all races, his vision-ary world seemed to exclude the real world of police, bombings and detentions. He said that apartheid was dead and the corpse must be buried, and he appealed to Botha to take bold action, but he not specify the details. He resented any international interference, and after he had angry disagreements with President Botha he was con-cerned not to offend him further. He remained stubbornly optimistic, and liked to repeat the observation that the Chinese symbol for crisis also meant opportunity. He still saw white South Africans as playing a unique role in Africa. 'We are sometimes cursed but we are always respected,' he said in his annual report after the emergency in August 1985. 'Southern Africa is waiting on us. If we succeed in our task we shall command respect from the world and, like a magnet, attract much-needed capital. Does this appear to be a flight of fancy? May I then remind you that "He who does not believe in miracles is not a realist".'*

The more conventional Afrikaner tycoon was Fred du Plessis, the head of the conglomerate Sanlam which, based on life insurance, had extended itself through property, banking and industry. Ostensibly, he firmly rejected the policy of closing Afrikaner ranks and moving towards isolation, an option which he called 'slow stagnation and death'; he insisted that a growth rate of 4 percent was essential to produce enough new jobs for the growing population, and that this was impossible without foreign participation. And he now denounced the past policies of apartheid which had misused South Africa's mixture of peoples: 'We used that very diversity to force the population into tight little compartments of self-interest – racial, linguistic, cultural and tribal.' But du Plessis too remained a true Afrikaner. As President of the SA Foundation he was exposed to criticism from the world's businessmen including Roger Smith's Corporate Council, but he could discount most of it as uninformed. He described in March 1986 how the foreign businessmen at one meeting had 'enumerated a few changes that would ease their situation in South Africa and they were then dumbfounded to be told that most of their stated requirements had already been embodied in official policies'. He conceded that there has been 'a hardening of attitudes towards South Africa in business circles abroad', but he looked to foreign governments, particularly the British government, which showed more 'realism and understanding' than the businessmen, and welcomed Mrs Thatcher's opposition to sanctions.

* Rembrandt Group: Chairman's address, August 29, 1985. *See also* speech on 'Free Enterprise in Africa' to the South Africa Club, London, April 16, 1986

And as the Afrikaners felt more embattled, du Plessis was inclined to agree with Botha on the need for stronger action against black rebels, whatever the international cost.

Rupert and du Plessis, like most other Afrikaner businessmen and President Botha himself, put much of their hope on the emergence of a black middle-class of small businessmen or professionals to counter the radicalism of the ANC and provide a bridge with the black world. But as the crisis continued the black businessmen were also being rapidly radicalised. Their moderate chief spokesman was Sam Motsuenyane, chairman of the African Bank and president of the National African Federated Chamber of Commerce (NAFCOC) who had been hopeful about President Botha's reforms; but even he was now very disillusioned. In July 1985, after the emergency had been declared, he led a business delegation to see the foreign minister Pik Botha, to press for Mandela's release and for dialogue with the ANC: but he was bitterly disappointed by Botha's 'Rubicon' speech – 'a major political and economic disaster' – which ignored all his proposals; and in 1985 he and other businessmen paid a visit to see Tambo in Lusaka, from which they came back encouraged that the ANC foresaw a major role for free enterprise. The black businessmen were visibly distancing themselves from their Afrikaner counterparts: when Fred du Plessis opened the annual meeting of NAFCOC in July 1986 he explained, somewhat disingenuously, that the Afrikaner's business success did not depend on their political power; but Motsuenyane quickly replied that the blacks' position was quite different: 'The Afrikaner has never been deprived of the right to vote in his own country.'*

The younger Afrikaner businessmen felt more inclined to mix with the wider white community as the common danger gave them a common purpose, while Afrikaners felt more concerned to embrace the free-enterprise ethic,

* Barry Streek in *Weekly Mail*, July 18, 1986

partly to counter the 'communist onslaught', partly from
a greater sense of their own opportunity. 'As Afrikaner
business people became more numerous and more successful,' wrote Leonard Thompson, 'they became committed
to the market economy, and consequently less dependent
on political patronage and less tied to the rigid racial
ideology of the past.'* And in political calculations the
arithmetic suggested that President Botha or his successor
could only preserve their leadership in parliament by ap-
pealing to more English-speaking voters to compensate for
the loss of the Afrikaner right-wing – surrendering some
of the exclusiveness of Afrikanerdom in exchange for the
broader white support. 'The real question is whether the
Afrikaners can hold on to their monopoly of power,' said
the Afrikaans journalist Stanley Uys in November 1985.
'Whether they can continue to exclude the English-
speaking population from any role in the decisions. So
long as they maintain that monopoly, they won't be able
to make any real concessions to the blacks.'†

But though Botha periodically wooed English-speaking
voters and businessmen he showed little desire to open up
the citadel of Afrikanerdom which had provided such rich
rewards for his people over forty years. This white tribe,
insulated by political power and patronage, was more
exclusive than any of the black tribes whose separateness
it sought to encourage; and Afrikaners talked about their
ethnicity with a mystique which European nations, like the
Dutch and English, had long ago abandoned. The special
hold of their Afrikaans culture was evident even in Breyten
Breytenbach, the dissident Afrikaans poet and painter who
had broken out to marry a Vietnamese princess, lived in
exile in Paris and then joined the underground group
Okhela, loosely linked with the ANC. When he secretly
returned to South Africa to establish an underground
resistance, he was betrayed and served seven years in jail,

* Thompson, *op cit.*, pp. 191–2
† Interview with author, November 19, 1985

surrounded by brutal Afrikaner warders. He vowed that 'Nothing can ever bridge the gap between the Afrikaner tribe and myself'; and when he was moved from Pretoria jail 'I swore then – as I still swear today – that never will I freely set foot again in Pretoria. Let that bloated village of civil servants and barbarians be erased from the face of the earth.'* Yet nine years afterwards in April 1986 Breytenbach returned to Pretoria to receive a literary prize, where he warned his Afrikaner audience: 'We are culturally incapable of initiating, accompanying or accommodating the imminent transformation of our society. Our rottenness is unique and our self-destruction will certainly also be unrepeatable.'†

By March 1985 all President Botha's authority and Afrikaner pride were being challenged by the mounting international pressure, and the confrontation with black rebels at home. In the black townships the 'comrades' and street committees were taking the initiative, and moderate black leaders were increasingly under pressure. Even Winnie Mandela, who was a heroine to the young black activists in spite of her relative restraint, had suddenly burst out with a call to take necklaces and matches into the white suburbs. The ANC leaders were appalled, knowing that she would be said to represent Mandela's own views, which she did not: she was persuaded to keep quiet for the following weeks, and then effectively withdrew her previous call: 'I wasn't advocating violence: I was saying that the time would come when people shall be called upon to defend themselves . . . The panicking racists say I advocated violence. I have not done so yet.'‡ But her outburst had been an ugly warning of horrors ahead.

The main political battleground remained the black schools. As the three-month ultimatum by parents in December came close to expiring the government had

---

* Breyten Breytenbach, *The True Confessions of an Albino Terrorist*, London, Faber and Faber, 1984, p. 255

† Johannesburg *Sunday Times*, April 13, 1986

‡ Speech at Orlando Stadium, May 1986

appeared conciliatory. They lifted the state of emergency, and the minister of education Gerrit Viljoen appealed for black children to go back to school. At the end of March 1,500 parents, teachers and pupils attended a second National Education Conference in Durban, and decided to advocate a return to school, while also planning major demonstrations on May Day and June 16, the anniversary of Soweto. The parents' generation appeared to be regaining their control; and an important keynote address, carefully prepared by a committee, was delivered by Zwelakhe Sisulu, the son of the ANC veteran Walter Sisulu who was now editor of the black paper *New Nation*. It explained how:

> In any struggle it is extremely important to recognise the critical moment, the time when decisive action can propel that struggle into a new phase. It is also important to understand that this moment does not last for ever – that, if we fail to take action, that moment is lost. This particular moment has several important features.
> * The State has lost the initiative to the people. It is no longer in control of events.
> * The masses recognise that the moment is decisive and are calling for action.
> * People are united around a set of fundamental demands and are prepared to take action on these demands.
> Having said this, I want to strike a note of caution. It is important that we don't mistake the moment or understand it to be something it is not. We are not poised for the immediate transfer of power to the people. The belief that this is so could lead to serious errors and defeats. We are, however, poised to enter a phase which could lead to the transfer of power. What we are seeking to do is to shift the balance of forces in our favour decisively . . .

The balance did seem to be shifting. The black activists in the UDF and elsewhere were building up their 'alternative structures' which mocked the government's own hierarchies, and their most striking victory came on May Day when they organised their first successful one-day strike: in Port Elizabeth and most of the Eastern Cape nearly 100 percent of the workers stayed away, and even in the gold-mines the workers went out on strike: Anglo-American reported 83 percent absent.* May Day had become a highly politicised festival: in Soweto 20,000 blacks attended a rally of the trades union group COSATU, while in Durban Buthelezi's party Inkatha launched its own United Workers Union of South Africa (UWUSA) at a rally of 60,000 Zulus. It was the first time black South Africans had made their own calendar.

The government were now being threatened not only by black school-children, but by right-wing Afrikaners who were rapidly becoming highly-publicised, through their extreme group the Afrikaanner Weerstandsbeweging (AWB) led by the ex-policeman Eugene Terre'Blanche. On May 22, when the foreign minister Pik Botha was scheduled to speak at Pietersburg in the Northern Transvaal, Terre'Blanche successfully took over the meeting with his 'storm falcons' waving their flags with the emblems of the three-armed Swastika. The AWB's own political policies were puerile: its 'programme of principles' was openly anti-semitic and anti-capitalist, blaming Jewish capitalists and Anglo-American for allowing blacks to flow into the cities and promising to free Afrikaners from 'spiritual and economic enslavement by Anglo-Jewish money'. The actual following of the AWB was much exaggerated by its publicity and melodrama; but it clearly had many supporters among the Afrikaner police who refrained from moving against the invaders, and it was appearing ominously like the paramilitary wing of the conservative party under Andreas Treurnicht: when several Afrikaner right-wing groups assembled at the Voortrekker monument in June, Terre'Blanche was the most acclaimed speaker.† It provided a pretext if not a reason for Botha to take bolder action against black rebels.

* *Weekly Mail*, May 2, 1986
† *See* Patrick Laurence in *Weekly Mail*, June 6, 1986

By the beginning of June the political tension was mounting rapidly as the tenth anniversary of Soweto approached. The government had put forward two new bills, the Public Safety Amendment Bill and the Internal Security Amendment Bill, to enable the Minister of Law and Order to declare 'unrest areas' and to give the police special powers including ordering detention without trial for 180 days – thus making a state of emergency virtually unnecessary. But the bills were opposed not only by the Progressive Federal Party but also by the Indian and coloured MPs elected under the new constitution, who insisted on sending the bills back to the standing committee – thus delaying their passing until after June 16. As the critical date came closer the minister for law and order, Louis Le Grange, was pressing for emergency powers; and Botha himself was increasingly impatient of international pressure and the threat of sanctions.

On June 12 Botha declared his second, and much more far-reaching, state of emergency which would precipitate a more fundamental crisis, and would drive a deeper wedge between South African businessmen and their Western counterparts.

17

Crackdown

We are tired of having to govern South Africa under the threat of sanctions.

President Botha

No factory or mine can work without us. No city can function without us. Nothing in this country can work without blacks. We are no longer simply hewers of wood and drawers of water.

Chief Buthelezi in his address at Jabulani
Amphitheatre,
Soweto, June 29, 1986

In its centenary year Johannesburg showed all the outward signs of triumphant permanence and prosperity since its wild beginnings as a mining camp in 1886. The city centre was scarcely recognisable from the bleak grid of rectangles where I had worked thirty years before; and only a few corrugated rooves and gingerbread balconies still jostled next to the sheer office towers. A many-faceted mirror-building, shining like a giant diamond, had sprung up on the site of the old Indian markets along Diagonal Street, to provide yet another building for the Anglo-American Corporation. A cylindrical glass tower had risen up next to the stone law courts, containing the newest luxury hotel, the Johannesburg Sun. The names of the world's multinationals glittered from the tops of the tower-blocks.

Banners and posters now advertised the 'city with a heart of gold', 'our strength is our people'; and a romantic television serial had just been launched to commemorate the centenary. 'On this site was to rise one of the greatest cities in Africa . . . a city of the future, with so little time to look back.' Johannesburg had prepared for a programme of celebrations, and a rush of tourists. But the plans and slogans – 'a hundred cheers for a hundred years' – had gone sour in the course of the year: the black Community Support Committee had warned the sponsors that they would 'incur the wrath of the black people', and proposed their own slogan 'a hundred years of oppression'. The business sponsors had admitted defeat. The white woman selling centenary souvenirs at the kiosk near the town hall told me she had not sold enough in one day to pay for her bus-fare.

And on Monday June 16, 1986, the blacks were celebrating their own anniversary – ten years after the Soweto uprising. The government said it would be a 'normal working day', but the city centre was as empty as if it had been visited by a plague: the station and bus-termini, which usually teemed with black commuters, were deserted. Only a few white people were walking the streets and some were actually *carrying* their own parcels out of the Johannesburg post office, watched by a group of blacks sitting on the steps. There was no reliable news since the State of Emergency had been declared four days before: the newspapers gave bare reports from the government, the radio provided cheery items including a romantic travel talk by Laurens van der Post. No one could go in and out of Soweto, or knew how many people had been imprisoned. In a black newspaper office the journalists told me that a four-year-old girl in Soweto had been shot in the back, and a whole church congregation arrested: it was not till the end of the week that both reports were confirmed. Rumours reverberated about the success or failure of the one-day strike: the government radio news ('brought to you with the compliments of Nissan South Africa'), insisted that most blacks had gone to work against all the evidence of the streets. By the next morning it was clear that for the second time in the year the blacks had shown they could assert their own sanction: to withdraw their labour. Anglo-American had already made a virtue of necessity, following the Premier Group by declaring it a half-holiday: 'South Africa's calendar of public holidays,' announced Gavin Relly, 'no longer reflects the full spectrum of national sentiment.'

The only centre of activity was the brown stone cathedral which had seen so many protests in the forty years of apartheid. Before midday it filled up with all races, including some familiar faces of liberals, academics and do-gooders but only two prominent businessmen – both of them Jewish. The service opened with a reading from Isaiah, beginning: 'Shout without restraint,' and continued with hymns. Then Bishop Tutu delivered his sermon, insisting that he would never agree not to mix religion with politics, and warning that the emergency was 'grossly insensitive and highly provocative'. He asked 'why are we allowing this country to be destroyed?' and ended with his arms stretched out to heaven while the cameras whirred. As the service ended a black woman in red began singing the ANC anthem – Nkosi Sikelele Africa – holding out her clenched fist, while half the congregation joined in.

From their glittering new buildings and suburban estates, the Johannesburg tycoons now surveyed the most testing political crisis of their city's lifetime. The second emergency which President Botha had declared on June 12 was far more rigorous than his first one eleven months earlier; and he was determined to rally the business community behind him in an atmosphere of crisis. At each previous crisis – 1952, 1960, 1976, 1985 – radical politicians and journalists had always tended to exaggerate the extremity of the repression, leaving no words to describe the next turn of the screw. This crackdown was undoubtedly more thorough and efficient than anything before: it gave

far greater freedom to the police to arrest, detain and
interrogate whoever they wished, with unprecedented censorship to prevent any reporting of their actions. (After I
wrote a report on detainees for the London *Observer*, I
was informed that the minister of home affairs had with-
drawn my exemption from a visa.) It was not until two
months later that the government revealed that 8,500
people had been detained under the regulations (which
many lawyers still thought was only half the full number).
And only in August, when the courts found that censorship
had been illegally imposed, could a few glimpses of police
activity be revealed behind the censors' blanks – though
in the words of the *Weekly Mail*: 'The black lines camou-
flaged only those few areas not already covered by a mass
of other legislation affecting reporting on prisons, police
and the Defence Force.' This was one report which
emerged uncensored in August, about the township of
Zwelethemba near Worcester in the Cape which had been
the scene of earlier consumer boycotts (*see* Chapter 12);
it provided a glimpse of the new kind of military apartheid
which was being enforced in the midst of an advanced
industrial system.

> Zwelethemba is a township virtually under siege; a South
> African Defence Force camp is pitched on its borders,
> and within walking distance is a police station, hastily
> erected during the last State of Emergency. Searchlights
> from towers that encircle the township span the streets
> nightly, frequently coming to rest on the front doors of
> known activists or anyone else suspected by the police.
> A 7 pm to 7 am curfew imposed the weekend the current
> emergency began is still in force.*

The major battleground was once again the schools, where
new regulations forced pupils to re-register and to carry
special identity cards, and forbade them to take part in

* *Weekly Mail*, Johannesburg, August 22, 1986

any non-educational activities in the school buildings, while soldiers and police were sent into schools to enforce order. There were accounts of security forces beating the school-children, taking them out of class, and even acting as teachers to provide their own version of history and geography; there was one report of a whole class being arrested and detained. The new generation of schoolchildren was growing up alongside the police state in its most literal everyday form: their chief daily experience of whites was of uniformed men carrying guns and sjamboks. The children retaliated with school boycotts in some areas, sometimes attending with their own underground schools. They were still in the vanguard of the revolt, with older politicians on every side trying to mobilise and control them. While the ANC and the UDF were trying to keep them within their parents' discipline, Chief Buthelezi furiously attacked the ANC in exile for exploiting the children, at a massed 'prayer meeting' which he addressed in Soweto, with police protection at the height of the emergency:

> Our children will yet be turned into cannon fodder unparalleled in the history of mankind if we continue to allow others to employ our anger as though it was their property . . . Nowhere in the history of the world have young people of school-going age achieved the liberation of their country on their own . . . Those who sit in exile and use our young folk as storm troopers as they seek personal glorification, or the glorification of narrow sectional interests, must be rejected by every black South African.*

But there was little sign that the schoolchildren needed any encouragement from outside to spur them against the police. The real danger as the emergency bit harder was that they would accept no allegiance, that their fury could not be contained, and that the internal feuds between warring black factions would descend into anarchy.

* Speech at Jabulani Amphitheatre, June 29, 1986

There was no doubt that the government was determined
to use the new emergency to smash the networks of political groups, particularly youth groups and offshoots of
COSAS which were linked to the UDF, that had grown up to
challenge their power in the previous two years; and the
police were clearly encouraging the growing tensions between the UDF and its rival AZAPO. Nearly half the detainees
were youth leaders, and the security forces had clearly
been closely watching the new 'alternative structures':
there were suspicions that they had deliberately allowed
them to flourish over the previous year, in order to identify
their leadership and then cut them down.

The UDF kept up a bold front, and the ANC was certainly
more famous than ever. 'For the government to say that
the ANC is banned is laughable. You know it and we know
it,' Zwelakhe Sisulu, the resilient editor of *New Nation*
told the Afrikaans journal *Die Suid Afrikaan* in June
before he was himself detained. Several key black leaders
evaded arrest. On the third anniversary of the UDF in
August 1986 its publicity secretary Murphy Morobe, who
had been in and out of hiding for a year, reappeared to
maintain that 'the UDF has not only survived the most
severe repression but has grown into a mass movement
. . . our organisations are stronger and deeper than before
and are thus better able to replace activists detained, killed
or forced into exile.' And by early October the leaders of
the UDF, together with COSATU and the National Education
Crisis Committee, all emerged from hiding to announce a
'momentous' campaign for 'national unity against apartheid and the emergency'. The government responded a
week later by forbidding the UDF to receive funds from
abroad, which had been contributing half its finances.* But
the resistance groups had undoubtedly taken a battering: as
Shaun Johnson, having interviewed a wide range of young
black leaders, described them in July 1986:

* *Weekly Mail*, August 22, 1986, October 3, 1986, *Financial Times*,
October 10, 1986

Today youth organisations are in disarray. Leaders are incarcerated, others are underground and unable to supervise day-to-day organisational business, meetings are impossible, and there is a distinct air of directionlessness and despair. I do not believe that the Emergency can destroy the complex, deeply entrenched youth structures. But it can certainly set back what was seen to be a linear process of growth.*

The businessmen in Johannesburg faced the two extremes of black fury and white repression with still greater bewilderment. Most of them, I found, agreed that the state of emergency was necessary: they had dreaded a new outburst of violence on June 16, and many believed the government's warnings that the ANC had prepared a national revolt. The declaration of the emergency had been followed by a local boom and a flurry of economic activity stimulated by the finance minister Barend du Plessis with a new package. At the Reserve Bank Governor de Kock was able to revive the value of the rand, partly by massive selling of dollars; and he explained that: 'When investors realised that South Africa was not on the verge of revolution – no matter how serious the situation was – it was natural that both the financial and commercial rand should appreciate.' The censorship contributed to the boom. 'The sparseness of news,' said Max Borkum, the former chairman of the stock exchange, 'has helped to give people euphoria.' Exchange controls had helped to bolster the domestic economy. As businessmen said: 'We are randlocked.' The government used the mini-boom to show that business appreciated a tough, decisive stand, and by the end of the first week of the emergency de Kock was claiming that South Africa was now 'on top of the debt crisis'.

But the mini-boom, most businessmen agreed, was full of illusions. Capital was still leaking out of the country,

* Shaun Johnson, *op. cit.*

whether through Swiss banks which were laundering rand or through South African companies doing their own disinvesting through their subsidiaries abroad. Estate agents reported that 10 percent of all property in city-centres was empty – even though Indians and others were now allowed to buy properties in some white areas. Unemployment was hitting not only blacks but whites; and under a government relief scheme 250 whites were now working in Johannesburg's city parks, digging ditches for $2 a day. Nor did de Kock's optimism stand up for long. Two months after the emergency began he revealed in the Reserve Bank's annual report that the gross domestic product (adjusted for inflation) had grown by only 1 percent in 1984–5, and in 1986 it would not be more than 2 percent – compared to an average of 4.9 percent in the long heyday between 1946 and 1974; and he admitted that economic recovery had been slowed by 'domestic lack of confidence and foreigners' strongly negative perceptions of South Africa's political stability and economic prospects'.

The businessmen – particularly the retailers and manufacturers – knew they would have in the end to gain the consent of the black workers and customers. Boycotts and mini-strikes still continued despite the regulations, and the middle-class black employees came under much greater pressure from radicals in the townships. And Botha's policies showed no real consistency or reassurance: his oscillations between reform and repression provided the most dangerous combination, first raising black expectations, then dashing them and provoking resistance: it looked almost like a deliberate formula for revolution. Five years earlier Botha had yielded to the pressure of industrialists to allow black unions: now his police had arrested most of their leaders, in the middle of crucial wage negotiations. Even without their leaders, the unions could still keep some shop-workers away, in protest against the detentions.

Some businessmen did publicly oppose Botha's crackdown. The Federated Chamber of Industries, presided over by John Wilson of Shell, made a statement which 'strongly disapproved of the state of emergency and the further detention and disassociated itself from the strategy of political repression and economic isolationism to which the South African government is apparently committed'. Many business members of the Chamber angrily dissented from the statement, and President Botha wrote a furious private reply to Wilson saying it was 'quite ridiculous' and that the government was already committed to negotiation and conciliation.

> Kindly do not trouble me with your points of view if you are not prepared to take the trouble of familiarising yourself with mine. Unless you too come to grips with the realities of the security situation in this country and act accordingly you are bound to pay a heavy price. This is not a threat – it is a considered warning. Instead of criticising the government in the most irresponsible fashion you should be helping it. That is your duty as a South African . . .

'But with whom is government negotiating these reforms?' Wilson asked in an article just afterwards: 'The identifiable black leaders are specifically excluded from the negotiation process . . .'* Botha, after his earlier conciliatory talks, was now spelling out much more brutally his attitude to foreign investors, insisting that they must knuckle down or get out. And in spite of his protests, John Wilson had rashly insisted just after the crackdown that Shell would continue to invest heavily in South Africa with 'the full backing of its international shareholders'.†

A few businessmen went further. Tony Bloom of the Premier Group and Chris Ball of Barclays took part in a candid radio discussion with two leading members of the ANC, Thabo Mbeki and Mac Maharaj, and later lunched with Oliver Tambo (*see* Chapter 1). They were fiercely

---

* *Business Day*, Johannesburg, July 4, 1986
† *Sunday Tribune*, Durban, July 20, 1986

attacked for talking to terrorists while more bombs were
going off, and the government-controlled *Citizen* called it
a 'Blooming shame'. Gavin Relly of Anglo-American was
now lying lower, well aware of his company's vulnerability
in the current political mood. 'With the rise of the right-
wing in white politics,' wrote *The Citizen* with a nasty
implied threat, 'the last thing Anglo should want is a revival
of the Hoggenheimer canard which was fortunately buried
several decades ago.'* Most companies preferred general-
ised protest to specific actions, and many multinationals
and others joined to sponsor yet another advertisement,
prepared by J Walter Thompson, showing black and white
hands stretching towards each other. It said 'Instead of a
State of Emergency, let's declare a State of Urgency to
remove all discriminatory legislation without delay . . .'
and asked the government to free political detainees and
negotiate with acknowledged leaders about power sharing.
But Afrikaner businessmen were notably absent from the
signatories.

   Faced with the choice of decisive police repression and
an uncertain black mob, most businessmen were more
concerned with their short-term security than their longer-
term survival. They put some hope once again in President
Botha; and as sanctions loomed closer they were pressed
to rally more closely behind the government to defeat
them. Botha was again promising a major new speech, this
time at a special Federal Congress of the National Party
in Durban in August; and the world leaders, including
Thatcher and Reagan, were again assured that if they
would refrain from provocative pressure Botha would push
through his own reforms. But the Congress was preceded
by a mood of defiance encouraged by the apparent effec-
tiveness of the emergency and by the internal mini-boom.

   The Johannesburg stock market was now hitting record
levels while gold and platinum prices were pressing upwards, partly *because* of the South African crisis: the

* *The Citizen*, June 3, 1986

prospect of chaos and catastrophe could be good news for many speculators in a country with so many key minerals in short supply; and the platinum price had already shot up in anticipation of cut-backs and sanctions. Just before the Congress de Kock had announced that the higher gold price would ensure that South Africa would have a surplus on the current-account balance of payment of over four billion rand.

Botha's speech proved yet another anti-climax for the world, and revealed much more clearly that the basic structure of apartheid would still remain intact. He produced two new proposals: that major black townships such as Soweto could be given a special status as autonomous city-states, which he compared to Europe's city-states like Monaco; and that South Africa could join in high-level talks with the major Western nations to discuss stability in Southern Africa. His minister for constitutional affairs, Chris Heunis, discussed a new Council of State which would bring together homelands and the city-states with parliament. But Botha insisted that apartheid would prevail in residential areas and in schools, that he would not negotiate with the ANC or make any concessions to world opinion: 'Granting concessions under conditions bordering on blackmail merely encourages the raising of demands.' And he ended his speech by reasserting the mystical role of the Afrikaners to lead the subcontinent: 'I look at the constellations in the sky at night and what are the words I see written there? Southern Africa for Christendom.'

His speech totally contradicted the beliefs of Western leaders – most of all Mrs Thatcher – who had insisted that the Afrikaner government, if left to itself, would dismantle apartheid and genuinely begin to share power with black leaders. The government emphasised that reforms would continue, but within the context of strict control of the black movements: and the emergency now appeared, as Allister Sparks of the *Washington Post* described it, as 'a desperate attempt to stem those forces and get the logs

back in place while the limited reforms are completed'.*
President Reagan rushed in to welcome the idea of talks
about apartheid – which gave a new fillip to Botha at the
Congress – but the State Department quickly back-
tracked, explaining that the meeting would 'focus on re-
gional issues, rather than apartheid'; while the British
Foreign Office was now more forthright, insisting that
Mandela must be released and the ANC unbanned: 'We are
disappointed that President Botha showed no signs of
taking the quantum leap forward which is so clearly necessary.'

More riots and repression followed the Congress, with
growing evidence that the army as well as the police were
using systematic torture to try to cow all opposition. The
security forces, with the help of censorship, were beginning
to give the impression of order and calm. But behind
Botha's show of strength the reports from the townships
suggested that they were moving still further out of control;
Soweto remained a battleground as the government tried
to enforce the payment of rents; and the white director of
housing, Del Kevan, had her house in a white suburb
bombed with a limpet-mine after which she resigned. The
more leaders were detained, the less the prospect of limiting and controlling the violence. Some members of the
ANC, which had called to render South Africa ungovernable
eighteen months before, was beginning to worry that it
might become ungovernable by anyone.

And even the communists, the persistent advocates of
revolution, were becoming more concerned about the
potential loss of control. Six weeks after the emergency
the South African Communist Party – now coming more
into the open – celebrated its sixty-fifth anniversary in the
Conway Hall, the traditional meeting-place of the Left
in London. In the packed hall tough stewards frisked
everyone: old-style British communists, young anti-
apartheid idealists, South African exiles of all colours. A

---

* *Observer*, August 16, 1986

black choir in red shirts sang the old Congress songs, punctuated with the names of Mandela, Tambo, Slovo. Round the hall hung photographs of the martyrs – Bram Fischer, Ruth First, Moses Kotane. On the platform, above pictures of Lenin and Marx, the red flag was draped alongside the black, green and gold flag of the ANC; and the chairman of the SACP, Joe Slovo, sat with the Secretary-General of the ANC, Alfred Nzo.

The British communists seemed exhilarated by the prospect of a real revolution complete with the kind of heroes, martyrs and complete commitment which had long faded in Europe. 'The dreams which inspired the founders of the party are about to be realised,' said the secretary of the British Communist Party, Gordon McLennan. But the South Africans were more guarded. The ANC pledged friendship with the Communists and Alfred Nzo said 'Our banners flutter together at the head of the columns'; but he took care to explain that 'The ANC will defend the right of anyone who chooses to belong to the SACP, or to any party of their choice, so long as they are not a vehicle for racism or fascism'; and he recalled how Churchill, Roosevelt and de Gaulle emerged as giants during the Second World War when they fought the forces of Nazism.

The key speech was by Comrade Joe Slovo, the chairman of the South African Communist Party who was also on the ANC executive: a lawyer from Lithuanian Jewish parents – like so many successful compatriots – he had practised as a lawyer in Johannesburg before he went into exile for twenty-five years, where his wife Ruth First was killed by a letter bomb. He still sported a blazer, South African style, and a throaty South African accent. He paid tribute to the Party 'which brought into existence the first modern national liberation movement in Africa'. He was convinced that the factors for revolutionary advance were now coming together: the rulers could not rule in the old way, the people were discovering people's power, the ANC were in the vanguard. 'The South African masses are on the move as never before: we vow to help them finish the job.'

But his speech was muted, theoretical and cautious. He described how South African communists had to work out their own indigenous theory of revolution; and how they could never be separated from the ANC – which 'has no competition as the alternative power in our land'. He explained that the SACP, unlike Congress, owed its allegiance solely to the working people: 'The road which was taken when the liberation flag eventually flew in Pretoria would depend on the correlation of class forces which came to power.' After they had achieved majority rule there would still for some time be a role for private property and a mixed economy, including 'managers and business people of goodwill'. He explained that: 'Enough experiences have been accumulated of disastrous great leaps forward to teach us to be wary of baking slogans rather than baking bread during the transition phase.' And he warned against the 'Pol Pot philosophy' which thought you could 'pole-vault into socialism and communism the day after the overthrow of white rule . . .'

Many members of the ANC were surprised by Slovo's caution, and his lack of a practical programme. 'He was trying to calm down the young hotheads,' one ANC veteran said after the meeting. 'It looks as if the ANC has swallowed the SACP,' said another. I asked Slovo afterwards how far his speech represented new thinking. 'Well, it represents thinking. We've been catapulted into a new situation. We've been used to being an agitational opposition, not an alternative power. Now we've been forced to formulate our approach.' How close did he see the possibility of chaos? He replied:

A lot of the future depends on Pretoria: if the government digs in its heels, chaos may make negotiation impossible, and a bloody struggle would leave a lot of historical debts to be paid. Of course the so-called chaos has already caused the crisis, which is a positive happening: but there are manifestations which we don't like, as the kids begin to say: what can we do today? I've never believed that it's the job of a revolutionary to make a revolution: only to lead it. There are lots of situations which have no control. I've never relished the escalation of violence: we didn't go into it with any *élan*, but because it was the only option, the last option: and we want to get out of it as soon as possible.

While President Botha continued to blame the communist onslaught for any resistance, many communists were already dreading an anarchy in the black townships which could go far beyond their influence: most of the 'comrades' who set the necklaces on fire owed no allegiance to the ANC or the SACP. The old Afrikaner mythology of the fight against communism was beginning to lose its relevance to the rest of the world; and as America and Europe began finally to move towards sanctions the Afrikaners were having to re-think their old assumption that the West would always support them in the final anti-communist crusade; and some were beginning to see American capitalists as an enemy more threatening than Soviet communists.

18

The End of a Road

I would be more impressed with those who made no bones about the reason they remain in South Africa and said honestly: 'We are concerned for our profits' instead of the baloney that the businesses are there for our benefit. We don't want you there. Please do us a favor: Get out and come back when we have a democratic and just South Africa.

Bishop Tutu, *New York Times*, June 16, 1986

Botha's crackdown had defied world opinion, and the issue of apartheid and sanctions exploded across America and Western Europe. South Africa was now more than ever the caricature of the world's problems, reviving dormant fears about race and chaos and bringing back the old arguments about poverty and inequality and the conflict between business and morality. But the clamour for sanctions also showed all the difficulties of taking effective steps. South Africa's gold and precious metals were still interlocked with the world's money and high-technology industries: half the continent depended on its exports and trade. How could you isolate and cut out a malignant growth in the midst of the world's intricate trading system? And what happens after disinvestment?

The chiefs of the multinational corporations – with General Motors, IBM and Shell in the forefront – watched

their own justifications and diplomacy being overtaken by
the public outcry which was pushing their governments
towards the sanctions that would undermine their investments. Sanctions also drove a wedge through the Western
political world. The two key leaders, Ronald Reagan and
Margaret Thatcher, still passionately opposed them, and
still hoped that the apartheid problem would solve itself.
But both were now under much heavier bombardment
until slowly and reluctantly they were compelled to change
course.

After Botha's crackdown Mrs Thatcher still resisted
pressure from the European Community, the Commonwealth and growing numbers of conservatives. Parliament
held an emergency debate, and the British government
undertook to work actively 'for effective measures which
will help achieve a peaceful solution in South Africa'. Soon
afterwards the twelve prime ministers of the European
Community held a summit which called again for the
release of Mandela and the unbanning of the ANC, and
agreed to send out the British Foreign Secretary Sir Geoffrey Howe for a final attempt at dialogue before imposing
sanctions. Sir Geoffrey reluctantly agreed on his unpromising mission, explaining that apartheid was 'not Christian,
not civilised and certainly not in the interests of the West
that it should survive'. But Mrs Thatcher seemed determined to undermine Howe's leverage on Botha by attacking the immorality of sanctions in a succession of
interviews. Nearly all black leaders, including Mandela,
Tambo and the churchmen Tutu and Boesak, refused to
see Howe, insisting that his visit was merely a delaying
tactic against sanctions: Botha eventually agreed to see
him, but then himself slammed the door, and Howe returned empty-handed. He had been sent (said the Tory MP
Robert Adley) 'up the creek without a paddle and then
brought home without a canoe'.

The House of Commons was now much more vocal.
Denis Healey, the shadow foreign secretary who had just
visited South Africa, called for comprehensive mandatory

sanctions to bring the issue to a head; and Ted Heath
also supported the call for sanctions, while warning that
effective action would require a naval blockade. But most
of the Conservative Party was still resolutely opposed. The
Foreign Affairs Committee of all-party MPs produced a
rush report based on their hearings which had begun with
Tambo a year earlier. They could not agree whether wider
sanctions would strengthen or weaken the government:
they believed that after a while they 'would be likely to
bite very hard, and no South African government would
be able to ignore their effect in the framing of its policies'.
But they were pessimistic about the chances of peaceful
negotiation to a democratic system. In all the debates most
politicians shunned the basic issue of black majority rule,
and it was left to a diplomat, Lord Moran, to voice the
real fears of conservatives:

> There can be no half-way house in South Africa. Either
> you must have a white dominated society or you must
> have one man, one vote, which would lead to black
> majority rule and, in due course no doubt, a one-party
> regime, soon to come in Zimbabwe . . . I think one
> man, one vote would necessitate the departure of most of
> the 3 million whites, many of them to this country . . .*

It was still the Commonwealth more than parliament that
made trouble for Thatcher; and after Botha had so
decisively rebuffed the eminent persons they were on the
warpath for sanctions. Malcolm Fraser from Australia
insisted that sanctions were essential to bring South Africa
not to its knees but to its senses: he agreed they might only
have a 50 percent chance of success; but said the alternative
was the total destruction of Western interests in South
Africa. General Obasanjo burst out publicly against
Thatcher's 'misguided tribal loyalty'; and Brian Mulroney
of Canada and Bob Hawke of Australia joined forces with

* House of Lords, July 4, 1986

the black states. British conservatives and white South Africans quickly pointed out that Canada and Australia would suffer little, and might gain something from imposing sanctions; but Mulroney and Hawke both argued that the British were too preoccupied by the short-term to see their long-term interests ahead.

Through July, while the South African police were mopping up the black resistance, the sanctions issue reverberated through Britain with furious rhetoric on both sides. It easily lost touch with any serious consideration for the interests of either business or blacks; and South Africa became darkly related to immigration and race riots in Britain: 'Do you want another Brixton?' The attacks on sanctions soon overspilled into attacks against the Commonwealth, on its secretary-general Sonny Ramphal, and eventually on the Queen herself, who was accused of supporting the Commonwealth against Mrs Thatcher – an assumption which even briefly threatened to cause a constitutional crisis.

But while politicians insisted that sanctions were against Britain's commercial interests, many businessmen were now much less sure that they wanted to be part of an anti-sanctions crusade. Their spokesman at BICSA Sir Leslie Smith charged into the fray, mustering a posse of companies to make a statement against sanctions which was widely publicised in South Africa, protesting that they 'would retard rather than accelerate the process of change'. But sixteen of the fifty member-companies including the biggest banks, Barclays and Standard, refused to sign it, and many members with interests in black Africa, including Unilever and both oil companies, were now acutely embarrassed. Sir Leslie then tried to produce an agreed policy about South Africa which was passed from one company to the next like a hot potato, and was eventually issued with minimum publicity and contorted prose. It neither supported nor criticised sanctions: while condemning punitive pressures, it 'understood the frustrations' which had led the Commonwealth to call for sanctions, and was 'certainly not opposed to further pressures which support those working for non-violent change from within'.* Most British bankers were predictably fiercely opposed to sanctions: Sir Michael Butler, the right-wing diplomat who was now director of Hambros, even claimed that sanctions, by imperilling the repayment of the South African debt, could induce a world banking crisis. It was therefore interesting that Barclays, with a billion dollars at risk, were quite relaxed about sanctions: preferring to seek profits elsewhere.

The United States Congress was now a much more militant force for sanctions than the British parliament; and few American companies tried to oppose them. The House of Representatives had already passed a drastic bill for sanctions which had taken Washington and Pretoria by surprise; and Reagan's contradictory speech of July 22 (*see* page 19) which gave such succour to Botha, only provoked the Senators to stiffen their terms. They were led by two Republicans: Richard Lugar from Indiana, who was very conscious of the articulate black community in Indianapolis; and Nancy Kassebaum from Kansas, who chaired the Africa sub-committee, whose conservatism had turned to frustration. Both were influenced by Senator Kennedy, who provided a forum for Obasanjo and Fraser. In mid-August Lugar proposed his full sanctions bill, which included banning steel, airlines and government bank accounts, which was followed by a historic debate re-examining both American policy and the role of big business. Lugar gave credit to American companies' achievements: how Sullivan had established the first code of conduct, how Kelloggs corn flakes had first recognised a black union, how American companies had operated the first non-racial charities. But he insisted that his proposed sanctions were essential to combat apartheid. Senator Kennedy described the Americans' shame 'that our country is implicated in the terrible system that blights South Africa.

* British Industry in South Africa, BISCA, July 1986

Our corporations have benefited from the apartheid econ-omy, and our government has, for many years, indulged the leaders of apartheid.' Senator Proxmire invoked the Declaration of Independence to insist that when govern-ments suppress the people '. . . it is their right, it is their duty to throw off such government'. Senator Weicker remembered how '. . . When I first came to the US in 1970 everybody recognised that apartheid was wrong, but everyone said it would go away – let nature take its course . . . But the cancer did not go away. It has spread. It is worse today than it was in 1970.' And he urged Senators not to repeat the mistakes of the 'thirties when 'We chose to wait, and we chose not to act . . . The laws of Nazi Germany *vis-à-vis* Jews are identical to the laws of South Africa *vis-à-vis* black South Africans.'

The conservative senators counter-attacked with their own ideology, led by Jesse Helms from North Carolina who wanted an amendment that the United States would not negotiate with the African National Congress unless they abandoned violence and committed themselves to free and democratic government. He warned that the ANC was 'a Communist front controlled by the South African Communist Party, which itself is under the control of the Communist Party of the Soviet Union'. He came out with biographies of ANC leaders prepared by the CIA (but looking very similar to Pretoria's own reports*) which its director William Casey had especially de-classified; and his views were supported by Senator Denton from Alabama, who had held hearings on terrorism in 1982 and who compared South Africa to Vietnam, Cambodia, Iran and Nicaragua. But Helms was rebutted by Weicker who quoted the report of the eminent persons and Mandela's own statement in 1964 that 'the creed of the ANC is and always has been African nationalism'. After some bargaining Lugar and

* Compare the CIA notes published in the debate of August 14, 1986 with 'Talking to the ANC' published by the government in Pretoria earlier in 1986.

Helms agreed to a modified amendment, calling on both government and the ANC to renounce violence, but maintaining the package of sanctions, which went through by sixty-seven to thirty-one.

The Senate was now openly confronting the White House, and their two courses were set for the biggest collision on foreign policy of Reagan's presidency. In September Reagan was determined to veto the sanctions bill, and hoped that he could bring enough Senators over to his side – with the help of promises of aid and a black ambassador to Pretoria – to reduce the two-thirds majority. But most of the House and the Senate were now adamant; and at the beginning of October the two houses of Congress finally voted on the bill. The South African foreign minister Pik Botha telephoned Senators during the debate to warn them that Pretoria would retaliate against American farmers: and Chief Buthelezi called them more discreetly to insist that sanctions would hurt the blacks. But Pretoria's intervention only rallied most of the Senators, and on October 2 the Senate voted by seventy-eight to twenty-one to pass 'The Comprehensive Anti-Apartheid Act of 1986'. It was almost a complete alternative foreign policy: it spelt out conditions to both sides, calling for Pretoria to release Mandela and for the ANC to condemn 'necklacing'. But its overriding purpose was to impose sanctions which would be stepped up if Pretoria made no substantial progress in twelve months towards a non-racial democracy.

The European governments had also stumbled towards sanctions, more reluctantly and less convincingly. At the Commonwealth meeting in early August Mrs Thatcher had already agreed to go along with the other Europeans, and she was glad to shift the burden of opposing fuller sanctions to Helmut Kohl in West Germany – who wanted to continue importing South African coal and who was pressurised by a pro-Pretoria lobby including Franz-Josef Strauss in Bavaria. In the final meeting of the twelve European nations in September, the Germans and the Portuguese defeated the proposals for coal sanctions; but the rest of the package went ahead, including bans on steel and on new investment, but not on airlines. The European sanctions were less comprehensive than the American; and both sides of the Atlantic had shown deep divisions. Yet the agreement to impose sanctions, however divided and incomplete, represented the first complete break with earlier policies over the last forty years of apartheid.

It also marked a tragic admission: that investment and economic improvement would not in themselves lead to peaceful change and the achievement of black rights. It was the end of that long road of the love-affair between South Africa and Western capitalism, which had begun in earnest a century before with the discovery of gold in Johannesburg. The recriminations would continue. Christians and Marxists would blame the corporations for having built up apartheid; Western industrialists would insist that their commercial interests were against any colour bar, and many would argue that they were now resisting apartheid as far as they could. Certainly the demands for disinvestment had produced some spectacular improvements in black wages and conditions from companies which were justifying their presence. But the heroic confrontations with apartheid which they advertised abroad were a long way from blacks' own day-to-day perceptions of white companies, whether they were confronting an Afrikaner *baas* on the shopfloor, or observing the white executives retreating back to their white suburbs. And few businessmen would willingly give up a life-style which combined nineteenth-century servants and leisure together with twentieth-century comforts and technology.

As South Africa began moving closer to civil war the attempts by the multinationals to take on apartheid – whether by desegregating washrooms and canteens, promoting black executives, funding black education or even practising civil disobedience – were looking more trivial compared to the build-up of the military and police machine, which itself owed much to Western technology, and which was now demanding a mounting tribute of

obedience, taxes and intelligence from the industrialists.
Multinational managers would be compelled to provide
fuels, equipment and personnel to help the army and police
beat down the black resistance, and they would have to
keep military secrets even from their own headquarters in
London or New York; while the country-wide network
of Joint Management Centres bound them still closer to
Pretoria.

The governments' moves towards sanctions were soon
followed by a dramatic exodus – at least on the surface –
of American corporations. Already over two years the
numbers of American companies in South Africa had gone
down from 325 to 265; and the retreat included Procter
and Gamble and Coca-Cola (though it still sold its syrup).
At General Motors, Roger Smith had become increasingly
uneasy since visiting South Africa in April 1986, as a
member of George Shultz's advisory committee: 'Something happened to that government there that changed
their mind,' he said later, 'and they are not doing what I
hoped they would. Maybe the world did it to them: maybe
the siege mentality has set in.' GM was also, Smith said,
'struggling desperately' against the declining car-sales; and
he was keeping the local company under constant review.
Then on October 21 he announced that GM was finally
pulling out, after six decades in South Africa: it had been
losing money for several years, he explained, and 'we have
been disappointed in the pace of ending apartheid'. 'We
had no alternative,' said the outgoing chief executive in
South Africa, Bob White, 'we were flirting with technical
bankruptcy. We had all the grief of being here with none
of the profits.' On the Sunday after GM's announcement,
Leon Sullivan preached at his Zion Baptist church in
Philadelphia: 'When we initiated our effort in South Africa
ten years ago,' he told his congregation of a thousand,
'people said discrimination would stay for another 300
years. But they didn't realise God was there.' And he went
on to explain: 'When GM decided to get out of South
Africa, God lifted the mountains and said: Leon, walk . . .

I want you to know that God is in everything that is happening in South Africa'. The chairman of IBM John Akers followed suit, blaming the 'deteriorating political and economic situation'. The withdrawal of the two giants – the biggest in the world by sales and market capitalisation respectively – knocked on the head any lingering belief in Washington that corporations could be the main agents of change against apartheid: though the State Department spokesman Charles Redman complained that the withdrawals would weaken American influence, and would hurt black workers.

The disinvestments were not quite what they looked. Both GM and IBM were selling out to local South African managers, to whom they would lend the money to buy the subsidiary, and for whom they would still supply their technology; and they would even put in some more capital before new American investment was banned after November 12. 'They're not cutting us off so much as they are cutting us loose,' said a local IBM executive; and IBM had taken similar steps to cease investing in India and Nigeria. 'All our customers will continue to get the service excellence which is associated only with IBM products,' said an advertisement just afterwards. Robert Price, the new chief executive of GM in South Africa – soon renamed Nuco – soon made clear that they would have little patience with the unions, and no inhibitions about selling to the military. And as a sign of their toughness the company appointed as chairman Sir Michael Edwardes, the South African who had been responsible for turning round the ailing auto company British Leyland in Britain in the 'seventies with a legendary detachment from his managers and workers. The American headquarters could be thankful they would soon have no assets, no employees and no visible presence in the country, so that they could avoid the world's criticisms, while still profiting from sales under their agreements. They would come closer to the Japanese, who had never invested in South Africa but profited from selling cars or computers.

There was some gloating in Pretoria about the innocu-
ousness of the disinvestment, and some recrimination
among anti-apartheid campaigners: 'These companies are
not withdrawing from South Africa,' wrote Duncan Innes
in the *Weekly Mail*, 'they are simply changing the form of
their involvement in this country.' But the loss of support
from those magic initials IBM and GM was a more visible
symbol of the break with the West than any government
sanctions.

The exit of General Motors left a wake of bitterness.
Three thousand workers promptly went on strike in
protest against the 'secret and mysterious dealings',
insisting on safeguards and benefits under the new
owners, thus delaying the introduction of a new car, the
Opel Monza. When GM fired some of them and hired
more workers from the great pool of unemployed the
strikers angrily picketed them, allegedly threatening them
with necklaces, until police dispersed them with dogs.
After three weeks of striking the management issued an
ultimatum, and most strikers returned sullenly to work.
The black union federation COSATU insisted that the
strike had been against the non-consultation, not against
disinvestment itself: and GM was a special case since the
future of its South African plants was very uncertain
anyway. But the anger over GM's precipitate departure
caused some gloating among the opponents of disinvestment who had warned that it would cause loss of jobs;
and it put the politicised black union leaders – who
wanted both to stop Western support for Pretoria and
to safeguard jobs – in a more extreme quandary. It gave
a new poignancy to the old saying: 'if there's one
thing worse than being exploited by a multinational
corporation, it's *not* being exploited by a multinational
corporation.'

American capital would remain deeply involved in South
Africa's future, even if it preferred not to be – whether
through past investments and responsibilities, through the
interdependence with the rest of Africa, or through the

indispensàble precious metals and gold. Disinvestment was the end of one road, but it now raised more acutely the question of the American role in the post-apartheid era, and whether Western capitalism could come to terms with a future black government, and vice versa. Without pressures from Pretoria, the American multinationals now felt freer to make contact with black leaders, including the African National Congress. Could the multinationals change sides, as Gulf-Chevron had swiftly jumped when Angola had become independent, or as Mobil had switched in Rhodesia–Zimbabwe? Or would the aftermath of South Africa's civil war be so bitter and destructive as to exclude even the oil companies, despite all their skills at surviving? Much of the answer would depend on whether the multinationals could exercise their own long-term diplomacy, and follow up disinvestment with more positive steps to associate themselves with a future black majority.

The most far-reaching of all disinvestments came from Britain, when the chairman of Barclays, Sir Tim Bevan, after visiting Johannesburg, announced on November 24 that Barclays was selling out the whole of its 40 per cent interest in its South African subsidiary Barclays National to Anglo-American, together with De Beers and the Insurance group Southern Life. Sir Tim still publicly insisted that it was primarily a commercial decision that 'it was not the job of businessmen to get involved in politics', and that the bank was neither for nor against sanctions. The directors had in fact decided to sell out at a board meeting the previous May, largely because they had been losing business from protesting depositors in Britain: the anti-apartheid campaigners and students in Britain could rightly claim a victory after sixteen years of campaigning. Barclays' disinvestment, like General Motors', caused no immediate economic damage: the London board had to sell its 40 per cent interest for about £82 million, at the low exchange rate of the financial rand; the new owners would be glad to maintain the profitable network of branches, still keeping a 'working relationship' with London; and the

London board was still saddled with its billion dollars of
South African debt. But the Barclays withdrawal, following its decision a year earlier to stop all lending – and
coming in the same week as the disinvestment by two more
North American groups, Kodak and Bata shoes – was the
most significant of all the West's gestures of its dissociation
from apartheid policies. For it marked a withdrawal not
so much of technology or management but of confidence
and credit, in the literal sense of trust, which is the bankers'
life blood: it discouraged other foreign corporations, including Barclays' many clients; and it left the remaining
British companies, including the rival bank Standard, more
exposed to attack. The argument continued about the
political impact; but if the Western financial community
had wanted to show that, after sixty years lending and
investing, they had finally written off Pretoria they could
hardly have made it clearer than by selling their stake in
the biggest bank in the country.

Predictably, many British critics soon insisted that the
withdrawal was not thorough enough; that the pull-out
was 'cosmetic' and maintained a relationship with the
South African bank. The Anti-Apartheid Movement was
divided: many campaigners wanted to maintain the boycott
until Barclays moved out more completely; others wanted
to accept Barclays as a victory and move onto other targets.
Barclays was anxious to have the boycott called off, and
to regain student accounts: they invited campaigners to
meet them to explain that they had genuinely taken sides
against Pretoria, and the chairman-elect, John Quinton,
visited the ANC in Lusaka. In May the campaigners finally
called off the boycott. In South Africa in the meantime,
Chris Ball remained chief executive of the bank under its
new ownership; he was now still more caught between
opposing pressures, and made contradictory statements.
He worried that Barclays' withdrawal 'would remove the
leverage of foreigners'; while he quickly organised advertisements proclaiming 'The Bank' was returning to its
long-lost national independence. 'At last, ownership of

The Bank has come home to South Africa . . . What might
have been an awkward situation for the country as a whole
now becomes a real opportunity . . .' But Ball remained
a thorn in Pretoria's flesh, and kept in touch with the black
opposition.

Most of the British multinationals remained. A few
companies including the Prudential and Hill Samuel cut
back their involvement, but the biggest insisted that they
would not follow the Americans, and could improve conditions by staying. Shell remained the ANC's chosen scapegoat, and was increasingly worried: 'Shell is the only
company having to handle an international campaign
against it,' said John Wilson in an anguished address to his
staff in August. He admitted that businessmen had been
naïve in trusting Botha, and 'were oblivious of the extent
to which co-operation between the state and business in
fact repressed black aspirations'.* He saw more trouble
ahead: 'Shell's position is not comfortable. The threat
of disinvestment is real.' In October the Dutch senior
managing director of the Shell group, Lo van Wachem,
responded to pressure by condemning Pretoria's policies:
in a much-publicised letter to senior executives round the
world, he gave a gloomy view of South Africa's future and
said that Pretoria's concept of change was 'far removed
from the aspirations of the majority'. He denied that
business by itself could induce Pretoria to change, while
still insisting that Shell must stay, to help prepare black
South Africans for the end of apartheid. Yet Shell's position, like that of other European companies, remained
suspect to blacks; and the ANC and the UDF still saw them
as the allies of Pretoria's military clampdown: for while
Shell clearly saw the dangers ahead, they were not able
effectively to identify themselves with 'the aspirations of
the majority'.

President Botha was stepping up his pressures on

* Keynote address to Senior Staff Conference, Cape Sun Hotel,
August 4–5, 1986

companies to rally behind the government, and in November 1986 he summoned his third major meeting in seven years with South African business leaders. Some dissidents were not invited, including Chris Ball of Barclays National and (until the last minute) John Wilson of Shell. Others, including Gavin Relly and Tony Bloom, arranged to be out of the country. But most companies were represented, including Anglo by Zach de Beer. Several speakers at the conference reiterated the need for political reform – though carefully not spelling out specific needs such as the release of Mandela. President Botha, who opened the conference with an appeal for 'realistic idealism', was able to conclude that the meeting was 'full of goodwill'. But the uncritical presence of the businessmen, with no fundamental reforms in sight, was inevitably seen by blacks as a return to the traditional alliance between business and apartheid.

Many liberal white South Africans remained baffled that the West could impose sanctions and thereby set back blacks' economic prospects. Dr Bethlehem, the respected economist of Johannesburg Consolidated Investments, had reckoned in September 1986 that sanctions would drastically reduce the blacks' share of the national income, from a projected 36 percent to 20 percent by the year 2000.* It was true that sanctions were the bluntest of blunt weapons, which would hit many others beyond its target. But they were also, as Senator Lugar explained, one of the very few ways in which foreign nations could intervene, short of war.

They certainly came as a shock to Pretoria, in spite of the long forewarnings. For forty years the Afrikaners had dismissed most Western rhetoric against apartheid, with good reason, as mere posturing; they had remained confident that the West would back them up against the communist onslaught when the chips were down. Now for the first time the Western rhetoric had been backed up by

* Sanctions and the Process of Adjustment, JCI, September 12, 1986

governments as well as by bankers and corporations, in an unmistakeable dissociation.

But more significant than sanctions was the West's shift of policy towards the African National Congress. In September 1986 Sir Geoffrey Howe talked for the first time to Oliver Tambo, following his junior minister Lynda Chalker, in a two-hour discussion at his country house. They had the usual argument about violence; but Sir Geoffrey emphasised that he wanted to keep in touch with the ANC, which in turn welcomed the British government's acceptance that they were central to any South African solution. Four months later George Shultz received Tambo in Washington. Pretoria responded to these new openings with angry outbursts; not surprisingly, for they marked the defeat of their strategy to portray the ANC as the tools of Moscow, and to isolate them as pariahs and terrorists like the PLO; while they were a victory of the ANC in *their* strategy to isolate Pretoria. The West's talks with the ANC added the critical political dimension to sanctions: for they indicated that the West was not only withdrawing support from the South African government, but beginning to change sides.

Could these half-hearted sanctions have any real effect? South Africa was theoretically acutely vulnerable as an industrial state heavily dependent on trade; but its interlocks with the world system also made it hard to hurt it without hurting others – or the whole system. Gold still provided half South Africa's trade; and the neatest sanction would deliberately depress the price of gold. *The Economist* on July 19 recommended with apparent seriousness that the central banks should threaten to start selling their gold unless Mandela was released – a suggestion which Senator Orrin Hatch took up in Washington. But it was never politically plausible: it needed the support of conservative central bankers, and it would also hit other gold-producers in North America and Australia. And gold was up to its old tricks: as the world economy looked more uncertain the gold-price began to move up, providing a fillip to Pretoria's finances which looked like temporarily compensating for sanctions. Some black politicians were now dreading that the worse their repression the higher the gold price would climb, in eager anticipation of riots, strikes and shut-downs which would reduce the supply.

Arms had been the first target for sanctions; but the UN embargo of weapons since 1977 had often been breached. It was not true, as Pretoria often boasted, that the embargoes had made South Africa virtually self-sufficient in weaponry: the intricate technology of advanced weapons systems now included many crucial components for which there were serious shortages, particularly in electronics; a confidential government report in 1985 had warned that 'any move towards disinvestment from South Africa would have a particularly severe effect on the electronics industry'.* But the profits to be made from selling components to Pretoria were irresistible to middle-men and suppliers: the French who had theoretically obeyed the arms embargo were still supplying spare parts for Mirage planes, while the new South African-made fighter the Cheetah which Botha launched in 1986 was based heavily on French and Israeli technology and components. Only if Western governments began monitoring the arms embargo much more rigorously could they prevent key components getting through.

An oil embargo had been proposed by anti-apartheid campaigners since the early 'sixties; for South Africa had no oil of her own, and the oil-from-coal plants of SASOL could not keep pace with the growing consumption. An embargo by OPEC became more effective after the fall of the Shah of Iran in 1979, who had been Pretoria's loyal ally; and South Africa had to pay high premiums to buy oil through Oman, Brunei and other embargo-breakers. By 1983 (President Botha revealed three years later) South Africa sometimes had only enough oil for a week; and the

* Gavin Cawthra, *Brutal Force*, London, International Defence and Aid Fund, 1986, p. 102

premiums over ten years had cost 22 billion rand.* But the
oil glut after 1985, like the climbing gold price, came to
Pretoria's rescue, making producers more desperate to sell
surplus oil; and in early 1986, when the oil-price collapsed,
South Africa rapidly replenished her stockpile of oil which
was stored in disused mines and elsewhere. Oil tankers
continued to arrive at South African ports, many of them
commissioned by the embargo-breaking companies Trans-
world in Rotterdam and Marimpex in Hamburg: the Shipping Research Bureau in Amsterdam, which monitored
the oil embargo, identified eighty-three tankers delivering
crude oil during 1983 and 1984, including seventeen from
Brunei, thirteen from Saudi Arabia and thirteen from
Oman. The European Community agreed in September
1985 to cease oil imports to South Africa, but did little to
implement the ban.† A serious oil embargo still appeared
the most obvious stranglehold on Pretoria; but Western
governments were still far from having the will or the
means to enforce it.

   A ban on airlines flying to and from South Africa had a
special attraction to sanctioneers, including Andrew
Young who had advocated it for many years. It would
have an immediate psychological impact on white South
Africans – even if they could still fly to Europe via neighbouring states – while leaving blacks relatively unscathed.
The enlarged airports in Zimbabwe or Botswana would
become vital to South Africans, thus providing potential
hostages against Pretoria's reprisals, while airlines could
begin to connect up an alternative air traffic system for the
sub-continent. But international airlines – which always
see themselves as the special champions of free trade and
free movement – strongly resisted any disruption. British
Airways, the biggest foreign carrier, had some worries
about their dependence on South African airports, and in

   * Speech at Vereeniging, April 25, 1986
   † *See* Newsletter on the Oil Embargo, February 1986 and September
1986. Shipping Research Bureau, P.O. Box 11898, Amsterdam

July 1986 they applied for landing-rights in Botswana. But
they were loth to loosen their long-established links; their
daily flights to and from South Africa brought in almost a
fifth of their total profits – all the more welcome when
transatlantic traffic had fallen and BA was about to be
privatised – and their combative chairman Lord King had
firmly lobbied Mrs Thatcher to resist airline sanctions.
Both BA and Lufthansa insisted that if they stopped flying
to Johannesburg, Swissair and El Al would gladly take
over their business; but when American sanctions prevented South African Airways from flying to New York
Lufthansa and Swissair added extra flights.

It was the Swiss, who belonged to neither the UN, nor
the European Community nor NATO, who were portrayed
as the weak link in nearly every chain of sanctions: determined that their money must be neutral and secret, prepared to lend, to swap gold or to get capital out of the
country with equal impartiality. The more threatening the
sanctions, the greater the profits to be made out of breaking
them. But the Swiss, together with the Taiwanese, the
Israelis and other identifiable sanctions-breakers, were
also convenient scapegoats and excuses for other Europeans to cheat. In Britain officials of the Department of
Trade zealously briefed businessmen how to compete with
the Swiss in evading sanctions, with the slogan 'one man's
sanctions is another man's opportunity': while the Swiss
ambassador in Pretoria was privately assuring the black
opposition that his country would not increase its trade.

As the Western governments voted for sanctions, Pretoria prepared its own extensive sanctions-busting machinery, with a department of experts – many of them with
experience from Rhodesia twenty years before – working
with industrialists and importers. Sanctions-busting became part of the new patriotism, to which businessmen
had to show their loyalty. But this did not mean they would
be ineffectual, nor did Pretoria think so. As the bills were
going through they lobbied furiously against them, and Pik
Botha made a much-publicised tour to find new trading

links in the Far East – where he was well received by Taiwan but got short shrift from Japan. Pretoria would certainly be able to circumvent most sanctions, but at great extra cost; and in the meantime the ban on new investment and the bankers' own sanctions underlined the most serious fact – that there was little prospect of more foreign capital on which to build future growth.

The crucial question about sanctions was not economic but psychological and political: how would white South Africans react to the West's signal? The first impact would certainly provide a challenge and stimulus, to prove themselves and defy the world – like Rhodesians twenty years earlier. But the sequel would be less exhilarating: for whatever the success of the sanctions-busters, apartheid was already hitting many whites' pockets, and some of their jobs; and the future looked much more dismal. However successful the repression of blacks, it could not generate a lasting internal economic recovery, while the armed forces and police would become a still larger drain on the economy.

It was true that white South Africans had inherited from international investors a remarkably dynamic economic system, which was close to self-sufficiency in many areas. But could they maintain and develop that system, with more and more black consumers as well as factory-workers, while denying them political and human rights and turning the townships into armed camps? Or would the imperatives of industry inevitably press the society towards more individual freedom? There was no lack of depressing precedents, in Nazi Germany, in parts of Latin America or in Eastern Europe, for industrial expansion thriving on minimal rights; and Asia had its own mutations of Western capitalism, like Korea's, which could prosper without genuine democracy. But there was no real parallel for a racial minority in an advanced industrial state depending for their prosperity on an overwhelming majority which was rallying against them. Even before the crackdown white industrialists were already worried in their own factories by the alienation, the lack of incentives and the industrial sabotage which was slowing their productivity. Botha's policy of recognising black unions while stamping out their political role presented a more fundamental contradiction than existed, for instance, in Poland: for apartheid had pressed the black workers into a much more distinctive solidarity, which identified blackness with alienation from the state.

Many Afrikaners were now depicting themselves as 'a first world inside a third world' and liked to believe that their white islands could survive securely and prosperously, while drawing their labour and servants from townships which could be fenced-off in their own separate world of anarchy, repression and black-on-black violence. But could these white bastions remain immune from black-on-white violence, when their factories and homes depended on them? The Afrikaners still clung to the mythology of their tribe, in the midst of their industrialisation: and many conservatives abroad liked to admire the toughness of this 'white tribe of Africa' and to predict that, in a continent of tribes, the strongest would win. But South Africa's unique industrial development had already forged a much more integrated economic system than anywhere in Africa, which was drawing both blacks and whites away from their tribes; and no amount of fencing off could remove their basic interdependence.

Certainly the immediate future must still depend on the decisions of the most powerful tribe. Are the Afrikaners really prepared to pay the price of their economic growth and Western security to defend their own tribal stronghold? Do they have the cohesion – which the Southern States in the civil war ultimately lacked – to sustain a second civil war in defence of their privilege? They had proudly clung to their mythology since the Boer War, and many Westerners including Mrs Thatcher saw them as stubborn to the last. But myths are never a clear guide to future behaviour; and even the 'Iron Lady' was outwardly most defiant when about to give way. The Afrikaners had

never really been tested since 1902. They had never had
to choose between economic expansion and white domination because they had comfortably got both: 'The ox
wagon was also a bandwagon,' as Conor Cruise O'Brien
put it.* Through the 'sixties the multinationals had been
glad to help extend both the economic and the military
state. However much Western governments had huffed
and puffed against apartheid they had always played in
with yet more delaying tactics from Pretoria, while their
military and intelligence teams had encouraged the Afrikaners to believe that they stood together against the
communist menace.

But Western bankers and governments had now brought
home the choice between apartheid and prosperity, to the
point where whites as well as blacks were being put out of
jobs. Verwoerd's 'grand apartheid' may always have been
an intellectual sham, which dressed up domination with
religious and anthropological trappings; but while it was
accompanied by spectacular economic growth in the 'sixties it could convince Afrikaner intellectuals and even
some Westerners. It was its economic failure in the 'seventies that began to discredit that apartheid theory: and it
was not the political theorists, but the bankers and the
blacks between them who pushed Botha into declaring
apartheid outdated and abolishing the pass-laws. Botha's
policies now had no real consistency: at the end of 1985
he had come very close to releasing Mandela under pressure from Western governments and bankers; six months
later he switched 180 degrees, slammed the door on Mandela and declared a more ruthless emergency. With such
changeability no one could confidently claim that the Afrikaners were immune to pressure: their government was
visibly confused, indecisive and inconsistent, their reforms
prompted by international demands – though they would
not admit it.

The theological basis for apartheid was itself crumbling

* *Atlantic Monthly*, March 1986

under both internal and external pressure. In October 1986 the Dutch Reformed Church, which still claimed 38 percent of South Africa's whites among its members, reached a muddled compromise by which they would admit all races to membership, while still not merging with black or coloured reformed churches; and they also accepted a policy document announcing 'racism is a sin, which no person may defend or practice' – which effectively undermined the religious basis for all past apartheid laws.

The whites no longer had any grand design to maintain white supremacy over a fast-growing black majority, no new blueprints to replace the tattered schemes for tribal homelands; while Botha has discredited his own tricameral parliament by overruling it to declare the emergency. Pretoria still clung to the strategy of dividing black tribes, which enabled Afrikaners to argue that there was no real black majority; but the revolts within the homelands and the defections of their leaders were already undermining those assumptions. The Afrikaners' special language of power-sharing, group rights and consultation looked more obviously bogus as the government became more desperately pragmatic, determined to maintain its power with brute force like any other police state.

For the younger generation of Afrikaners – and of all white South Africans – the long-term future under sanctions must be bleak: slow economic growth, if any, which cannot keep pace with the rising black population and costs of defence; factories which depend on markets abroad, which are increasingly denied to them; an expectation and pride which had been nurtured on widening horizons and rapid development, now facing contraction; and above all a degeneration into a brutal civil war. Pretoria's current counter-attack against the black resistance may well produce for a time a new appearance of white calm and black divisiveness, with the help of mass detentions, unleashing black vigilantes and encouraging tribal conflicts: but the government can offer no convincing scenario of how they can gain any long-term black consent.

Without it, military priorities will take over from economic incentives, while whites will face much greater personal dangers and strains. The argument will continue as to whether the Afrikaners will be stubborn to the end; whether (in the Boer War terminology) they will be 'hands-uppers' or 'bitter-enders'. But as the choices become harsher, mythologies will clash with realities. It is quite true that the Afrikaners, unlike the French in Algeria, have nowhere else to go; but for that reason, they will in the end – like the whites in the Deep South – face the realities of compromise, as the French colonists never did.

In the light of past history it is absurd for Western governments or companies to expect Pretoria to make reforms by itself, to dismantle the structure of apartheid. The context and assumptions which Pretoria has set distort all the perspectives inside South Africa, where the roads only meet off the map and the communities look less and less like a single nation. The South African union seventy-eight years ago now looks like a dangerous experiment which has reached the point of explosion and semi-civil war which can tear the country apart. And as Keppel-Jones warned forty years ago, just before the apartheid government came to power: 'The salvation of this country can lie only in a reversal of historic tendencies so thorough as to constitute a revolution.'* The interest of the West must lie in making that revolution as bloodless and manageable as possible: in preserving the continuity of human rights, the respect for the law and civilised values; and in making their own links with a future non-racial or black government.

To achieve that, Western governments must follow their own road-map and ignore Pretoria's dead end. Western businessmen and diplomats talk about the precipice and the abyss, but prefer not to contemplate how they might cross over them: with all their protestation against apart-

* *See* p. 82.

heid, they try to avoid the question of 'one man, one vote', or who will hold power in the end. Yet the character of the future black government, and its relationships with Western governments and corporations, will depend crucially on the nature of the transition, and on the bridges that the West can build across the ravine. The longer the West refuses to face up to a future black majority, the more anti-Western it is likely to be. The complaints that the black opposition is communist can all too easily be self-fulfilling, if the West refuses to provide its own support; but the evidence inside South Africa suggests that it is home-grown nationalism and anti-capitalism which present a much greater force than external communism.

The Western corporations must be decisive actors in this drama, as much as governments. Their interests are crucially threatened; their behaviour, more than their governments', will determine black attitudes to the West; and they can act more decisively and quickly than governments (as Kissinger said).* Many more American companies will certainly disinvest, rather than endure attacks at home for the sake of an unpromising future inside South Africa; and disinvestment is preferable to the kind of passive playing-in with Pretoria which has accompanied so much investment over the forty years of apartheid, and which has so damaged the relations between blacks and business. But disinvestment is in itself a purely negative policy, which all too easily leads to a general writing-off of the future of Southern Africa, white or black. There remains, I believe, a potentially crucial role for Western corporations which choose to stay – provided they face up to the long-term implications and responsibilities, as actors not spectators in the drama. This narrative has, I hope, shown how often in the past corporations have undermined their own future by assuming political impotence, and not daring to pursue their own long-term interests, whether by publicly dissociating themselves from apartheid, by

* *See* p. 29.

educating and promoting their black employees, or by breaking down internal segregation, for fear of reprisals or a white backlash which are often illusory. Today the necessity to take a political role is far more urgent. To safeguard their own future the corporations will have to distance themselves from the short-term pressures which push them towards Pretoria, and look ahead to a future black government. If they are to convince blacks that they are on their side they will have to make a much more decisive commitment to their community and political groups: they cannot merely provide 'neutral support' in the form of black education, housing or welfare – which will always be compromised by the constraints of the apartheid system.

Within South Africa the military-political offensive and the polarisation on both sides will lead to a still more ferocious confrontation, which will make it harder for companies to change sides. The peaceful movements for black rights, including consumer boycotts of shops and protests of labour unions, become more difficult as their leaders are detained and the young activists call for more ruthless action. The government is once again determined, as it was in 1960 and 1977, to show that it can achieve what Britain and France failed to achieve in their colonies in the fifties (with very few exceptions such as Malaya); to permanently crush the opposition with their counter-revolutionary offensive and to make the ANC more ineffective than the PLO. The severity of the emergency laws and the effective clampdown on news may well give the appearance of success for some time in military and police terms. But the government's military obsession continues to distort its thinking, as it did in previous crises. No military strategy, as General Malan used to admit, can ever succeed without capturing 'hearts and minds': and it is not only black hearts and minds that have become more rebellious, but those of many administrators, theologians and business executives who cannot contemplate a permanent military solution.

The context of the conflict is now rapidly extending to the neighbouring countries as Pretoria takes reprisals against them: while the two ex-Portuguese states, Angola and Mozambique, are rent by civil wars in which the rebels are supported by South Africa; and the death of President Machel has brought a new danger that Mozambique will be split in two. No one should underestimate Pretoria's scope for destabilizing the whole region, thus both extending their influence and appearing to prove their point that blacks are incapable of self-government. But the wider conflict presents an opportunity as well as a danger for the western governments and corporations: for the solution to many deadlocks can be found by changing the context (as Jean Monnet insisted when he overcame the deadlock between France and Germany in 1950 by taking the first steps towards a European Community). The western nations can only begin to resolve the South African deadlock, and to intervene effectively to reach a peaceful solution, in the wider context of the surrounding states which are beyond the reach of the apartheid system: and they will have to pick up this challenge in the most positive way. For the front-line states will become the real bases of opposition, through which the West can maintain its presence and continuity untainted by Pretoria; and they will desperately need to build up their alternative infrastructure of air, rail and road links independent of Pretoria's control, if they are not to become dragged further into the South African disaster. Only by providing support in this wider region can the western governments and companies break away more completely from the fatal associations with apartheid which have so seriously damaged their future prospects of maintaining their influence in a black South Africa.

19

Postscript: The White Verdict

How would the white South Africans perceive their own problem after two years of internal emergencies and external pressure? At the beginning of 1987 President Botha called a general election for May to renew his mandate and justify his policies to his people. For the next months the all-white election campaign provided a test of whether the whites were able (as Botha had put it himself after he came to power) to 'adapt or die'.

The campaign took place against a background of continuing repression. The police and the army patrolled the black townships, still with almost unlimited powers under the state of emergency, with detentions, intimidation and torture largely unreported under the censorship laws. The police made more use of black 'vigilantes' to help them, and began recruiting black 'special constables' who were given only three weeks training before policing the townships. The security forces extended their influence through their secretive National Security Management System which co-opted civilians, including businessmen, to connect up the web of joint management centres across the country, and helped to provide intelligence and control of black activities.

The black political structures in the townships which had been set up before the first emergency were still further undermined as their leaders remained in detention or on the run. The young activists still managed to launch a new South African Black Youth Congress (SAYCO) in April 1987 to replace the banned student body Cosas, which aimed to 'unite and politicise working youth, the unemployed and student youth, regardless of race, colour, sex or religion'. Led by a former guerrilla trainee, Peter Mokaba, it adopted the ANC colours – black, green and gold, with the addition of red – and compared itself to the ANC Youth League in 1944, whose members had included Mandela and Tambo. It proclaimed the militant slogan 'Freedom or death: victory is certain'.

But it was the black labour unions which now emerged in the front line of politics as the only legal organisations – apart from the churches – which could provide expression for black grievances. The union leaders were emerging as major political figures, rivalling the ANC in their status. In the weeks before the election the unions began to show their strength: the black transport workers who had hitherto been passive went on strike and railway coaches were set on fire. The Johannesburg headquarters of Cosatu, the biggest black union federation, became literally a battleground in April, when black demonstrators who had been attacked by the police took refuge in the building. The police and army then surrounded the building, claiming that it contained 'trained terrorists', while the union leaders insisted they were having a peaceful meeting. The police charged into the building, whipping and kicking the black workers, killing at least three and detaining four hundred. The following week, after four black transport workers had been found 'necklaced', the police again surrounded the Cosatu building and arrested suspects. Then a week later two powerful bombs exploded inside Cosatu house, wrecking elevators and printing machines and cracking the walls so that the building was declared unsafe. Cosatu offices in other cities were also destroyed. The blast, said Cosatu, was 'part of a co-ordinated campaign to break the power of the labour movement'.

The idea that black unions could develop without political involvement now looked still less likely. A few businessmen publicly deplored the persecution of Cosatu. John Wilson of Shell explained that he still clung to the hope of a negotiated solution, but went on: 'As violence, high-handed and strong-arm tactics are employed in what is transparently an attempt to crush an increasingly powerful government opponent, one's belief in that negotiated future becomes even more fragile'.

But during the election campaign most South African businessmen were reluctant to defy a government which appeared to be restoring law and order. 'Faced with the choice between chaos and injustice' as one director of Anglo-American put it, 'it may sometimes be necessary to choose injustice'. President Botha played up the revolutionary threat from the African National Congress, and accused Chris Ball of Barclays of having helped to finance advertisements calling for the un-banning of the ANC. When Ball denied it, Botha appointed his friend Justice Munnik as a one-man commission to investigate, who reported that Ball had provided an overdraft to a 'Mr Z' knowing it would be used to pay for the advertisements. In the meantime Ball was unveiling the new name of the bank since Barclays had sold it: the 'First National Bank', with the symbol of a tree in front of the sun. The government seemed determined to use Ball to scare other businessmen away from the ANC, and only a few businessmen publicly protested against the government's intimidation. One of them was Murray Hofmeyr of the Anglo-American group who had taken over as chairman of its subsidiary Johannesburg Consolidated Investments after Gordon Waddell had resigned in some despair about the government's policies. Hofmeyr attacked the government's 'deliberate smear campaigns followed by the all too familiar technique of guilt by association' and went on to criticise his business colleagues: 'it should be a matter for serious reflection how readily businessmen are duped by these manoevres'. Other business leaders were reluctant to make public criticism, and Raymond Ackerman of Pick 'n Pay supermarkets retorted angrily: 'We are hard at work behind the scenes trying to work for change. We are not seeking headlines but looking for action, and Hofmeyr's statements have no foundation'.* But the victimisation of Ball did cause more businessmen to rally round him, and he retained his job as chief of the First National Bank.

Multinational executives were now much less hopeful of achieving any fundamental change. In March 1987 Leon Sullivan held a further meeting of chief executives at Leeds Castle, once again with Ted Heath as co-chairman. The mood in the castle was now much more pessimistic, and the Americans were less prominent, as several major corporations had disinvested: IBM and Burroughs stayed away, and Roger Smith of GM sent a deputy who spent most of his time taking notes. Judge Steyn, from the South African Urban Foundation, praised Sullivan fulsomely for having ennobled the cause of commerce and industry, but Sullivan himself seemed dispirited. He was looking for some 'quantum leap' from Pretoria which would enable him to withdraw his demand for total disinvestment at the end of May, but there was no sign of any such leap. The businessmen discussed how they might stop the momentum of disinvestment. One South African pointed out that only the blacks – perhaps only Archbishop Tutu – could do that. Three months later Sullivan formally called for all American companies to disinvest within nine months.

But disinvestment was leading to some disenchantment among its activists, both inside and outside South Africa. The bankers' withdrawals had undoubtedly helped to undermine international credit and confidence in South Africa; but the selling of industrial plants to local owners at knock-down prices was much less obviously damaging to Pretoria, particularly if the western corporations still supplied their technology. Among the exodus of American companies only Kodak was thought to have thoroughly

* *Weekly Mail*, April 15, 1987

broken its links, by cutting out technology and making no profits: the blacks talked about 'Kodaking' as the model of genuine disinvestment; but even Kodak provided a windfall for its new South African managers. It was hard for any American company to sell out without enriching white South African businessmen. Schemes were initiated to enable blacks to buy disinvested companies, but they caused rifts between the political groups, with the Left attacking black leaders who wanted to join the capitalists. Many black labour unionists were worried that their new local white owners would be far more ruthless than the multinationals; while in the United States there were signs that the withdrawal of investments was being accompanied by a general withdrawal of concern. The *threat* of disinvestment had been very effective in drawing attention to the connivance of corporations with apartheid, and pressing them towards a bolder confrontation; but massive withdrawals would remove the leverage, and could easily lead to a mood of 'to hell with Africa'. Total disinvestment was like the nuclear deterrent, more effective as a threat than an act.

In the meantime South African businessmen were stimulated by the short-term economy, which looked more hopeful than in the dark days of August 1985. The immediate response to sanctions had predictably been an internal boom. The local savings and pension funds, under strict exchange controls, had nowhere else to put their money; the 'siege economy' encouraged inward investment; and the Johannesburg stock exchange soared again. The state of emergency and censorship, by removing scenes of violence from overseas television screens, had provided an appearance of calm abroad as well as at home, and some foreign investors began to put money back into South African shares and property – now at knock-down prices – thus pushing up the 'financial rand' by nearly 30 percent during March 1987. The gold price still went up in response to the falling dollar and global uncertainties, bringing a rapid improvement in South Africa's balance of payments.

As a debtor-nation, South Africa was beginning to look more reliable to foreign bankers, who in March reached a new and more lenient agreement which gave South Africa three years in which to repay interest plus 13 percent of the capital on its loans.

But the longer-term prospects for businessmen still looked very bleak, above all because of problems of man-power. They would still need more skilled black workers, even in a recession, but they faced much less promising prospects of recruitment and orderly negotiations since the second emergency. The black unions which they had persuaded Botha to legalise eight years earlier were now inevitably becoming politicised, and increasingly harassed and circumscribed by the government. And companies were also very short of the white skills they needed. Each month thousands of white South Africans – including ac-countants, engineers and computer experts who were es-sential to industrial growth – had been voting with their feet by leaving the country. Many of them dreaded being constantly liable to call-up for military duty, which could now involve fighting not on a far frontier, but in the townships outside their own white cities. The official figures for emigration under-estimated the totals, for they included only those who applied to take money out, while many of the most valuable potential employees were the young graduates who had gone abroad after taking their degree in order to avoid or postpone military service, and who then decided to settle abroad. The disappearance of such people, trained at great expense, was an incalculable loss to the South African economy.

Already the problems of the South African economy were very visible. The standard of living for average whites was lower than in 1970 and inflation was running at 16 percent. The gross national product had gone up by only 0.5 percent in 1986, while fixed investment had gone down by 16 percent. The country needed massive foreign loans and investment to finance higher growth-rates, but it was now exporting capital through its debt repayments. 'If

South Africa were a "normal" country', wrote the *Financial Times* correspondent Anthony Robinson, just before the election, 'the government would be facing a humiliating defeat'. But South Africa was far from normal, and the white electors were becoming increasingly obsessed by a single issue – security.

The election campaign itself was less embattled against world pressure and opinion than many liberals had feared. It revealed the biggest rifts in the Afrikaners' camp since their National party came to power forty years ago. Afrikaner academics, theologians and businessmen, who had been part of the core of the party, defected in droves. The University of Stellenbosch, which had once been the heartland of apartheid, became the centre of dissent; and the rifts appeared to contradict the warnings of western conservatives, led by Mrs Thatcher, that sanctions would only drive the Afrikaners further into the laager. The election campaign had never developed into an anti-American crusade like John Vorster's campaign of 1977 which ferociously attacked President Carter's interference.

Three 'independent' candidates – Wynand Malan, Denis Worrall and Esther Lategan – defected from the National Party because it was not reforming fast enough. They were far from meeting the aspirations of the black opposition, but they represented the first serious challenge to the ruling party from the left; and significantly they gained strong support from interests who stood to lose heavily from the imposition of sanctions. Most leading South African sportsmen, already suffering acutely from the international sports boycott, supported the independents. 'That changed my view of the influence of international pressure', said one of their campaign managers. Denis Worrall, the former ambassador to Britain who stood against Botha's favourite minister Chris Heunis in Helderberg, was financed by Cape wine-growers and fruit-farmers who were worried about their overseas markets; and also by the Afrikaner tycoon Anton Rupert, together with his son Johann, who headed the Rembrandt multinational tobacco empire.

But the election results dashed the hopes of any broad liberal swing, and revealed an emphatic lurch to the right. The National Party was returned with 123 seats, compared to 116 before the election. The right-wing Conservative Party, under Andries Treurnicht, took a quarter of the total votes, giving them twenty-one seats which made them the official opposition in parliament. 30 percent of all the white voters had voted for either the Conservative Party or the other right-wing party, the HNP, while nearly half the English-speaking voters supported either the Nationalists or the right-wing parties. The three independent candidates had some success: Wynand Malan was elected in the prosperous Johannesburg suburb of Randburg, and Denis Worrall was defeated by only thirty-nine votes. But the liberal party, the PFP, suffered a catastrophic defeat, with only 17 percent of the electorate, giving it twenty seats, one less than the Conservatives. It raised fundamental questions about the PFP's future viability – all the more since many white liberals had clearly abstained. The current leader, Colin Eglin, admitted that the vote was a major setback for 'the concept of a reform alliance developing into an alternative government . . .', while the previous leader, Van Zyl Slabbert, felt it vindicated his decision to give up his parliamentary role: 'parliament itself is trapped between the government and the extra-parliamentary opposition'. Archbishop Tutu had no doubts: 'Get out of parliament,' he told the PFP, 'you have given the world the impression that we have a multi-party democracy when it is now quite clear we have a total charade'.

The results appeared to show South African elections going the same way as elections in Rhodesia twenty years earlier, when liberal parties were constantly out-voted by right-wing parties, culminating in a solid majority for the Rhodesian Front. President Botha had refused to debate the question of reform during the election, and had done his best to emphasise the need for security, and to whip up the fear of black revolution – though this fear drove many voters still further right, to the Conservatives.

As for the blacks, they had dismissed the election as irrelevant, but not insignificant. They had made their own protest against the all-white vote by obeying a stay-at-home strike on election day, called by Cosatu, the UDF and the National Education Crisis Committee. The black newspaper, *The Sowetan*, conducted its own poll of readers, which showed Mandela at the top and Botha in 24th place. The white swing to the right had aborted any likely negotiations with a representative black grouping, and polarised the black and white leadership still further. Even Chief Buthelezi's hopes for continuing his 'Indaba' in Natal, with an agreement for power-sharing, were spectacularly dashed: the English-speaking voters in Natal moved decisively away from the more liberal candidates who had endorsed the Indaba, and provided the most spectacular shift to the right. Buthelezi said he was 'totally appalled' and expected a 'long, hard, costly political grind ahead'. Murphy Morobe, the acting publicity secretary of the UDF (most of whose leaders were still detained) said 'we are determined to ensure that this will be the last racist election in our country'. Oliver Tambo of the ANC called for an intensification of the armed struggle. Archbishop Tutu said that the results were 'the darkest age' in South Africa's history.

They certainly heralded a darker phase. In the first few days after the election, President Botha appeared determined to show the right wing that he could not be accused of being soft. His government warned businessmen that they would not now tolerate any infringement of the Group Areas Act by allowing black employees in white districts. The unions were harassed further, censorship tightened, and some foreign correspondents expelled.

What role was now left for Western governments or companies to exert pressure? The opponents of sanctions were quick to explain that the elections had proved that sanctions *were* counterproductive. South African businessmen, including Anglo-American, argued once more that what was needed was more investment, and more aid for black welfare and education, to ensure economic growth and better communications which would gradually liberalise attitudes. And in London the British Industry Committee on South Africa, BICSA, was responding by pressing for a new 'Marshall Aid' for Black South Africans. But it was hard to visualise, in the light of the past experience of 'constructive engagement', how lifting sanctions, relaxing pressure and injecting massive funds could conceivably moderate Pretoria's attitude. Nor had the election campaign proved that white South Africans would be invulnerable to sanctions in the longer run: in fact it had given some signs to the contrary. The defections of Afrikaner academics, theologians and editors marked an evident weakening of the underlying confidence and faith of Afrikanerdom; and opinion polls before the election had suggested that nearly half the electors favoured the further dismantling of apartheid, including the Group Areas Act. It was the panic over security which had overriden all other perceptions at the election, but the government had little long-term prospect of maintaining security without some kind of settlement.

The economic pressures which had pushed Botha towards reform at the beginning of the 'eighties – even pushed him close to releasing Mandela – would still repeat the insistent message to him and his successors: that there was no prospect of economic improvement or lasting security without negotiating with the black opposition and re-entering the Western community. Without that, South Africa would begin to go into reverse. It was impossible to distinguish between the psychological impacts of domestic and international pressures in the future. Some existing overseas sanctions, including the closing of consulates in Australia and Canada, and the banning of flights to America, had an obvious immediate impact; others would take much longer. Perhaps the most devastating long-term sanctions would come from the white South Africans themselves – from deserters from military service, and from the brain drain of some of the ablest young white South Africans who were undermining the future basis of an advanced industrial state. The 'student-bashing' which appeared to be part of Botha's tactics during the campaign was expected to accelerate the trend, and some right-wing Afrikaners even welcomed the removal of potential liberal voters. But unless South Africa could provide more hopeful prospects for these key citizens it would be threatened with a de-industrialising process which would bring it closer to the rest of Africa, and remove the chances of sustaining high economic growth.

The most dangerous upshot of the elections would be for Western interests to give up hope and support for black South Africans. The more cynical Western conservatives enjoyed talking about South Africa as a third world country, with its white tribe becoming more like the rest of Africa. They concluded that the best thing that the West could do for South Africa was to leave it alone. Many campaigners for disinvestment, on their side, were inclined to assume that once they had compelled companies to disinvest they could do no more.

But any serious Western interest must call for more positive than negative pressures. Any flow of Western funds into South Africa itself will inevitably help to strengthen and justify the Pretoria regime; but the West can and must increase its active support for the surrounding front-line states which will increasingly become part of the battleground – most of all Mozambique as its civil war becomes the frontier between opposing troops, with the rebel army Renamo being backed by South Africa and the government's Frelimo troops discreetly backed by the West, particularly Britain. Only by strengthening their presence in these neighbouring countries, and by thus maintaining closer contact with the black opposition inside the Republic, can Western governments and corporations take steps to maintain their interests and survival in a future multi-racial South Africa.

The West cannot escape from its responsibility in a

region which it has helped to forge; whose industrial and military strength it built up with its investment and technology. Americans and Europeans have already encouraged black South Africans to demand their rights, and committed themselves to achieving a democratic and just society. No people can betray another people more completely than by first encouraging them to revolt and then, when they face the full force of repression, walking away.

Index

and disinvestment, 223
and Inkatha, 150
and Leutwiler, 53
and Mandela, 191, 246
and Reagan re-election, 218
and sanctions, 332
Slabbert on, 301–2
on state of emergency, 234
and Tambo, 191, 246

C. J. Fuchs, 267
Caltex, 160, 277
Cape Colony, 62, 63, 66, 71, 79
Cape Times, 88
Cape Town, 61, 63, 145, 236
Carlton Centre, Johannesburg, 125, 176
Carter, Jimmy, 166, 167, 188, 189
Cary, Frank, 169
Casey, William, 331
Caterpillar Africa, 119
Cayzer, Sir Nicholas, 119
Central Mining, 64–5, 72, 122, 123
Chalker, Lynda, 36, 272–3, 341
Chamber of Mines, 65, 80, 252
Chamberlain, Joseph, 67
Charter Consolidated, 123
Chase Manhattan Bank, 38–41, 46, 49, 114, 115, 158, 170, 247
Chatham House, 260, 271
Chemical Bank, 171
Chevron, 227
Choabe, Seretse, 253
Christian Institute, 147
Chrysler, 115, 119, 136
Church Commissioners, 228–9

Churchill, Lord Randolph, 63, 67
CIA (Central Intelligence Agency), 108, 109n, 331
Ciba-Geigy, 200
Cillie, Judge, 147
Cillie, Piet, 88
Citibank, 38, 41, 46, 171, 184–5, 228, 275, 277
Citicorp, 225
Citizen, 320
City Press, 189, 246
Civil Rights Commission, 218
Clark, Senator Dick, 168–9
Clausen, Tom, 171
Cleminson, Sir James, 273
Coca-Cola, 37, 277, 278, 334
Code of Conduct, 281
Coetzee, General, 195
Cole, Lord, 117
Colgate Palmolive, 86, 277
Collins, Canon, 140, 196
Colonial Office, 61
Comintern, 96
Commentary, 19
Commonwealth, 15–17, 20, 82, 89, 115, 120, 202, 258, 287, 288, 289, 327, 329, 332
'Commonwealth Accord', 289
'Commonwealth Group', ('Eminent Persons'), 15, 17, 34, 289, 293–5, 329, 332
Commonwealth Report on South Africa, 271
Community Support Committee, 312
'Comprehensive Anti-Apartheid Act, The', 332
Confederation of British Industries, 118, 133, 273